URBAN TRANSPORTATION FINANCING:
THEORY AND POLICY IN ONTARIO

Mark W. Frankena

Urban Transportation Financing: theory and policy in Ontario

PUBLISHED FOR THE ONTARIO ECONOMIC COUNCIL BY
UNIVERSITY OF TORONTO PRESS
TORONTO BUFFALO LONDON

© Ontario Economic Council 1982
Printed in Canada

ISBN 0-8020-3380-6

Canadian Cataloguing in Publication Data
Frankena, Mark W., 1943–
   Urban transportation financing
   (Ontario Economic Council research studies,
   ISSN 0708-3688 ; 26)
   Bibliography : p.
   ISBN 0-8020-3380-6
   1. Urban transportation – Ontario – Finance.
   2. Urban transportation policy – Ontario. I. Ontario
   Economic Council.   II. Title.   III. Series.
   HE311.C3205   388.4′042   C82-094305-3

This report reflects the views of the author and not necessarily those of the Ontario Economic Council or the Ontario government. The Council establishes policy questions to be investigated and commissions research projects, but it does not influence the conclusions or recommendations of authors. The decision to sponsor publication of this study was based on its competence and relevance to public policy and was made with the advice of anonymous referees expert in the area.

Contents

Preface

In writing this study I have benefited from the use of unpublished data provided by R. Allen Harvey of the Canadian Transit Association, Juri Pill of the Toronto Transit Commission, Gordon Arblaster of the London Transit Commission, and Gerry McMillan of the Ontario Ministry of Transportation and Communications. At the same time, I have concluded that the public would benefit from publication by the Ministry of Transportation and Communications of much more complete data on the province's transit subsidy programs, since much information about what is done with the tax-payers' dollars is not readily available.

I have also received valuable comments from the participants in two seminars held at the Ontario Economic Council and from Richard Arnott, Donald Dewees, George Fallis, David Gillen, Stephen Glaister, Herbert Mohring, Richard Puccini, and Enid Slack. Of course it should not be assumed that any of these people agree with my analysis or conclusions.

This study deals almost exclusively with urban transportation pricing and subsidy policies. Readers who are also interested in other urban transportation issues, such as modal choice behaviour, regulatory policies, and evaluation of investment decisions, may wish to read my textbook on *Urban Transportation Economics* (Toronto: Butterworths, 1979).

URBAN TRANSPORTATION FINANCING:
THEORY AND POLICY IN ONTARIO

1
Introduction

OVERVIEW

This economic analysis of urban transportation financing in Ontario has a double purpose. First, since few of the urban transportation policy-makers in Ontario are trained in economics, it tries to demonstrate the importance and usefulness of evaluating the economic merits of policy alternatives. Second, it attempts to determine whether existing policies waste resources or lead to undesirable transfers of income between different groups of people. When existing policies are found to be deficient, it suggests improvements in the ways people are charged for the use of roads and public transit and in the ways governments subsidize transit.

Resources are being wasted, for example, because use of urban roads is substantially underpriced during periods of peak demand. Furthermore, while there are sound economic justifications for substantial public transit subsidies, the allocation of subsidies by the Ontario provincial government on the basis of capital expenditures can be expected to waste resources. It is also concluded that maximization of ridership is not an appropriate objective for public transit systems because it is likely to lead to fare and service policies which waste resources.

On a number of other questions the information available was not sufficient to evaluate policy. For example, there was not enough evidence to determine whether the recent introduction of monthly transit passes in a number of urban areas in Ontario has wasted resources or not. Similarly, the merits of introducing in Ontario automated transit fare collection or honour fare systems of the type used in some West European cities could not be assessed. Nevertheless, the criteria of resource waste in these cases have been explained in light of the type of economic analysis needed in the future formulation of transportation policy.

OUTLINE OF THE STUDY

This study provides an economic analysis of the major issues involved in three areas of urban transportation financing policy: road pricing, transit fares, and transit subsidies. Rather than devoting equal resources to original research on each of the three topics, it was decided to concentrate on evaluation of transit subsidy programs and, secondarily, on transit fare policies. Extensive research has already been done on the economics of road pricing, while the literature on transit subsidies is quite meagre, and significant gaps exist in the literature on transit fare policies (such as on fare collection costs and monthly passes). Road pricing thus occupies only a single chapter (Chapter 2), whereas transit fare policies occupy two (Chapters 3 and 4), and transit subsidy policies occupy six (Chapters 5 to 10).

The reader must first be aware of the existing underpricing of road use in order to understand the issues involved in transit financing. The analysis of transit fares then makes the point that economically efficient transit fares will not raise enough revenue to finance an efficient level of transit services. This leads finally to the discussion of transit subsidies, which bridge the gap between transit revenues and costs.

Chapter 2 summarizes what economists have written about road user charges, including pollution and congestion charges. The discussion of this important topic has been deliberately kept brief because comprehensive road pricing was felt unlikely to win political acceptance in any urban area in Ontario in the foreseeable future regardless of its economic merits. Nevertheless, this question has important implications for a number of other policy issues such as the pricing of parking, gasoline, and public transit.

Chapters 3 and 4 provide an economic analysis of urban transit fare policies. Chapter 3 deals with the following topics: (i) efficient fare policies based on marginal social cost pricing principles, including peak / off-peak fare differentials, fares based on distance, and charging for transfers; (ii) fare policies which are efficient when the use of automobiles is priced below marginal social cost; (iii) fare policies which are efficient when the transit system is subject to a deficit constraint; (iv) the welfare gain from efficient fare policies; and (v) the economic costs of alternative methods of fare collection. Chapter 4 then deals with (vi) monthly transit passes; (vii) income distributional effects of transit fare alternatives; and (viii) a comparison of ridership maximization and economic efficiency as objectives for urban transit systems.

The remainder of the monograph is devoted to an economic analysis of urban transit subsidies. Chapter 5 explains and evaluates four arguments for subsidizing public transit in order to increase the efficiency of resource allocation, on the grounds that marginal cost is below average cost for public transit because of increasing returns to scale; private automobile trips are priced below their marginal social cost; there are external benefits associated with the form of urban development promoted by the existence of high-quality, low-fare public transit; and the knowledge gained from research and demonstration projects in urban public transit is a public good which benefits many urban areas. We also examine the justification for transit subsidies based on income distributional effects, how the level of subsidies should vary among cities of different sizes, and how the burden of subsidies should be allocated between local, provincial, and federal governments.

Chapter 6 describes the various federal, provincial, and municipal transit subsidy programs which have operated in Ontario during the past two decades, including capital and operating subsidies for subway, streetcar, and bus systems, the GO Transit commuter rail / bus system, and demonstration projects such as dial-a-bus. The chapter also includes a brief summary of subsidies available in other provinces and elsewhere.

Chapters 7 to 10 evaluate the effects of transit subsidies in Ontario on resource allocation and income distribution.

Chapter 7 surveys the many different consequences of transit subsidies, from the effects on fares and services, through the effects on capital intensity, labour contracts, and technical efficiency, to the effects on income distribution. It also looks at how provincial subsidy policies influence municipal government subsidies.

Chapters 8 to 10 focus on the effects of subsidies on fares, service, and ridership. Chapter 8 analyses the results of alternative transit subsidy formulas by means of an explicit theoretical model of a transit system under alternative assumptions about the objectives of the transit firm.

By contrast to the analysis in Chapter 8, which is entirely theoretical, Chapters 9 and 10 are empirical studies of the effects of transit subsidies on fares, service, and ridership using two different sets of data. Chapter 9 uses data from nine urban areas in Ontario for 1950-78 to make a graphical analysis of the effects of subsidies. Chapter 10 uses data from London, Ontario, to make a statistical analysis with an explicit econometric model.

Chapter 11 presents the conclusions of the study and recommendations for urban transportation pricing and subsidy policies in Ontario.

2
Road pricing policies

Although a system of comprehensive road pricing in which road users are charged for the congestion and pollution costs imposed by their trips is unlikely to be established in the near future in any urban area in Ontario, there are two reasons that anyone interested in urban transportation problems should be familiar with the question. First, some simple measures to charge for the use of roads through parking or gasoline taxes might become feasible, particularly if more people understand their justification. Second, an understanding of the optimal road user charges allows one to appreciate the consequences of *not* collecting such charges. One cannot analyse urban transit fare policies or evaluate the case for urban transit subsidies without understanding the complications that arise because of the failure to charge for road use on the basis of marginal social cost.

EFFICIENT URBAN ROAD USER CHARGES[1]

If the government wishes to achieve an efficient allocation of resources (including efficient use of existing urban roads and urban land), road user charges should be set so that road users pay the marginal social costs of their trips. The marginal social cost of a trip is the value of the other goods and services (including leisure) that are given up by all members of society because that trip is produced.[2] If road users pay the marginal social costs of their trips, they will take

1 For a more detailed discussion of this topic, see Frankena (1979, chap. 4).
2 The marginal social cost of a trip on an existing urban road normally consists of the travel time and the vehicle operating costs of the person making the trip, the congestion and pollution costs imposed on others, and the wear and tear of the road.
    The analysis of the efficiency of marginal social cost pricing for road use applied in this chapter rests on three assumptions. First, collection of road user charges is costless.

only those trips for which their willingness to pay is at least as much as the amount that all affected parties would be willing to accept as compensation for giving up all the goods and services forgone when scarce resources are allocated to the production of road trips. In this case, the allocation of resources will be efficient. By contrast, if road users pay less than the marginal social costs of their trips, they will take some trips which they value at less than the marginal social cost. In this case, the allocation of resources will be inefficient.

The marginal *social* cost of an extra road vehicle trip on an existing road consists of five elements: (i) the value of the travel time of the people in the vehicle making the extra trip; (ii) the operating costs of the vehicle making the extra trip; (iii) the marginal *congestion* costs imposed on other road users because the extra vehicle trip increases the density of traffic on the road and hence increases travel times, vehicle operating costs, and the risk of accidents for other road users due to congestion; (iv) the marginal *pollution* costs imposed on others because the extra vehicle trip increases air and noise pollution damage; and (v) the marginal *road maintenance* costs imposed on the government because the extra vehicle trip increases wear and tear of the road and increases requirements for road administration, police, and court services.

In the absence of road user charges, the marginal *private* cost of using an urban road includes only the first two of the preceding five elements.[3] Consequently, the marginal private cost of vehicle trips would be less than the marginal

---

Second, there are no distortions in related sectors of the economy which interfere with the efficient allocation of resources, e.g. other goods and services such as urban transit rides are priced at marginal social cost. Third, there are no costs involved in raising revenues to finance the road system in the event that the revenues from road user charges are not adequate for this purpose.

3 The marginal *private* cost of a trip is the cost of the trip which is actually borne by the person who takes the trip. In the absence of road user charges, the person who takes a trip bears the cost of his own travel time and vehicle operating expenses but does not bear the congestion and pollution damage or the maintenance costs imposed on others by the trip. The congestion and pollution damage and the maintenance costs are the marginal *external* costs of a trip. The marginal private cost and the marginal external costs add up to the marginal social cost of a trip.

There are two reasons that the marginal private costs of vehicle operation may understate the corresponding category of marginal social costs. First, automobile insurance premiums in Ontario typically do not depend on current automobile use, except to the extent that they depend on whether an automobile is used in an urban area, whether it is used for work trips, and whether it is driven more than 10000 miles per year. Second, in recent years gasoline has been priced below its marginal social cost as a result of federal government policy.

social cost in circumstances in which an additional vehicle trip increases congestion, pollution damage, or wear and tear of roads. As a result, some people would take road trips which they value at less than the marginal social cost, and road use would be inefficiently high. In addition, the level of pollution damage per vehicle trip would be inefficiently high.[4]

In these circumstances the government could reduce road use to an efficient level, and also reduce the level of pollution per vehicle trip to an efficient level, by imposing appropriate road use and pollution charges. These charges per vehicle trip would be equal to the sum of the three marginal external costs imposed by an extra vehicle trip, that is, the marginal congestion costs, the marginal pollution costs, and the marginal road maintenance costs. Imposition of these user charges would raise the marginal private cost per vehicle trip to the level of the marginal social cost.

The manner in which these charges might be applied will be discussed further below. But first we will consider how they are calculated.

MODEL OF ROAD CONGESTION CHARGES

For the sake of simplicity, we will assume in this example that road users do not impose pollution damage or wear and tear on the road. Because of this assumption, the only marginal external cost of road vehicle trips is the marginal congestion cost imposed on other road users.

Suppose that the relationship between the marginal private cost (including time and vehicle operating costs) of travel per vehicle mile and the number of vehicle trips per hour on an existing road is given by the curve labelled MPC in Figure 1.[5] In this case there is no congestion, and hence MPC is horizontal, as long as the number of vehicle trips per hour is less than OA, but congestion begins, and hence MPC slopes up, when the number of vehicle trips exceeds OA. Since there is no congestion if the number of vehicle trips per hour is less than OA, in this range an extra vehicle trip does not impose any marginal congestion costs on other road users. Consequently, the marginal social cost (MSC) per vehicle mile is identical to the marginal private cost, i.e. the MSC and MPC curves coincide.

However, when the number of vehicle trips per hour exceeds OA, an extra vehicle trip imposes marginal congestion costs on other road users. Consequently, the MSC curve lies above the MPC curve. The vertical distance between

4 Unless emissions were restricted to the efficient level by regulatory policies.
5 It is implicit in this relationship that all vehicles have the same value of travel time per hour. Appendix A deals with a model in which there are two income groups with different values of travel time.

Figure 1
Model of a congested road

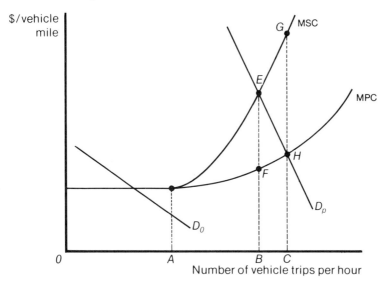

the MSC and MPC curves at each level of vehicle flow measures the marginal congestion costs per vehicle mile imposed on all other road users combined by an extra vehicle trip. The distance between the MSC and MPC curves increases as the number of vehicle trips per hour increases, reflecting the fact that as the road becomes more congested the marginal congestion cost imposed by an extra vehicle trip increases. Figure 1 makes it clear that at any level of road use the marginal social cost per vehicle-mile of an extra vehicle trip consists of the marginal private cost per vehicle mile borne by the vehicle that makes the trip plus the marginal congestion cost imposed on other road users.

We can now use Figure 1 to demonstrate the nature of the inefficiency which will result if the government does not charge for the use of congested roads. Suppose that during periods of peak demand the demand curve for vehicle trips per hour is represented by D_p in Figure 1. The equilibrium number of vehicle trips would be OC, where D_p and MPC intersect. This is an equilibrium because at the trip level OC the marginal private cost per vehicle mile is equal to the price per vehicle mile at which people would take OC trips.

The level of road use at OC is inefficient, because a number of people would be taking trips they value at less than marginal social cost. For example, when OC trips are being taken, one of the road users values a trip at only CH dollars per vehicle mile, but the marginal social cost of the last trip produced would be CG dollars per vehicle mile. Thus, production of the trip for the person who values it at only CH dollars per vehicle mile involves a net waste of resources of HG dollars per vehicle mile.

In fact, the efficient number of vehicle trips would be OB, where D_p and MSC intersect. When OB trips are being produced and are taken by the people who are willing to pay the most for them, only those people who are willing to pay the marginal social cost of an extra vehicle trip (BE dollars per vehicle mile) would be taking trips.

The dollar value of the gain in efficiency from restricting the number of trips per hour from OC to OB would be the area of the triangle EGH.[6] The area EGH is equal to the marginal social cost of increasing the number of vehicle trips per hour from OB to OC minus what people would be willing to pay for the BC extra trips.

The underlying source of the inefficiency in road use is that in deciding whether to use the road people ignore the marginal congestion costs imposed on others. They compare the value of trips to the cost they bear personally rather than to the marginal social cost.

One way to achieve efficient use of the road would be for the government to impose on all vehicles a congestion charge per vehicle mile equal to the marginal congestion cost, i.e. the vertical distance between MSC and MPC, at the level of road use where D_p and MSC intersect. In the present example, the charge would be EF dollars per vehicle mile.

The preceding analysis applies to hours of the day during which there is congestion. Now consider a time, such as the middle of the night, when the demand for trips is so low that the number of vehicle trips per hour is less than OA and there is no congestion. Suppose that during such periods the demand is represented by the curve labelled D_o in Figure 1. Since the MSC and MPC curves coincide for low numbers of vehicle trips per hour, the equilibrium number of trips that will be taken (which is determined where D_o and MPC intersect) and the efficient number of trips (where D_o and MSC intersect) are the same. Consequently, if it wishes to achieve an efficient allocation of resources, the government should not impose any road user congestion charge during hours when there is no congestion.

It can be concluded that in this model the charge the government would have to collect in order to achieve efficient use of roads varies with the extent of congestion. It would be relatively high on downtown streets and in the direction

---

6 This assumes that trips are taken by the people who are willing to pay the most for them and is only an approximation since we should be using an income-compensated demand curve.

of peak flow on urban arterial roads during rush hour, and it would be low or zero on suburban residential streets, on rural roads, and during non-rush hours generally.[7]

ESTIMATES OF EFFICIENT URBAN ROAD USER CHARGES

Congestion charges
Dewees provides estimates of the marginal congestion costs imposed by an additional morning rush-hour automobile trip in each direction on a number of different roads in an area about seven miles from downtown Toronto. The estimates take the existing transportation system as given and consider time costs alone. The marginal congestion costs range from zero to over one dollar per vehicle mile. On average, the marginal congestion costs were 25 cents per vehicle mile for all automobiles combined, 38 cents per vehicle mile for inbound automobiles, and 4 cents per vehicle mile for outbound automobiles.[8] Dewees also estimates that at mid-day the marginal congestion costs averaged 1.4 cents per vehicle mile for inbound automobiles (Dewees 1978).

The preceding figures exceed the efficient congestion charges relevant to time costs alone for the existing transportation facilities in Toronto. This is because the marginal congestion costs calculated by Dewees during peak periods correspond to the distance HG (i.e. the marginal congestion costs that would be observed in the absence of congestion tolls) rather than the distance FE (i.e. the marginal congestion costs that would be observed if efficient congestion tolls were imposed) in Figure 1.[9]

In a study for expressways in a large U.S. urban area, Keeler and Small (1977) find that, if the level of investment in expressways were efficient, then considering only time costs the efficient congestion charge for private automobiles would be about 0.1 to 0.2 cents per vehicle mile on all expressways at night; 0.3 to 1.2 cents on all expressways between 9 a.m. and 4 p.m.; 2 to 9 cents on rural and suburban expressways in the peak direction at rush hour; and 6 to 34 cents on central city expressways in the peak direction at rush hour.[10]

---

7 These comments are based on a simple model of road congestion in which there is assumed to be no pollution damage and no wear and tear of roads. In the real world it would sometimes be efficient for the government to impose pollution charges and road maintenance charges on road users even when there is no congestion.
8 Dewees (1979). The value of travel time is assumed to be $3.75 per vehicle-hour.
9 However, the calculations assume no rain or snow, no accidents, and no road repairs, so that they tend to understate average congestion costs.
10 Keeler and Small (1977). The value of travel time is assumed to be between $2.25 and $4.50 per vehicle-hour. Road construction costs are in 1972 dollars.

In a similar study, Kraus, Mohring, and Pinfold (1976) calculate that the efficient congestion charge on private automobiles would be 0.2 to 0.5 cents and 1 to 3 cents per vehicle mile for daytime non-peak and peak hours respectively on rural expressways; 0.5 to 1.5 cents and 3 to 9 cents for non-peak and peak hours respectively on typical medium-cost urban expressways; and 1 to 3 cents and 5 to 15 cents for non-peak and peak hours respectively on high-cost urban expressways adjacent to the central business district (CBD).[11]

Pollution charges
Motor vehicles emit pollutants, chiefly hydrocarbons, carbon monoxide, and nitrogen oxides, which are both irritating and damaging to health and property. Small (1977) estimates that on average air pollution costs would be at least 0.4 cents per vehicle mile in U.S. urban areas for a car without emission controls. This is a lower-bound estimate because it assumes that the cost of illness and death is equal to direct medical expenditures plus forgone earnings, and because it does not include a number of forms of damage, such as the effects of lead emissions, discomfort, and household cleaning costs. Also, this is an average cost; according to Small, 'it is certainly plausible to argue, for example, that damage of at least several cents per mile is caused in high-density central business districts by automobiles in slow-moving congested traffic.' In another study, Dewees (1974) suggests a figure of about 1 cent per mile as the average air pollution cost in urban areas for a car without emission controls. Zerbe and Croke (1975) estimate that in Chicago the average air pollution cost imposed by cars (some of which had pollution control devices) was less than 1 cent per vehicle mile. The pollution damage figures in these three studies are in current dollars from the mid-1970s.

Since pollution damage is one of the marginal social costs of automobile travel, charging road users for their pollution damage would lead to a more efficient allocation of resources. However, even if Dewees's estimate of pollution damage is correct, it would not be efficient simply to charge passenger cars an air pollution tax of 1 cent per mile. Such a policy would not give motorists an incentive to reduce the amount of pollution per mile, for example by installing and maintaining emission-control devices or by having regular tune-ups. An efficient pollution charge would be related to the level of effluent damage per mile, or at least to the type of pollution-control device installed, as well as to the mileage driven. This would give drivers an incentive to select a level of emission that would minimize the social cost of pollution per mile driven (including not

11 Kraus, Mohring, and Pinfold (1976). The value of travel time is assumed to be between $1.50 and $6.00 per vehicle-hour.

only pollution damage but also the costs of installing and maintaining emission-control devices and increased fuel consumption) as well as to drive an efficient number of miles.

Assuming, hypothetically, that a typical automobile without emission controls would cause air pollution damage of 1 cent per vehicle mile and that it would be efficient to reduce air pollution to 20 per cent of the uncontrolled level, the efficient air pollution charge would amount to 0.2 cents per mile for passenger cars. Of course, the charge per mile might amount to several times this in circumstances where marginal pollution costs would be unusually high.

The preceding discussion has ignored the fact that the Canadian government has imposed emission-control standards on new automobiles for the past decade. These standards require that new automobiles emit not more than 19, 30, and 76 per cent respectively of the uncontrolled levels of hydrocarbons, carbon monoxide, and nitrogen oxides respectively. While emission control standards might in principle be used to achieve an efficient reduction in the level of pollution per vehicle mile, they do not provide an incentive to reduce the number of miles driven to the efficient level because they do not make automobile users pay for the pollution damage they cause. Thus, even if the most efficient possible emission controls were in effect, there would still be an efficiency argument for charging road users for the marginal pollution costs of their trips. Moreover, in practice, emission control standards deviate considerably from the controls that would be necessary to achieve an efficient reduction in the level of pollution per vehicle mile. This is because existing emission control standards apply only to new cars and have only a limited effect on emissions from older cars. Consequently, the efficiency argument for imposing pollution charges is important despite existing emission control standards. On the other hand if road users were charged for their marginal pollution costs, emission control standards would be redundant.

So far we have considered only air pollution. Noise pollution provides an additional basis for pollution charges imposed on road vehicles.[12]

Road maintenance charges
In a study using 1968 prices for Ontario, Haritos (1973, 111) estimated that marginal road maintenance costs for passenger cars amounted to 0.2 to 0.6 cents

12 Keeler and Small (1975, 54) suggest a figure (in 1972 prices) of 0.1 cents per vehicle mile for noise pollution, in addition to a figure of 0.5 cents per vehicle mile for air pollution. Straszheim (1979) uses a figure of 0.57 cents per vehicle mile as an estimate of what he calls right-of-way externalities of road use, including noise, smell, and aesthetic effects. This is in addition to 0.5 cents per vehicle mile for air pollution externalities.

per vehicle mile. The most important cost elements related to pavement maintenance, snow ploughing, sanding, and salting.

In a study using 1972 prices for California, Keeler and Small (1977, 10)
estimated that marginal road maintenance costs related to such things as pavement maintenance were 0.05 cents per vehicle mile. At least part of the discre-
pancy between the estimates by Haritos and those by Keeler and Small may be
explained by the fact that winters are milder in California than in Ontario.

Keeler, Cluff, and Small (1974, 25) estimated that the *average* cost per vehicle
mile for local government services, including highway administration, police,
and courts, was 0.45 cents. This leaves open the question of how much these
costs would be increased by an additional vehicle mile.

Based on these studies, it appears that during the early 1970s a reasonable
figure for marginal road maintenance costs, including both wear and tear and
government services related to road use, would have been about 0.5 cents per
vehicle mile.

Summary
The preceding survey of efficient urban congestion, pollution, and road maintenance charges indicates that these charges would be highly variable, depending particularly on the extent of congestion and pollution. Available studies
suggest that during the mid-1970s marginal social cost pricing of urban road
use by private automobiles would have involved a variable charge of 0 to 35
cents per vehicle mile for congestion, a variable charge for air pollution which
would probably have averaged around 0.5 cents per vehicle mile, and a
charge of around 0.5 cents per vehicle mile for road maintenance. Because of
inflation since the mid-1970s, the charges which would be required to achieve an
efficient allocation of resources in the early 1980s would be about double
these charges.

Consider a family which drives 2500 miles a year in urban areas under
congested conditions and 3500 miles a year in urban areas under uncongested
conditions. Suppose that the efficient congestion charge is $0.15 per mile under
congested conditions and zero otherwise, and that efficient pollution and road
maintenance charges combined average $0.015 per mile. This family would pay
$465 a year for urban road use with efficient user charges, compared to the $150
or so they would pay with existing provincial motor fuel taxes and registration
fees. In short, the dollar magnitudes involved in moving to efficient urban road
pricing would be far from trivial for urban families. (Of course, increased
government revenues would also be far from trivial, and the government would
be able to cut taxes on incomes, retail sales, property, etc.)

COLLECTION OF URBAN ROAD USER CHARGES

Many ways have been proposed in which the government could collect road user charges that would approximate the efficient charges described above. The basic problems are that the efficient congestion charge per vehicle mile varies with the extent of congestion, and the efficient pollution charge per vehicle mile varies with the level of emissions from the vehicle as well as with the severity of pollution problems. Alternative methods of collecting road user charges are discussed below.

Registration, gasoline, and mileage taxes
Taxes based on such things as automobile purchase and registration, drivers' licences, total vehicle mileage, and consumption of fuel and tires are at best crude approximations of efficient road user charges because the amount of tax paid would not depend in any direct way on the amount of congestion and pollution costs imposed on others.

In spite of this, in the absence of other forms of road pricing, a case might be made on efficiency grounds for charging higher automobile registration fees and fuel taxes in larger urban areas than in other parts of the province, or perhaps for charging a tax based on total vehicle mileage for vehicles registered in larger urban areas.

In addition, a reasonable way to collect the pollution charge would probably be to base it on total vehicle mileage, place of registration, and either actual emission per vehicle mile for the particular vehicle (which would have to be measured periodically) or average emission per vehicle mile for the type of vehicle. Also, a tax based on vehicle mileage and weight would probably be a reasonable way to collect the road maintenance charge.

Toll booths
Manual toll collection at conventional toll booths offers a practical way of collecting user charges in the case of limited-access expressways and major tunnels and bridges, but it would not be an efficient way of collecting general road user charges in the typical urban area. The land, capital, and labour costs of the toll booths themselves would be high; the toll booths would be unsightly; and payment of tolls would involve a significant cost in terms of increased travel time, vehicle operating expenses, and pollution damage because of the delays imposed on road users.

On-vehicle meters and automatic vehicle identification

A number of proposals have been made for use of special meters or electronic equipment to record the mileage each vehicle travels on congested roads. Walters (1961) has suggested that vehicles be equipped with meters, similar to those used by taxis, which would record mileage when the 'flag' is up. Street signs would indicate when the flag should be put up, and fines would be imposed on vehicles that failed to do so. Vickrey (1963) has suggested that vehicles be equipped with electronic identifiers. Roadside scanning devices would measure the mileage of each vehicle in congested zones as well as the extent of congestion. In either case, billing could be handled by mail on a monthly basis.

While experts have argued that there is no fundamental technological barrier to implementing a road pricing scheme using electronic identifiers, the technology in question has not yet been tested in the field. Moreover, there remain numerous questions concerning costs and very serious objections to the threat to privacy posed by electronic surveillance of travel, which could be used for purposes other than charging for road use.

Supplementary licences

At present the most popular proposal for collecting road congestion charges would require vehicles travelling in the downtown area during congested periods to display on their windshields a special supplementary licence sold by the city government.

A version of this scheme has been in operation since 1975 in Singapore, which is the only city in the world which has ever collected the type of road user charges discussed in this chapter (see Watson and Holland 1978). A recent plan for road pricing in London, England, was also based on a version of this scheme, but that plan has now been shelved (May 1978). Finally, the Urban Institute in Washington D.C. and the U.S. Urban Mass Transportation Administration have developed proposals for a road pricing demonstration project based on windshield stickers, but so far they have been unable to find any urban area in the United States willing to undertake a demonstration project even though federal subsidies are available (see Bhatt 1974; Bhatt, Eigen, and Higgins 1976).

In the Singapore case, daily licences to enter the two-square-mile downtown area in the morning rush period were sold for about $1.50 in 1975. In London, England, daily licences required in the ten-square-mile central area from 8 a.m. to 6 p.m. would have been sold for about $2.50. Finally, the Urban Institute proposals generally assume that daily licences would be priced around $1.15 in medium-sized cities such as Berkeley, California (population 116 000), or Madison, Wisconsin (population 200 000).

The principal shortcoming of supplementary licences is that the charge does not vary with the number of vehicle miles of travel in congested areas once the licence has been purchased.

Parking surcharges
Another way of collecting road user charges is to impose a surcharge on parking. Before considering this possibility, however, we will discuss how parking should be priced if one wishes to achieve an efficient allocation of resources and if use of roads is already priced at marginal social cost by one of the technologies described above.

Marginal social cost pricing of parking
In the case of automobiles, transport facilities include not only road rights-of-way but also parking space. Widespread provision of parking space below marginal social cost in congested areas contributes to excessive use of parking spaces and congested roads.

Municipal governments frequently permit curbside parking at a low or zero price and subsidize publicly owned lots, sometimes from revenues raised by special local improvement taxes levied on nearby businesses. Municipal governments also use zoning bylaws to force the owners of commercial and other buildings to provide more parking spaces than they would choose. This raises the supply of parking spaces and hence reduces their monthly rent. Firms, governments, and universities often supply free or subsidized parking to employees and customers. This practice is encouraged by provincial and federal tax laws, which enable firms to deduct from their taxable income the cost of parking spaces provided to employees and do not require employees to pay income tax on this fringe benefit.[13]

The significance of free parking is suggested by several studies. A 1967 survey found that 48 per cent of a sample of 132 people who commuted to central Toronto by automobile were provided with free parking by their employers (Recon Research Consultants 1968, 80). A 1972 survey found that 40 per cent of peak hour commuters who drove to work in Vancouver parked free (Brown 1972). A 1974 study found that 29 per cent and 3 per cent of commuters who drove to work in central Ottawa received free and subsidized parking respectively from their employers. The same study found that 46 per cent of all cars

---

13 City of Toronto, Department of Public Works (1973, 12) and Segelhorst and Kirkus (1973).

parked in downtown Ottawa (a one-square-mile area) parked free (Wilbur Smith and Associates 1975, 27, 89). However, a large share of these drivers worked for the federal government, which adopted a policy of providing fewer parking spaces and charging for parking in 1975.

If one wishes to increase the efficiency of use of roads and of the resources allocated to parking facilities, government policies which lead to overinvestment in parking facilities should be ended and fees for the use of parking spaces should be set to reflect the marginal social cost of those spaces. Among other things, this means governments should eliminate the existing tax incentive to provide free employee parking by including the value of parking provided by employers in taxable income.

The marginal social cost of using an existing parking space takes the form of additional congestion. When a parking space is occupied and the number of vacant parking spaces decreases, motorists are forced to search longer for spaces and to park farther from their destinations. Moreover, when a car parks along a curb, it imposes delays on road users generally by removing road space and by holding up traffic while entering and leaving the parking space. The fee for use of a parking space should equal this marginal social cost if one wishes to achieve an efficient allocation of resources and if road use is already priced at marginal social cost.

Parking surcharges as road user charges

If road user charges are not collected by one of the other methods described above, one might attempt to collect them for the use of congested roads at the same time as parking fees. In congested areas of the city, the charge for parking could consist of two parts: a basic parking charge equal to the marginal social cost of using a parking space and a road congestion charge equal to the marginal congestion costs imposed on other road users by a vehicle on its way to and from the place it parked. This policy could be implemented by imposing an excise tax equal to the road congestion charge on the use of spaces in privately owned parking lots and by fixing appropriate fee schedules for use of publicly owned parking spaces. For example, the daily parking fee for the public in the garage under Toronto's City Hall is $1.50 higher if a vehicle enters between 8:15 and 9:15 a.m. or leaves between 4:30 and 5:30 p.m. In 1970, San Francisco imposed a 25 per cent tax on parking throughout the city (reduced to 10 per cent in 1972). Alternatively, it has been proposed in Toronto that the Metropolitan Council be empowered to regulate the rates of public and private off-street parking facilities. (Ontario Royal Commission on Metropolitan Toronto 1977, 248).

Apart from the case of Toronto's City Hall, parking charges in urban areas in Ontario do not vary with the time of day, with two general exceptions: lower or zero charges for parking after 6 p.m. and prohibitions on parking or higher fines for parking violations in some areas during rush hours.

An important limitation on using parking surcharges as a means of collecting road congestion tolls in the downtown area is that a substantial share of the vehicles entering the downtown of the typical urban area now pass through without parking. According to Kulash (1974d), if the downtown area is defined to include about one square mile, about 15 to 30 per cent of the cars entering the area do not park. If the downtown is defined more narrowly to include about one-quarter square mile, about 40 to 60 per cent of the cars entering the area do not park.

A second limitation arises because cars parked in the downtown area travel different distances on congested roads coming downtown. Unless the portion of the parking fee reflecting the road congestion charge is related to trip length (say by a system of vehicle stickers indicated the distance of the driver's residence from the central business district), parking fees would be either too high for short trips or too low for lone ones. Another limitation, suggested by Gillen (1977b), is that an increase in core area parking fees due to imposition of a road congestion charge might simply induce people to park outside that area rather than to reduce their use of congested arterial roads by switching to public transit or by travelling at a less congested time of day.

Costs of alternative road pricing technologies
An Urban Institute study of Bhatt et al. (1976) compares costs and other characteristics for a hypothetical application of road pricing using four alternative technologies (Table 1). The calculations assume that charges of approximately $0.50 per vehicle mile will be imposed on morning and evening peak trips in a four-square-mile central area, that the average vehicle trip in the priced area is one mile long, and that 200,000 vehicle round trips are made daily in peak periods.

It should be noted that the costs in the table do not include time costs imposed on road users by the road pricing scheme, i.e. time spent paying tolls, purchasing licences, etc. If these costs were included, both toll booths and supplementary licences would presumably have significantly higher costs.

An important reason that most proposals for road pricing now involve supplementary licences is that the initial investment cost for a supplementary licensing scheme is very low. The major cost of the scheme is not equipment but the wages of enforcement personnel. This makes supplementary licensing most suitable for demonstration projects that may be abandoned. Also, unlike on-vehicle meters and automatic vehicle identification, supplementary licensing can be applied easily to out-of-area users and does not pose a threat to individual privacy.

TABLE 1

Comparison of road pricing technologies for a hypothetical application

	Toll booths	On-vehicle meters	Automatic vehicle identification	Supplementary licences
Potential for fraud and theft	Low	High	Low	High
Difficulty for occasional and out-of-town users	None	Great	Great	Little
Enforcement difficulty	Little	Some	Little	Some
Difficulty of application with complex charges varying by time-of-day and zones of operation	Some	Little	Little	Some
Other major problems	Waste of space and time	Distraction of drivers	Invasion of privacy	Counterfeiting
Total annual cost for permanent, long-run implementation	$1 800 000	$3 500 000	$3 000 000	$2 500 000
Initial investment cost	$70 000 000	$4 000 000	$8 000 000	$18 000

SOURCE: Bhatt, Eigen, and Higgins (1976, 14)

EFFECTS OF URBAN ROAD PRICING

Travel patterns, land use, and congestion levels
Introduction of substantial congestion charges would deter use of vehicles on congested roads. An increase in the money cost of travel on congested roads would encourage people, particularly low-income motorists, to advance or postpone vehicle trips to times when congestion and user charges would be lower, divert vehicle trips to less congested routes, combine vehicle trips by the formation of car pools, substitute public transit trips for trips by private automobile, choose residences and jobs which are closer together, and make fewer trips. Similarly, congestion charges would increase the incentive for firms to locate in less congested areas or to operate during off-peak hours in order to reduce transport costs for customers, employees, and freight.

Thus, introduction of congestion charges would lead to changes in travel and land use patterns which would reduce congestion in areas and at times where it is most severe. This would reduce the pressures to expand the capacity of urban roads to accommodate peak demands.

In Singapore, where daily licences to enter the downtown area in the morning rush period were sold for about $1.50, the number of automobiles entering the downtown area between 7:30 and 10:15 a.m. declined by 74 per cent, and the number of vehicles of all types entering the downtown area during the same period declined by 44 per cent. Four effects accounted about equally for the decline: people switched from cars to buses, formed car pools, drove to work before the peak period, and (in the case of cross-town commuters who previously travelled through the downtown area without stopping) by-passed the downtown area. The change in the distribution of traffic in Singapore apparently led to an increase in morning peak-hour speeds of 20 per cent in the central area and 10 per cent on inbound radial roads and a decrease in the morning peak-hour speed of about 20 per cent on the circumferential by-pass route.[14]

Gomez-Ibanez and Fauth (1980) estimated that in Boston, peak-period supplementary central area licences costing $0.50 to $2.00 a day would reduce peak-period automobile vehicle trips to or through the central area by 15 to 57 per cent, increase transit trips to the central area by 16 to 43 per cent, and increase traffic speeds in the central area by 23 to 173 per cent.

In London, England, it was estimated that a charge of $2.50 a day for a supplementary licence would reduce peak-hour automobile vehicle miles in the central area by 37 per cent and increase peak-hour speeds by 40 per cent (May 1978, 32).

---

14 Watson and Holland (1978). Part of these changes are attributable to a doubling of central area parking fees, higher taxes on vehicle ownership, and recession.

Using 1964 data for Toronto, Gillen (1977b) estimates that the elasticity of automobile use with respect to parking costs was -0.31 for people who drove to work in the downtown core. In a subsequent study using the same data base, Westin and Gillen (1978) estimate that a 34 per cent increase in the average parking fee would have induced roughly 17 per cent of the people who drove to work in the downtown core to switch to public transit or car pools. Using 1975 data for federal government employees in Ottawa, Gillen (1977a) estimates that a 1 per cent increase in parking fees would have led to a 0.23 per cent reduction in automobile use for the journey to work. A study for Ottawa found that during the year 1974-5, when the federal government raised the parking fee for employees from zero to $20 to $24 a month, there was a 21 per cent reduction in federal employees who drove automobiles alone to work (see Table 2), though at least one-third of this reduction appears to have been due to factors other than the increased parking fee, such as improved transit service.

Based on a review of the experience of several urban areas, Kulash (1974d) concludes that the price elasticity of demand for number of downtown parking spaces for work trips is about -0.3, assuming that parking fees are increased for a large area. He suggests that if a parking tax increased the parking fee from $2.30 to $4.60 per vehicle a day in a one-square-mile downtown area, there would be a reduction of about 20 per cent in the number of cars parked downtown by commuters and a somewhat higher percentage reduction in the number of cars parked downtown for non-work trips. However, the reductions in vehicular traffic downtown would be considerably less than 20 per cent for three reasons. First, the parking tax would not deter through trips by cars, taxis, and trucks that do not park, or trips by vehicles which park in a space which would not be taxed (e.g. a space owned by the vehicle owner). Second, some people who formerly parked downtown would be dropped off downtown by other family members who would then drive back again, so that their use of roads would actually increase. Finally, any initial reduction in vehicle flow brought about by parking taxes would induce additional untaxed trips in the downtown area, such as more through trips and taxi trips.

Shoup and Pickrell (1979) conclude on the basis of a review of the literature on parking charges that in large urban areas at least 20 per cent of people who drive alone to work and park free would join car pools or use public transit if they were charged the market price for parking. To appreciate the magnitude of this effect, suppose that at first 20 per cent of all peak-hour automobile vehicle trips are accounted for by people who drive alone to work and park free. If imposition of commercial parking charges induced 10 per cent of these people to travel by public transit, 5 per cent to ride in cars that were already on the road,

TABLE 2

Changes in travel modes used by Canadian government employees in Ottawa

	Percentage of commuters	
Mode	Before withdrawal of free parking	After withdrawal of free parking on 1 April 1975
Drive alone	34.9	27.5
Car pool	10.5	10.4
Transit	42.3	49.0
Other	12.3	13.1

NOTE: 'Other' includes bicycling, walking, and taking taxis.
SOURCE: Transport Canada (1978)

and 5 per cent to share rides with each other at the rate of two people per automobile, there ould be a reduction of 3.5 per cent in the number of peak hour hour automobile vehicle trips.

Pollution levels
The introduction of a pollution charge related to the amount of pollution damage would reduce the level of automotive air pollution even if the government was already applying new car emission standards. First, a pollution charge would provide an incentive to reduce emissions per mile from cars after they were sold, by maintaining pollution control equipment, by having more frequent tune-ups, and by scrapping older cars. Secondly, a pollution charge would provide an incentive to reduce the number of miles driven by both new and old cars.

Efficiency gains
The basic economic argument for road pricing is that appropriate user charges would lead to an increase in the efficiency of resource allocation. Unfortunately, little is known about the dollar value of these potential efficiency gains.

Gomez-Ibanez and Fauth (1980) use a model of travel behaviour in Boston to estimate the net social benefits that would result from three alternative peak-period central area auto restraint measures: supplementary central area licences costing $0.50 to $2.00 a day, central area parking surcharges of $0.50 to $2.00 a day, and an eight-block auto-free zone. They conclude that efficiently priced central area licences would yield net social benefits in terms of reduced transportation costs (through changes in modes and routes of travel, with an assumption that the amount and time of travel would not change) of $20.5 million annually in 1975 dollars, apart from benefits related to reduced pollution and energy consumption. The corresponding net social benefits for parking surcharges and an auto-free zone were estimated at $23.8 million and $1.4 million annually.

Three studies have estimated the gains from efficient road pricing using simple simulation models. Arnott and MacKinnon (1978) conclude that the social benefits from efficient congestion tolls arising from a movement of residences closer to central business district work-places would be small even in long-run equilibrium, about $9 per household a year. In a similar study, Segal and Steinmeier (1980) conclude that the social benefits from efficient congestion tolls would be $0, $7.7, and $25.7 per household a year in cities with populations of 1/2 million, 2 million, and 5 million respectively.

Mohring (1981) concludes that in a large urban area the social benefit from efficient congestion tolls arising from their effect on mode of travel would amount to about 67 cents a person mile for travel in the direction of peak flow at rush hour. This very large benefit occurs because the road is assumed to be severely congested in the absence of congestion tolls. Efficient congestion tolls amounting to 69 cents a vehicle mile increase the share of person trips taken by bus from 10 per cent to 74 per cent and greatly increase the speed of travel. Part of the large gain from road pricing arises because the road is assumed to be narrower than would be efficient. If the road were widened efficiently, the gain from road pricing would be smaller.

Of course in evaluating the gains from efficient congestion tolls it is important to compare efficient tolls with alternative urban transportation policies which might be used, and not simply with the situation in which use of roads is not priced. Failure to do this would lead one to overstate the case for marginal social cost pricing of roads.

For example, one alternative to efficient road pricing would be a gasoline tax. Small (1976, Chap. 8) estimates the magnitude of the benefits arising from changes in the choice of mode of travel and accruing to both road users and the government from pricing the use of an urban freeway at marginal social cost rather than charging a tax of $.10 per gallon (in 1972 U.S. dollars per U.S. gallon) for gasoline used on the freeway. Small estimates that efficient road user charges would be 10.4 and 23 cents per vehicle-mile under conditions of light and heavy congestion respectively and that these charges would lead to net social benefits of 5 to 6.5 cents and 12.3 to 15.7 cents per vehicle mile respectively.

Another alternative to efficient road pricing would be a *uniform* road user charge that would not vary with the extent of congestion. The most efficient level for the uniform charge would lie somewhere between the charges that would correspond to marginal social cost pricing in a situation of high congestion and in a situation of low or zero congestion (Mohring 1970). Kraus, Mohring, and Pinfold (1976) tentatively suggest that the gain for a system in which roads are priced on the basis of marginal social cost so that tolls vary with the extent of congestion, compared to a system in which road user charges are set at the most efficient possible uniform level per vehicle mile regardless of congestion, might not be great. The gain could be less than 1 per cent of the resource cost of motor vehicle travel, i.e. around $5 per capita a year for Canada as a whole. However, they also found that under some reasonable conditions the gain might be much greater than this.[15]

Yet another possible alternative to charging for road use on the basis of marginal social cost would be to give buses preferential access over private automobiles to the road system, e.g. by providing them with reserved lanes on streets, expressways, and expressway access ramps and by giving bus drivers control over traffic signals. In two different studies, Mohring (1979) and Small (1976) conclude that a substantial share of the gains related to the allocation of trips between automobiles and buses that would be achieved by moving from the present system of road pricing to marginal social cost pricing under congested conditions in a large urban area could also be achieved by providing reserved bus lanes. Specifically, using a model that assumes that transportation policies affect only modal choice, Mohring concluded that under congested conditions reserved bus lanes could produce at least 80 per cent of the gains that could be achieved by marginal social cost pricing of road use. On the other hand the average social cost per trip would still be 12 to 16 per cent higher with reserved bus lanes than with marginal social cost pricing, and hence it is not obvious that the advantage of marginal social cost pricing is trivial.

In his similar study Small concluded that under the conditions which would be most favourable to schemes involving reserved bus lanes, these schemes would achieve only about half of the benefits that would be achieved by marginal social cost pricing of road use. Thus, while Small estimated the net social benefits from marginal social cost pricing of road use at 5 to 6.5 cents and 12.3 to 15.7 cents per vehicle mile under conditions of light and heavy congestion respectively, he estimated that under the most favourable conditions the net social benefits from reserved bus lanes would be 2.8 to 3.4 cents and 7.6 to 9 cents per vehicle mile respectively. Moreover, these results apply to the gains that would result from changes in choice of mode for travel. One would not expect bus priority schemes to rank as high as marginal social cost pricing in terms of effects on other resource allocation decisions, such as frequency and time of travel.

15 This study does not measure the gain that would result from moving from the present system of road pricing to the most efficient uniform road user toll.

It should be emphasized that each of the studies referred to here deals with only some of the benefits that would be achieved by efficient congestion tolls. Arnott and MacKinnon (1978) and Segal and Steinmeier (1980) consider only benefits arising from a movement of residences closer to workplaces in the central business district, and Gomez-Ibanez and Fauth (1980) consider only benefits arising from changes in mode and route of travel. By contrast, Mohring (1979) and Small (1976) consider only benefits arising from changes in the choice of mode of travel. None of these studies considers benefits related to changes in the frequency or timing of trips, changes in the location of employment and other trip destinations, or imposition of pollution or road maintenance charges.

Moreover, none of the studies referred to here considers the costs of collecting road user charges. In fact, little is known about how the costs of collecting road user charges would compare with the efficiency gains that such charges would generate. While many economists have advocated adoption of some form of comprehensive road pricing based on marginal social costs, there are undoubtedly many others who believe that collection costs would often outweigh the efficiency gains that would result from changes in travel and land use patterns.

Revenue
Road user charges have been justified here exclusively as a rationing device to achieve an efficient allocation of resources. I have not suggested that users of transportation facilities should be taxed in order to pay for the fixed costs of existing facilities, or to finance additional facilities, or to raise revenue to compensate people who are adversely affected by the congestion of the facilities or by the pollution caused by use of these facilities.

Nevertheless, these user charges would raise a substantial amount of revenue. This, in turn, would permit the government to reduce other taxes, such as property or sales taxes. The reduction of these other taxes would entail an efficiency gain because it would reduce the gap between prices and marginal social costs elsewhere in the economy. This efficiency gain elsewhere in the economy is an additional benefit from road user charges over and above the efficiency gain directly related to road use. In fact, of course, the government might use the additional revenue to finance new programs or growth of the bureaucracy. If the expenditure represented an inefficient use of resources it would seriously undermine the efficiency argument for introducing road prices.

It is of some interest to consider how the revenues from efficient urban road charges would compare to the costs of providing urban roads.[16] If road vehicle

16 For a review of the literature on how the revenues from *existing* road user charges compare to the costs of providing roads, see Dewees, Hauer, and Saccomano (1979). Studies have concluded that for Ontario as a whole revenues from road user charges were

trips are the only services produced on urban roads, if the production of road vehicle trips is subject to constant returns to scale, and if the capacity of the road system is at the efficient level, then the revenues from efficient congestion and road maintenance charges imposed on road vehicle trips will be equal to the costs to the road authority of providing the road system.[17] The costs considered here are the long-run opportunity costs per unit time of the resources used by the road system. These costs will not be the same as the historical costs of the road system; inflation and unanticipated developments in the urban area may cause historical costs to bear little relation to the current opportunity costs of using land and other resources. Also, the opportunity costs per unit time of the road system have no necessary relation to the expenditure per unit time of the road authority, since the latter will depend largely on the rate at which the road system is being expanded. Consequently, under existing accounting procedures, equality of revenues and costs would not necessarily produce a balanced budget for the road authority.

There are at least five reasons that the revenues raised by the type of user charges discussed in this chapter might not in fact equal the costs of providing the road system. First, the revenues discussed above do not include the revenues from pollution charges. As long as the road authority does not compensate non-users for pollution damage caused by road users, the revenue from efficient pollution charges would accrue as a profit to the road authority.

Second, the equality of revenues and costs will not generally hold if the capacity of the road system is not efficient. Since there is no apparent reason to expect that the capacity of the existing road system is efficient, one would not expect the revenues from the congestion and road maintenance charges which would be efficient for the existing road system to equal the opportunity costs of the existing road system.

Third, the equality of revenues and costs holds if there are constant returns to scale. If there were increasing returns to scale, the costs would exceed the revenues in question. If there were decreasing returns to scale, the revenues would exceed the costs. The best study on returns to scale for urban automobile systems is by Keeler et al. (1975). This study found that automobile systems are subject to constant returns to scale for output levels in excess of 1000 passengers

---

considerably less than the costs of the roads in the early 1970s. Since then road costs have risen considerably more than motor fuel taxes.

17 For a proof of this point see Mohring (1976, chap 2 and 3) and Henderson (1977, 151). A production process is subject to *constant returns to scale* if a doubling of all inputs would lead to a doubling of output. A production process is subject to increasing (decreasing) returns to scale if a doubling of all inputs would lead to an increase in output of more (less) than 100 per cent.

an hour. This suggests that in the case of urban expressways and other roads used heavily by commuters, revenues from efficient congestion and road maintenance charges would equal the costs of the road system if the capacity of the road system was at the efficient level. There would seem to be an important exception to this however. Where a road passes through a built-up part of the city, expansion of the road would face sharply increasing costs because of the need to demolish buildings. This would have the same effect as decreasing returns to scale. One would therefore expect the revenues from efficient congestion and road maintenance charges to exceed opportunity costs for many heavily used roads in older built-up areas of cities even if the capacity of the roads was efficient, in view of the high opportunity costs of expansions. Also, the finding that there are constant returns to scale would not apply to lightly used local residential streets in urban areas. Some of the major design parameters of these streets are constrained by the fact that one must provide a minimum of two lanes for traffic. This would have the same effect as increasing returns to scale. Indeed, on many such streets there would not be congestion. Consequently, one would expect the revenues from efficient congestion and road maintenance charges on local residential streets to fall short of the costs to the road authority of providing the streets.

Fourth, the equality of revenues and costs will hold if road vehicle trips are the only services produced on urban roads. If there are other demands for urban road use which would increase the size of efficient urban roads, the revenues from road vehicle charges alone would not cover the opportunity costs of urban roads. For example, if the width of roads is increased in order to reduce interference between road vehicles and pedestrians or bicycles, one would not expect revenues from road use charges applied to motor vehicles to cover the opportunity costs of the roads.

Fifth, the equality of revenues and costs holds if collection of road user charges is costless. However, since collection of road user charges is not costless, the efficient road user charges in practice would not equal the marginal external costs imposed by an additional vehicle trip under all circumstances. For example, supplementary licences (windshield stickers) would apply a crude form of marginal social cost pricing to certain categories of trips, but other categories of trips would not be covered even though they would entail some congestion.

As examples of revenues from the sale of windshield stickers, the Urban Institute estimated that at a price of $1.15 a day windshield stickers would raise $22 million a year in Madison, Wisconsin (population 200,000) (Spielberg 1978, 42). In London, England, it was estimated that at a price of $2.50 a day windshield stickers would lead to net revenues of $138 million a year, considering revenue from sale of licences, increased public transit revenues, and reduced fuel tax revenues (May 1978, 34).

Distributional effects
Thus far, the imposition of road user charges has been justified on the ground that they would lead to a more efficient allocation of resources, i.e. their aggregate benefits would outweigh their aggregate costs for all members of society taken together.[18] This argument is important because it suggests that if imposition of marginal social cost pricing for road use was accompanied by a system of income redistribution to compensate those who would be made worse off by the road user charges, everyone could be made better off (however, see Boadway 1974). Such a compensation scheme would involve use of the revenues from road user charges, and possibly also the revenues from supplementary taxes imposed on people who would be made better off by the road user charges, for the benefit of people who would otherwise be made worse off.

However, this compensation argument has two shortcomings as a rationale for ignoring distributional effects in deciding on the desirability of road user charges: it ignores the fact that compensation policies would inevitably cause distortions in resource allocation, and the government might not actually implement compensation policies.

In analysing the distributional effects of road user charges, we will consider two different situations. At first we will assume that road user charges do not change rents, property values, or land use, so that the relevant effects of road user charges depend on changes in the costs and levels of travel. Later we will consider the implications of changes in residential rents, property values, and location patterns in response to road user charges.

No changes in rents, property values, or land use
Assuming that there are no changes in rents, property values, or land use, the imposition of road user charges would have four major effects on income distribution: the money cost per vehicle of using roads would increase; road traffic and the time cost of using roads would decrease; the environment would become less polluted; and the increase in revenue from road user charges would allow other taxes to be reduced.

Ignoring any reduction in other taxes for the moment, one can identify four groups that would gain from road user charges: Non-travellers would gain from the reduction in pollution. Pedestrians, assuming they were not required to pay congestion tolls, would gain from the reduction in pollution and the reduction in road traffic at pedestrian crossings. Even if buses were required to pay road user charges, for bus riders the loss due to higher fares would probably be out-

18 This assumes that the costs involved in collection of road user charges would not offset the net benefits resulting from more efficient road use, land use, etc.

weighed by the gain due to reduced travel time on less congested roads. Similarly, for high-income motorists, or at least for those who value their travel time very highly, the loss due to road user charges would be outweighed by the gain due to reduced travel time.

Still ignoring any reduction in other taxes made possible by the increase in revenue from road user charges, one important group however would probably be made worse off by road user charges: middle- and low-income motorists, for whom the value of the reduction in travel time would probably be less than the road user charge.[19] This point is discussed in more detail in Appendix A.

Kulash (1974b) has estimated the net effect on members of different income groups in three large U.S. urban areas of the increased money cost and the reduced time cost of trips to work for motorists and bus passengers. Kulash concluded that the net incidence of the user charges *per trip taken* would be regressive, i.e. ignoring benefits from the distribution of road user tax revenues the net burden of the tax per trip taken would be larger *as a percentage of income* for low-income people than for high-income people. However, at least part of this regressive effect per work trip taken would be offset by the fact that higher-income people take more work and non-work trips.[20]

Using a model that takes account only of changes in travel costs resulting from changes in the mode of travel, Small (1976, 236-7, 243) concludes that if one ignores the benefits from the disposition of road user tax revenues the imposition of marginal social cost pricing in lieu of a gasoline tax of $0.10 per gallon (in 1972 U.S. dollars per U.S. gallon) would actually make people with family incomes of over $20000 (1972 U.S. dollars) significantly better off while imposing a small loss on people with lower incomes.

Changes in residential land use
However, the imposition of road user charges would lead to changes in rents, property values, and land use. In particular, one would normally expect road user charges to lead households to choose residences closer to their jobs. Assuming that jobs are more centralized than residences, and assuming that road user charges do not lead to a change in the location of employment, this would lead to a smaller, more compact city in which rents and property values would probably be higher in central areas and lower in suburban areas than in the absence of road user charges.

19 Richardson (1974). However, in the case of bottleneck congestion, even low-income motorists might be made better off.
20 Kulash does not consider the effect of number of trips on the incidence of road user charges.

In this case road user charges would have three important effects on income distribution not considered above. People would reduce the number of miles they travel, and hence transportation expenditures, by moving closer to their jobs; people would reduce the amount of land they would use in response to the higher rents in more central locations; and some people would gain while others would lose from the changes in rents and property values.

Segal and Steinmeier (1980) use a simulation model which allows for changes in residential land use to analyse the net benefits of optimal road congestion charges for different income groups. They conclude that, if toll revenues were distributed in proportion to household income, all income groups would benefit from the optimal toll, except that in medium-size cities (population ½ million) low-income households would receive no net benefit and middle-income households would be made worse off. They also conclude that regardless of city size high-income households would benefit most both absolutely and as a percentage of income.

Further considerations
The various alternative road pricing technologies would have somewhat different distributional effects. In particular, the charge involved in supplementary licences is independent of mileage for a person who has purchased a licence, while the charge involved in various metering schemes is proportional to mileage. Since higher-income people tend to travel more miles than lower-income people, the supplementary licence scheme would probably be more regressive than a metering scheme.

Imposition of road user charges is sometimes opposed because of its adverse effect on middle- and low-income motorists. While this is a serious problem, one should remember that middle- and low-income people would receive a number of benefits from road user charges even if the government did not adopt a deliberate compensation scheme. In particular, middle- and low-income bus riders, pedestrians, and non-travellers would receive benefits. Also, regardless of how the government used the revenues from road user charges to reduce other taxes or provide additional services, middle- and low-income people would almost certainly get some of the benefits.

Downtown businesses
A principal source of opposition to urban road user charges is the possible adverse effect on downtown businesses if road user charges increase the costs of transportation for employees, customers, and freight deliveries. For example, Kulash (1974a, 21) reports that 'San Francisco had a parking tax of 25 per cent at one point and then lowered it to 10 per cent. The reaction of downtown

businessmen and professionals with offices there had simply been too strong for the local government to withstand.'

Congestion charges would in fact have an adverse effect on some centrally located businesses and would induce some of them to relocate in less central locations. This would be true, for example, of a business if it derived little benefit from a central location and if its activities imposed a large amount of congestion. However, while city politicians may lament the relocation of such businesses, such moves would generally increase the efficiency of resource allocation. If any centrally located firm responded to the imposition of road user charges by moving to the suburbs, this implies that the advantages to the firm of locating in the central area were not enough to compensate for the costs to society of the additional congestion imposed by the firm's activities.[21]

On the other hand not all centrally located firms would necessarily be made worse off by congestion charges, and congestion charges might induce some firms to move to the downtown area. First, while congestion charges would raise the money cost of travel by automobile, they would reduce the time cost of travel. Consequently, for some categories of trips the overall cost of travel by automobile might in fact be reduced. Second, because of the decongestion of roads and/or expansion of transit services made possible by increased transit revenues, the cost of travel by transit would presumably decline. Third, the increase in government revenue due to congestion charges might lead the government to reduce some existing business taxes.

An analogy to water pricing

Much of the political opposition to urban road pricing arises because road pricing would make certain groups worse off unless the revenues were used to compensate the losers. In reviewing the political opposition to road user charges, Kulash (1974a, 22) makes an analogy which is worth repeating:

Perhaps a parallel can be found in the history of water pricing in New York. Water was once provided free there. No meters or billing of any kind were used. Incredible waste was being observed – it was estimated that half the water being supplied was leaking through faulty pipes or otherwise being wasted. When pricing was offered as a 'solution,' a debate raged for decades about the related efficiency and equity issues. Today the idea is accepted, but only after a heated and drawn-out controversy.

---

21 Of course it is possible that the location of the firm in the central area would confer external economies on others because of what urban economists refer to as 'agglomeration economies' (see Mills 1972, 16-17). In this case one might find that too few firms would choose central locations if there were congestion charges, unless there were also central location subsidies.

GASOLINE PRICING POLICY

Thus far we have implicitly assumed that automobile users pay the marginal social costs of the inputs required to operate their vehicles, including gasoline or diesel fuel. In fact, for several years Canadian automobile users have generally paid less than the marginal social cost of their fuel as a result of federal government policies (supported by the Ontario government) which maintained the price in Canada of both domestic and imported crude oil far below the world market price. However, following a number of tax increases, in mid-1981 the retail price of gasoline in Ontario was close to the marginal social cost, and hence pricing of gasoline was no longer an important cause of inefficient resource allocation in urban transportation.[22]

In mid-1981, the retail price of regular leaded gasoline at a full-service outlet in Toronto was 36.8 cents a litre. In order to determine the marginal social cost of gasoline, we make two adjustments to this price. First, we remove federal and Ontario provincial commodity taxes of 15.6 cents a litre.[23] Thus, the price of gasoline net of these taxes was 21.2 cents a litre. Second, we raise the price of crude oil in Canada by $25 a barrel, from the prevailing domestic price of $17.75 a barrel to the world price of equivalent crude oil of $42.82 a barrel f.o.b. Montreal. At 159 litres of gasoline in a barrel of crude oil, moving to the world price of crude oil would raise the price of gasoline by 15.7 cents a litre, to 36.9 cents a litre.[24] Thus, the marginal social cost of gasoline was about 36.9 cents a litre, or virtually the same as the retail price.

CAR POOLING INCENTIVES

It is often suggested that a significant reduction in congestion and/or road costs, pollution, and vehicle operating costs including energy consumption could be achieved if greater use was made of car pools instead of automobiles with one occupant. The average automobile occupancy rate for all trips in Canadian urban areas is about 1.4 people, and for work trips the rate is only about 1.2

22 The prices received by domestic producers of crude oil and the prices paid by users of petroleum products other than road vehicles remained seriously distorted.

23 These taxes do not include the federal and Alberta provincial taxes which were included in the $17.75 a barrel domestic price of crude oil referred to below.

24 Actually the price would rise somewhat more than 15.7 cents a litre, because a movement to world price for crude oil would raise private costs for oil refineries for two reasons not accounted for in the preceding calculations: production costs for refineries would increase because refineries burn petroleum as a fuel in the production process, and inventory costs of refineries would increase. Thus, the marginal social cost of gasoline would somewhat exceed 36.9 cents a litre.

people. However, pooling involves greater travel time for the individuals involved, less flexibility about time of travel, and less privacy and comfort. In order to determine the efficient level of car pooling, one must compare the marginal social benefits and the marginal social costs of increased car pooling.

If road user and parking charges were collected so that each vehicle was required to pay its marginal social cost, individuals would have the efficient incentive to form car pools. They would compare the savings from pooling in terms of reduced road user and parking charges and vehicle operating costs with the costs of pooling in terms of higher travel time and reduced convenience and comfort, and they would form car pools when it was efficient to do so.

It should be obvious to the reader that road user and parking charges based on marginal social cost considerations would be the same for any particular automobile regardless of the number of people riding in it, because the amount of congestion, pollution, and wear and tear caused by an automobile does not depend on the number of occupants. Thus, if there were efficient road user and parking charges (which would not depend on the number of occupants of a vehicle), any additional incentive for car pools would lead to excessive pooling, i.e. additional incentives for car pools would induce people to form pools even though the social benefits (reduced congestion, etc.) were less than the social costs (time spent forming the pool, collecting passengers, etc.).

However, if efficient road user and parking charges are not collected there is an argument for subsidizing car pools, for instance by charging reduced parking fees. In the absence of efficient road user and parking charges, the private incentive to form car pools will be less than would be efficient, and it is possible that a subsidy could encourage efficient pooling.

There are, however, serious limits to such subsidy policies. First, part of the gains from formation of efficient pools would be offset by the fact that subsidies for car pools would encourage excessive urban travel, particularly at rush hour, by all automobiles with high occupancy rates, since these automobiles would be charged less than their marginal social cost.

Second, subsidies for car pools would encourage diversion of trips from public transit to car pools. For example, between 1974 and 1977 Seattle introduced several incentives for car pools, including reduced parking fees and bridge tools and access to special bus lanes on a bridge and on a limited-access expressway ramp. A 1977 survey of people using the subsidized parking facilities found that former bus users outnumbered former single-occupant automobile drivers by almost two to one (Olsson and Miller 1978, 11).

Third, subsidization of car pooling for work trips will result in increased use of automobiles for non-work trips because of increased availability of automobiles during work hours for non-working members of a household. Ben-Akiva and Atherton (1977) estimate that increased non-work travel by auto would offset about one-third of the reduction in work travel by auto.

There is at present one example of a government subsidy for car pooling in Ontario. Two municipally owned parking lots on the fringe of the Toronto central business district have charged lower fees for car pools since 1974, when daily parking fees of $1.50 and $1.25 were reduced to $0.50 and $0.35 respectively for car pools. In this case a survey carried out one month after the car pool subsidy was introduced found that former single-occupant automobile users outnumbered former public transit users by almost three to one. (City of Toronto Parking Authority 1976).

On balance, however, the available evidence suggests to me that, in general, incentives for car pools probably would not increase the efficiency of resource allocation and might well reduce efficiency.[25]

CONCLUSIONS ON ROAD PRICING IN ONTARIO

Marginal social cost pricing of road use
It is very improbable that any scheme approximating marginal social cost pricing of road use will be politically feasible in Ontario in the foreseeable future. But in case this judgment should prove incorrect it is useful to add two further points. First, among the various technologies available for collecting congestion charges that would approximate those suggested by economic theory, supplementary licences (windshield stickers) probably have the greatest practical potential.

Second, the U.S. Urban Mass Transportation Administration (UMTA) has funds available for American urban areas to subsidize the design, implementation, and evaluation of a two-year demonstration project involving the requirement that drivers using congested urban roads purchase a windshield sticker. The UMTA funds are available for enforcement, stickers, and administrative expenses. Though no U.S. urban area has accepted the offer, if any of the larger urban areas in Ontario were interested in trying such a scheme, it would make sense for the provincial and/or federal governments to provide subsidies for the demonstration project.

The available evidence suggests that in the early 1980s the efficient price for windshield stickers to enter the downtown areas of Ontario's larger cities would be from $1.50 to $3.00 a day.

---

25 Small (1976, 257) concluded that, in the absence of marginal social pricing of road use, if buses were given priority access to roadway capacity it would make almost no difference for the efficiency of resource allocation whether car pools were given priority access to roadway capacity, unless reserved bus lanes were underutilized.

Road user charges

As suggested, motor fuel taxes and registration fees could be set at higher rates in large urban areas than elsewhere in the province as a crude way of imposing congestion charges in the larger urban areas. Another possibility would be to charge a tax based on mileage for cars registered in the larger cities.

I have also recommended that parking in urban areas should be priced on the basis of marginal social cost. Among other things, this means that the government should eliminate the existing tax incentive to provide free employee parking by including the value of parking provided by employers in taxable income. Municipal governments should also consider imposing parking surcharges on cars arriving at parking locations in congested areas during the morning peak period.

I recommend against provision of special incentives for car pools, on the ground that these are likely to promote inefficient car pooling, e.g. diversion from public transit to car pools, and hence are not likely to lead to positive net social benefits.

I have not dealt with the problem of accidental costs in urban motoring, but one comment on this topic is necessary.[26] Enforcement of the laws against drunk driving has been lax, and the legal penalties for drunk driving are absurdly mild. Because of the externalities involved, there are sound economic grounds for considerably tighter enforcement of the laws against drunk driving and heavier penalties for those convicted.

Taxi fares

In passing it is useful to add a few comments on another area of pricing in urban transportation not analysed in this study. Municipal governments use licensing to restrict entry into the taxicab industry and regulate taxi fares. These measures raise taxi fares above the efficient level and reduce the level of resources allocated to the taxi industry below the efficient level. Apart from reducing efficiency, these measures increase the inequality of incomes, because low-income people spend a larger share of their incomes on taxicabs than do high-income people. Thus, municipal governments could contribute to a more efficient allocation of resources and a more equal distribution of income if they would deregulate the taxicab industry (for further discussion see Frankena 1979, 73-5).

---

26 As a matter of interest, Small (1976, 116) estimates that the social cost of automobile accidents, including medical expenses, discounted forgone earnings due to injury and death, and the overhead expenses of operating the automobile insurance industry, averages 1.58 cents per vehicle-mile (in 1972 dollars) on urban freeways and 3.79 cents on other urban roads.

3
Transit fare policies: central issues

We turn now to urban transit fare policies. This chapter and the next investigate optimal fare policies and apply the tools of economic analysis to fare policy issues now being debated in Ontario: fare collection methods and monthly passes.

ANALYTICAL FRAMEWORK

Models of urban transit systems
We will normally assume that the transit firm's operating costs depend on the level of service offered and that the number of passenger trips demanded depends on the level of service as well as the fare. As we shall see later, under these conditions even if a transit firm offers only one type of service and charges a uniform fare a wide range of combinations of fare and service levels will be consistent with any given cost function, demand function, and budget constraint. With more than one type of service or more than one fare level, the feasible range of fare and service combinations can be very great.

Because of the complexity of this basic model, the analysis of transit fare policies will use several simplified models of transit systems which abstract from some of the complications involved in determinng optimal transit operating policies. For example, I sometimes assume that the transit firm's operating costs are uniquely determined by the number of transit passenger trips and that the number of transit passenger trips demanded is uniquely determined by the fare. These assumptions imply, among other things, that if a transit firm charges a uniform fare that fare will be uniquely determined by its cost function, its demand function, and its budget constraint.[1]

---

1 At most the transit firm would have a choice between a high fare with a low level of ridership and a low fare with a high level of ridership, and one would expect it to choose the latter.

Transit service levels

In order to discuss transit fare policies, one must make an assumption about how transit service levels are determined. For example, one could assume that transit service will remain unchanged at its present level, or that it will be adjusted to the level optimal for the fare policy selected. I generally make the latter assumption; for instance, in discussing efficient fare policies I assume that service levels are simultaneously determined at their efficient levels.

First- and second-best analysis

In order to analyse transit fare policies one must also make assumptions about how the capacity of the road system is determined and how use of roads is priced; whether the transit system operates subject to an exogenous political constraint on the size of its deficit, and if not how the deficit is financed; and whether the real resource costs involved in collection of transit fares depend upon the fare policy.

Decisions about fare policy should be made on the basis of an analysis which makes all these assumptions in a way which corresponds to conditions in the real world. However, in order to highlight the basic considerations involved in fare policy, it is useful to begin by considering simpler situations.

Consequently, we begin by considering the structure of urban transit fares which would lead to an efficient allocation of resources, assuming, first, that the capacity of the road system is efficient and that users of road vehicles pay the marginal social costs of their trips,[2] second, that the transit system is not subject to a deficit constraint, and that deficits are financed from revenues raised by pure lump-sum taxes, which are costless to administer and do not distort the allocation of resources, and third, that the costs of fare collection are independent of the fare policy. This set of assumptions permits us to analyse urban transit fares in an ideal or 'first-best' context and leads to conclusions about 'first-best-efficient' fare policies.

Some of the assumptions underlying this first-best analysis are unrealistic, and the implications of relaxing them will be examined in following sections. When the transit system's operating policies are subject to any constraint which makes it impossible to achieve the ideal allocation of society's resources the result is what economists call a 'second-best' situation. Thus, we see the transit fare policies which would be 'second-best-efficient' when automobile use is not priced at marginal social cost and the transit fare policies which would be second-best-efficient when the transit system is subject to a deficit constraint.

---

2 This implies, among other things, that transit vehicles using congested roads pay congestion tolls.

To determine an efficient fare policy one must compare benefits and costs. Consequently, we consider the efficiency gains from adoption of efficient fare policies and the costs of fare collection.

FIRST-BEST FARE POLICIES[3]

According to first-best analysis, transit fares should be set so that transit users pay the marginal social costs of their trips. In that case they will take those rides for which their willingness to pay is at least as great as the willingness to pay for the alternative forgone on the part of all affected parties when scarce resources are allocated to the production of transit rides.

To see how marginal social cost pricing would affect the structure of urban transit fares, we assume that the transit firm's operating costs depend on the number of vehicle hours of transit service supplied and that the number of passenger trips demanded depends on the travel time (including the waiting time) required per trip as well as on the fare. Under these assumptions, with any given number of vehicle hours of transit service the marginal social cost of an extra transit passenger trip consists of the value of the passenger's own travel time and the marginal congestion costs imposed by an extra transit passenger trip on other transit riders and on other road users.[4] In the absence of any fare, the marginal private cost of a transit passenger trip would be equal to the value of the passenger's own travel time. Thus, the first-best-efficient fare would be equal to the marginal congestion costs.

To elaborate, the marginal congestion costs of a transit passenger trip are of three types. If an additional passenger boards or alights from a transit vehicle, the average speed of the transit vehicle will be reduced. (The length of time a transit vehicle is delayed by the boarding or alighting of an extra rider is at least ten times greater if the vehicle must make an additional stop than if it would

3 The discussion in this section is based largely on Mohring (1972) and Turvey and Mohring (1975).
4 These are the short-run marginal social costs, assuming that the number of vehicle-hours of transit service is given. In the long run it might be efficient to increase the number of vehicle-hours of transit service, so that some of the marginal social costs might be borne by the transit firm rather than by other transit riders. However, if the number of vehicle-hours of transit service is efficient this distinction is not important, since short-run and long-run marginal social costs would be equal. For further discussion of the marginal social costs of transit passenger trips see Jansson (1979), who among other things questions the definition of the short run as a period in which the number of vehicle-hours of service is fixed but service schedules are not fixed. He analyses an alternative definition of the short run as a period in which schedules are fixed.

have stopped anyway.[5]) Thus an extra passenger trip increases the in-vehicle travel time for other transit riders. Moreover, given the number of vehicle hours and route miles of service, a reduction in the average speed of transit vehicles implies a reduction in average frequency and an increase in average waiting time for other transit riders. Furthermore, if an additional passenger boards or alights from a transit vehicle operating on a road shared by other vehicles, users of other road vehicles will be delayed.[6] Finally, if an additional passenger is on a loaded transit vehicle other riders will be less comfortable, and there will be an increase in the probability that someone else will be forced to wait for the next transit vehicle.

Peak/off-peak fare differentials

Peak vs off-peak travel times

Efficient resource allocation in public transit is complicated by 'peak-load' considerations. The demand for public transit varies greatly through the day and the week. However, the capital stock (essentially the number of vehicles) owned by the transit system is constant and adopting split shifts for labour involves costs. As a result, all vehicles are used (either to provide service or as reserves) during rush hours, though some are not used during non-rush periods.[7] Moreover, the marginal social cost per vehicle *hour* of transit service is higher during rush hours than during non-rush periods, partly because of the lower marginal capital and labour costs per vehicle hour during non-rush periods[8] and, in the case of buses, partly because of the lower marginal congestion costs imposed on other road users per transit vehicle hour of service during non-rush periods. For buses the marginal social cost per vehicle-*mile* of service is greater during rush hours not only because of the higher cost per vehicle hour but because of the lower speed of transit vehicles (for relevant data see Mohring

5 Mohring (1972, 599) reports a figure of eleven times greater. See also Allen (1975). Turvey and Mohring (1975, 284) report a figure of 19.5 times greater for London, England.
6 Allen (1975, 38, 42) reports that because buses are larger and accelerate more slowly than cars, a bus would impose 3.3 times as much congestion damage on other road users as a car would impose if they made the same number of stops. However, since buses generally make more stops, on average a bus actually imposes 5.5 times as much congestion damage per mile as a car.
7 However, some of the vehicles which are not 'used' during non-rush periods are actually undergoing maintenance and hence are productively employed.
8 During evenings and weekends, however, the marginal wage costs per vehicle-hour of service are greater than during the off-peak period between morning and afternoon weekday rush hours.

1979, 191). Finally, more transit passenger miles are produced per vehicle mile of service during rush hours than at other times.

Thus some components of the marginal congestion cost imposed by an extra transit passenger trip are higher during rush hours while other components are higher during non-rush periods. Since there are more people on each transit vehicle, more people waiting for transit vehicles, and more people using automobiles during rush hour, an additional transit rider will impose greater congestion costs on other transit riders (in-vehicle time, waiting time, discomfort) and on road users (time waiting behind buses at stops) during rush hours than during non-rush periods with a given number of transit vehicle stops (i.e. if the additional rider does not increase the number of stops during the rush or non-rush periods, or if the additional rider increases the number of stops by the same amount during both periods). Furthermore, since there are fewer riders per vehicle mile during non-rush periods than during rush hours, transit vehicles on average (with the exception of subways, which stop at every station regardless of demand) make fewer stops per mile during non-rush periods than during rush hours. Consequently, the probability that an additional rider will increase the number of times the transit vehicle stops is greater during non-rush periods.

It is thus not clear in the case of buses (though it is with subways) whether an additional transit rider imposes greater marginal congestion costs during rush hour or during non-rush periods. Empirical data are needed to determine the relation between efficient peak and off-peak bus fares.

In a study which uses the magnitudes of the relevant variables for a large American urban area, Mohring (1972) estimates that if the bus system followed efficient investment, operating, and pricing policies, the peak-hour fare would be 2.4 times the off-peak fare.[9] Thus, the best available information is that in ideal circumstances the efficient peak-hour bus fares would be substantially higher than the efficient off-peak fares.

Moreover, the ratio of the efficient peak to off-peak fares would probably be significantly higher for subways than for buses. This is because the marginal congestion cost imposed by an off-peak subway rider is very low, at least under current conditions in Toronto for instance. An additional rider does not increase the number of stops a subway makes. On average an additional rider does not have much effect on the length of time a subway train stops at a station because of the large number of doors per train and the fact that the rider does not pay his fare as he boards the vehicle. And finally an additional rider does not reduce the

9 Mohring does not consider the effects of bus pricing on road congestion. If the congestion imposed by transit vehicles on other road users were considered, the ratio of the peak-hour fare to the off-peak fare would be higher.

comfort of other riders because there are a large number of unused seats. It should be kept in mind, however, that adoption of lower off-peak fares would increase ridership and hence could increase the marginal congestion cost imposed by an additional off-peak subway rider. Consequently, the ratio of *efficient* peak to off-peak fares would probably be lower than the ratio of *current* peak to off-peak marginal congestion costs.

Peak vs off-peak travel directions
The theoretical considerations involved in determining the relative fares to be charged for transit trips in the direction of peak flow at rush hour and in the reverse direction on the same route at the same time of day are similar to the considerations involved in determining peak-hour vs off-peak period fares. In calculating fare levels for bus rides in the two directions along a route with five times as many people travelling in the main-haul direction as in the back-haul direction, Mohring (1972) found that first-best fares may be similar in the two directions or higher in the back-haul direction.[10]

Consequently, the best available evidence provides no support on first-best-efficiency grounds for a general practice of charging higher fares for *bus* trips in the direction of peak flow. However, Mohring evidently discounts this finding, because in a later paper Turvey and Mohring (1975) argue that first-best bus fares would be higher in the main-haul direction than in the back-haul direction.[11] Moreover, in the case of a subway there is no ambiguity. Since an additional rider does not increase the number of times a subway stops, the marginal congestion cost and hence the first-best-efficient fare are clearly lower in the off-peak direction than in the peak direction.

Fares based on distance
First-best efficient fares would be based on the distance travelled only if the marginal congestion cost imposed by an extra transit rider were different for

10 Ibid. However, this analysis ignores the effect of number of riders per vehicle on discomfort and on the probability that someone may be forced to wait for the next vehicle.
11 Turvey and Mohring (1975). One possible explanation for the difference between the conclusion in Mohring (1972) and that in Turvey and Mohring (1975) is that Mohring (1972) ignores the effect of an extra rider on the probability that someone may be forced to wait for the next vehicle while Turvey and Mohring (1975) take this into account. Since this component of the marginal congestion cost of a transit trip may be significant for the main-haul direction but not for the back-haul direction, consideration of this component makes it more likely that the main-haul fare would be higher than the back-haul fare.

short and long trips. Ignoring transfers, which will be considered below, one must distinguish between two types of transit routes in order to analyse the effect of distance. First, consider a 'steady-state route,' where the number of riders on a transit vehicle remains more or less constant as the vehicle moves along the route. On such a route the marginal congestion cost imposed by an extra passenger trip would increase with the length of the trip if and only if transit vehicles were sufficiently full that the longer an additional rider was on the vehicle the more discomfort he would cause to others and the more he would increase the chance that someone else would be forced to wait for the next bus. Given either prevailing or efficient patterns of transit service, this suggests that on a steady-state route the first-best-efficient fares would be positively related to distance in the peak direction during rush hour but not under other circumstances.

Second, consider a 'commuter route.' During the morning, commuters board at various points along the route and alight at the terminal in the central business district. During the afternoon, commuters board at the terminal and alight at various points. Assuming that the vehicle stops at a fixed number of points and that every passenger takes the same amount of time to board or alight, the total time required for the vehicle to cover its route will not depend upon where any passenger boards or alights. However, the closer to the terminal any passenger boards or alights from the vehicle, the more other passengers will be on the vehicle and the greater the marginal congestion costs in terms of increased in-vehicle travel time imposed on other riders will be. In this case, efficient fares would be higher for short trips than for long trips, unless the greater delay caused by a short trip was entirely offset by the greater discomfort caused by a long trip.[12]

Charging for transfers
An important component of the marginal congestion cost imposed by an additional transit passenger trip is the delay imposed on other transit riders and other road users when the rider boards or alights from the transit vehicle. Consequently, the marginal congestion cost imposed by an additional transit passenger trip will increase with the number of transfers. Thus, a first-best-efficient fare structure would not involve free transfers. In fact, each trip segment would be priced separately, so that the fare for a trip from point A to point C

---

12 For further discussion and examples in which first-best-efficient fares would be higher for shorter trips, see Turvey and Mohring (1975) and Mohring (1972, 597).

involving a transfer at point *B* would be the same as the fare for a trip from *A* to *B* *plus* the fare for a trip from *B* to *C*.[13]

Summary
Based on the above discussion, one might expect first-best transit fares for a steady-state route to look something like this:

$$F_{pp} = \alpha_o S + \alpha_1 D,$$
$$F_{op} = \beta_o S,$$
$$F_o = \gamma_o S,$$

where $\alpha_o, \alpha_1, \beta_o, \gamma_o > 0$; $\alpha_o > \beta_o > \gamma_o$[14]; and F_{pp} is the peak-direction, peak-hour fare; F_{op} is the off-peak-direction, peak-hour fare; F_o is the off-peak-hour fare; S is the number of trip segments (i.e. vehicles boarded); and D is the length of the trip. In contrast to the fare systems used in many Canadian urban areas, the first-best-efficient fare would depend neither on the age of the rider nor on whether the rider was a heavy user of the transit system.

It should be added, however, that in the absence of efficient peak / off-peak fare differentials an efficiency justification might be offered for reduced fares for those population groups whose use of transit is concentrated during off-peak periods. This might provide an argument for reduced fares for senior citizens, children, and (during the afternoon) for students. In Toronto, while 58 per cent of all transit rides are taken in off-peak periods, 76 per cent of trips by senior citizens and 69 per cent of trips by children are taken in off-peak periods (Joint Metro/Toronto Transit Commission Transit Policy Committee 1979a, 6, 19-20). In the case of students, morning travel is heavily concentrated in the peak period but afternoon travel tends to precede the peak.

---

13 If the costs of fare collection are lower for the single trip from A to C than for the two trips from A to B and from B to C, this would justify some discount in the fare for the single trip compared to the sum of the fares for the two trips. One might expect the costs of fare collection for the single trip to be lower than for the two separate trips if a person with a transfer boards faster than a person paying an initial fare, or if there is 'free body' transferring in a passenger control area.

14 $\beta_o > \gamma_o$ because the cost of slowing down a transit vehicle in the off-peak direction during the early part of rush hour is greater than the cost of slowing down a transit vehicle in an off-peak period. When a transit vehicle is delayed in the off-peak direction during the early part of rush hour, people waiting to travel in the peak direction will be delayed.

SECOND-BEST FARES WHEN AUTOMOBILE CONGESTION IS
UNPRICED

Introduction

We have looked at transit fares if no distortions interfered with efficient resource allocation elsewhere in the economy. However, as we have seen, one important distortion cannot be neglected in any discussion of fare policies: automobile users are not charged for the costs they impose on others when they use heavily congested urban roads.[15] Consequently, the private cost of automobile travel under heavily congested conditions is less than the marginal social cost, and the level of automobile use in such conditions is inefficiently high. This problem is most serious in the case of automobile travel in the downtown area and in the direction of peak flow on arterial routes at rush hour, particularly in larger urban areas. Similar arguments could be made about unpriced automobile pollution.

The problem of unpriced automobile congestion and pollution is relevant to transit fare policy to the extent that changes in fares affect the level of automobile use under congested and polluted conditions.

The most general case of this pricing problem considered by economists involves the following assumptions: (i) automobile use is priced below marginal social cost in peak periods but at marginal social cost in off-peak periods; (ii) the public transit firm can set different fares for peak and off-peak periods; (iii) all cross-price elasticities of demand between peak and off-peak travel by automobile and public transit are non-zero, and the cross-price elasticities are greater between times on a given mode or between modes at a given time than when both time and mode are different. In this case the 'second-best' efficient peak transit fare is below the marginal congestion cost imposed by an additional transit trip, i.e. below the level that would price rides at their marginal social cost, because of the efficiency gain involved in diverting automobile users to public transit during the peak. Moreover, the second-best-efficient off-peak transit fare is below the level that would price rides at their marginal social cost, even if off-peak automobile users pay their marginal social costs, because of the

---

15 Moreover, in the real world the capacity of the road system presumably is not at the level which would be second-best-efficient in the absence of road pricing. The level of transit service and the transit fare structure which would be second-best-efficient in the absence of road pricing will depend on how the capacity of the road system is determined, but the basic analysis presented here will apply in any case. For an analysis of second-best investment policies, see Wheaton (1978) and Henderson (1977).

efficiency gain involved in diverting peak automobile and transit users to off-peak transit (Glaister 1974). An example of second-best pricing of urban transit with unpriced automobile congestion is given in Appendix B.

The limitations of second-best pricing

There are, however, two limitations to second-best pricing of transit below marginal social cost as an alternative to marginal social cost pricing of automobile congestion. To begin with, second-best pricing of transit is less efficient. If both automobile use and transit use are priced below marginal social cost, people will be induced to do more than the efficient amount of travelling by both modes. In particular, when the transit fare is reduced below marginal social cost to attract automobile users to transit, the fare reduction also induces people who would not otherwise have travelled to take trips even though they value their trips at less than the marginal social cost of producing them. Available empirical studies suggest that the cross-elasticity of demand for automobile use with respect to public transit fares is low. According to Glaister and Lewis (1978) data for London, England, indicate that the elasticity of demand for peak-hour automobile use with respect to transit fares is only 0.025, and three other studies estimate the elasticity of demand for automobile use with respect to transit fares to be in the range between 0.05 and 0.07 in large urban areas. Based on information about typical modal splits for large urban areas (twice as many person trips by car as by public transit) and about typical fare-elasticities of demand for transit for large urban areas (-0.2 to -0.3), one can conclude that in response to a reduction in the transit fare the number of automobile person trips will decline by about half of the number of additional transit person trips.[16]

Furthermore, it is conceivable in principle that in some situations even complete elimination of transit fares might not offset the effect on modal choice of failing to collect congestion tolls for automobile use; in other words, the second-best transit fare could be negative. (This is the case in Mohring (1981), and it would be so in Appendix B, Figure B.1a, if the intersection of D_t and MPC_t was to the left of the intersection of MSB_t and MSC_t.)

16 This conclusion may be clarified by a numerical example. Suppose that 3000 people are travelling, 2000 by car and 1000 by transit. If the fare elasticity of demand for transit is -0.2, a 1 per cent reduction in the fare would lead to an increase in the number of transit riders by 2. If the cross-elasticity of demand for automobile use with respect to the transit fare is 0.05, the same fare reduction would lead to a reduction in the number of automobile travellers by 1. See Glaister and Lewis (1978, 347) and Frankena (1979, 21-2) for data.

Empirical estimates of second-best fares

Glaister and Lewis (1978) have estimated the bus and rail (subway/commuter rail combined) fare structures that would be justified by second-best efficiency considerations to deal with road congestion in the absence of road pricing in London, England. They make the following assumptions. (i) The marginal congestion cost per passenger mile of peak-hour automobile travel would decline linearly from 39 cents at the current level to 29 cents at half that level, i.e. they take the capacity of the road system as exogenously given at its current level. (ii) The marginal social cost of bus travel (excluding the passengers' own time) is 37 cents per passenger mile during peak periods, including 16 cents in bus operating costs, 8 cents in bus capital costs, and 13 cents in road congestion costs, and the marginal social cost of bus travel is 16 cents per passenger mile during off-peak periods, consisting entirely of bus operating costs. (iii) The corresponding marginal social cost of rail travel is 26 cents per passenger mile during peak periods and 2.6 cents per passenger mile in off-peak periods. They estimate that the second-best efficient bus fares would be 18 cents per passenger mile during peak periods and 8 cents per mile during off-peak periods, and the corresponding rail fares would be 16 and 1.4 cents respectively.

The study by Glaister and Lewis leads to two important conclusions. The second-best-efficient fares would be only about half the levels of the first-best-efficient fares that would be suggested by the principle of marginal social cost pricing if efficient road user charges were being collected. For example, the first-best-efficient peak period bus fare would be 37 cents per passenger mile, whereas the second-best-efficient fare would be 18 cents. Moreover, the ratio of the second-best peak-hour bus fare to the second-best off-peak bus fare would be about 2.25, and the corresponding ratio for rail fares would be 11.3. Thus, even if automobile congestion is not priced, the efficient peak-hour fares are substantially greater than the efficient off-peak fares.[17]

17 Glaister and Lewis (1978). British pounds have been converted to Canadian dollars at the rate of $2.60. See Allen (1975, 72-85) for another empirical study of second-best transit fares. The latter study reaches the conclusion that the second-best peak transit fare would be *below* the second-best off-peak transit fare. There are two differences between the Glaister and Lewis and Allen analyses which help to explain these differences in findings, apart from the fact that their data are drawn from different sources. First, Glaister and Lewis determine second-best bus fares subject to the constraint that auto congestion tolls are zero during peak and off-peak periods. Allen determines both second-best bus fares and automobile congestion tolls subject to the constraint that auto congestion tolls must be the same during peak and off-peak periods. As a result, in Allen's analysis, automobile use is priced below marginal social cost during the peak but above marginal social cost during off-peak periods. Secondly, Glaister and Lewis assume that the marginal social cost of bus use is higher during the peak than during off-peak periods. Allen

IMPLICATIONS FOR FARES OF SUBSIDY COSTS AND CONSTRAINTS

Thus far we have considered transit fares purely as devices for inducing people to take the efficient number of transit rides. We have ignored the problem of financing the transit system. We will see later that the revenues generated by efficient fares in a first-best context or in a second-best context when automobile congestion is unpriced would fall far short of the amounts required to finance the transit system. The fare policies discussed above therefore imply substantial subsidies for the transit system. This fact raises two important points which have a bearing on the efficient fare structure.

In order to finance transit subsidies, the government must levy taxes. These taxes lead to a reduction in the efficiency of resource allocation elsewhere in the economy, because they raise prices above marginal social costs for other goods and services. Consequently, in order to justify a fare reduction on efficiency grounds, it is not sufficient to prove that the fare reduction would increase the efficiency of resource allocation in urban transportation. One must also prove that this increase in efficiency in urban transportation would more than offset the decrease in efficiency elsewhere in the economy when a tax is raised in order to finance the increase in the deficit of the transit system which would be brought about by the fare reduction. One must consider as well the administrative costs of raising tax revenues.

Consequently, efficient public transit fares would actually be higher than those suggested above. While all transit fares would be higher, the increases would not be uniform dollar or percentage amounts. The general pattern of fare increases is discussed below.

Second-best fares with a deficit constraint
For political reasons there may be a limit to the subsidies that can be made available to the transit system. In that case the transit firm can run only a limited deficit. Suppose that this limit would be exceeded if fares were set so that the private costs of trips would equal the marginal social costs at the efficient levels of output. This situation presents another problem in second-best-efficient pricing: How should the transit firm adjust its fares to satisfy the deficit constraint with the minimum sacrifice of efficiency?[18]

---

reaches the reverse conclusion, evidently because an additional bus rider is more likely to cause a bus to make an extra stop during off-peak periods and because the value per hour of automobile users' travel time was assumed to be higher during off-peak periods than peak periods, due to differences in the mean incomes of travellers in the different periods.

18 Of course efficient adjustment to a deficit constraint would include changes in service as well as fares.

We shall consider circumstances in which the deficit-constrained second-best-efficient fare system would involve (1) a two-part tariff, (2) different fares for different services, and (3) fare discrimination. For the sake of simplicity we shall assume that automobile users pay the marginal social costs of their trips. Later we shall consider how these results would have to be modified in the real world, where automobile users do not pay for their marginal congestion costs.

Two-part tariffs

Suppose that a transit firm subject to a deficit constraint offers only one type of service and cannot practise fare discrimination among riders. Suppose, however, that it can charge a 'two-part tariff,' which requires a transit user to buy a monthly permit for use of the transit system at a price P and also to pay a fare F for each trip.[19]

Based on what is known about transit demand elasticities, it is reasonable to assume that (in the relevant range) an increase in either P or F would reduce the transit system's deficit. However, an increase in P above zero or an increase in F above the marginal congestion cost imposed by an additional transit trip would bring about an efficiency loss because either of these deviations from first-best-efficient pricing would deter people from taking some transit trips that they would value at more than the marginal social cost of production.

In order to understand the nature of these efficiency losses, we will consider how one would measure the efficiency loss due to an increase in F above the first-best-efficient level in a simple model of an urban transit system, assuming that P is held constant at zero. We will consider the case in which the demand for transit rides depends only on the fare, not on travel time or income, and the marginal social cost of producing transit rides is identical to the marginal private cost for the transit firm.

Consistent with these assumptions, suppose that the demand and marginal cost curves are represented by D and MC respectively in Figure 2. In this case, the first-best-efficient fare would be OS. Suppose, however, that the transit firm is required to produce an excess of fare revenue over variable costs, and that it will accomplish this by raising F above OS. The loss in efficiency due to an increase in F is measured as consumers' willingness to pay for the rides forgone due to the fare increase minus the value of inputs released when these rides are no longer produced. Thus, if the fare is raised from OS to OT, the loss of efficiency is equal to the area VUW, which is area $YUWL$, the consumers' willingness to pay for the rides forgone, minus area $YVWL$, the value of the inputs released. The increase

19 For a discussion of the two-part tariff which would maximize monopoly profits, see Oi (1971). Of course the two-part tariff that would maximize profits would be different from the two-part tariff that would be second-best-efficient given a deficit constraint.

Figure 2
Efficiency loss and increase in net revenue due to a fare increase

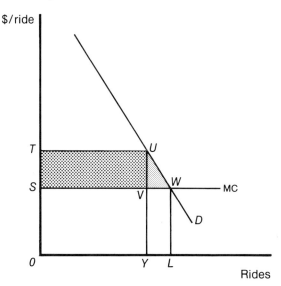

in transit fare revenue net of costs due to this same increase in the fare would be measured by the area *STUV*.

It is evident from the geometry in Figure 2 that when *F* is equal to the first-best-efficient fare, the *marginal* efficiency loss due to a (small) fare increase would be zero. Also, for a linear demand curve, the marginal efficiency loss due to a 1 cent increase in *F* would increase, and the marginal net revenue due to a 1 cent increase in *F* would decrease, as *F* was increased above the first-best-efficient level. Consequently, the marginal efficiency loss per dollar of extra net revenue due to a fare increase would be zero for *F* equal to the first-best-efficient fare and would increase as *F* is increased above the first-best-efficient level.

The fact that this loss would increase as *F* is increased above the first-best-efficient level suggests that reliance on increases in *F* alone might not be the most efficient way for a transit firm to satisfy a deficit constraint. It might be more efficient for the transit firm to introduce a two-part tariff, i.e. to set *P* greater than zero, to reduce the necessary increase in *F*.

Of course, setting *P* above zero would bring about an efficiency loss similar in nature to the one caused by setting *F* above the first-best-efficient level. However, the overall efficiency loss associated with satisfying the deficit constraint might be reduced by relying partly on increases in *P* above zero. For example, assume that demand behaviour is such that the marginal efficiency loss per dollar of extra net revenue due to a fare increase is zero if F equals the first-best-efficient fare and then increases as F increases and that the marginal efficiency loss per dollar of extra net revenue due to an increase in P is zero if $P = 0$ and then increases as P increases.

Given these assumptions, in order to maximize efficiency subject to a deficit constraint the second-best-efficient pricing rule would be as follows: starting with P equal to zero and F equal to the marginal congestion cost of a transit trip at the efficient level of output, raise P and F in such a way that the marginal efficiency loss per dollar of extra net revenue due to increases in P and F are kept equal. Stop raising P and F when the deficit constraint is satisfied. One implication of this pricing rule is that under the assumptions made here the second-best two-part tariff would involve a level of P greater than zero, i.e. in the face of a deficit constraint it would be more efficient for a transit system to introduce a two-part tariff than to rely on an increase in the fare alone. (Of course we are ignoring collection costs.) Similarly, the second-best two-part tariff would involve a level of F above the marginal congestion cost imposed by an additional transit rider.[20]

Different fares for different services
Suppose now that we change the assumptions and consider a transit firm that cannot charge a two-part tariff but offers two different services for which it can charge different fares.

There is a large body of economic theory dealing with the issue of second-best-efficient pricing by a multi-product monopolist operating under a profit or deficit constraint.[21] This theory is directly relevant to the problem at hand.

Consider a simple case in which the demand for transit rides on each service depends only on the fare for that service, not on income, the fare for the other service, or travel time on either service; the marginal social costs of producing transit rides on both services are identical to the marginal private costs for the transit firm; and the marginal social costs per ride for the two services are constant and equal.

Consistent with these assumptions, suppose that the demand curves for service A and service B are represented by D_a and D_b respectively and that the

20 To avoid excluding occasional users of the transit system, people might be allowed to ride without a 'permit' upon payment of a fee higher than the 'fare' charged for people with permits.
21 Standard references are Ramsey (1927), Boiteux (1956), Baumol and Bradford (1970), and Mohring (1970). These sources implicitly assume away the possibility of competitive entry induced by second-best prices which involve cross-subsidization: see Faulhaber (1975) and Braeutigam (1979).

Figure 3
Second-best fares for a two-service transit system
with a deficit constraint

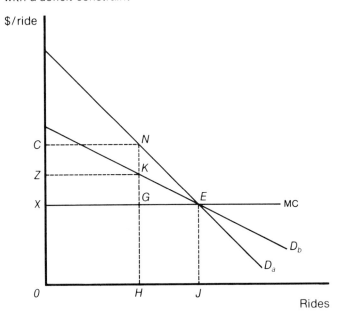

common marginal cost curve is represented by MC in Figure 3. In this case the first-best-efficient fare policy would be to set both fares equal to OX, and both output levels would be OJ.

Suppose, however, that the firm is required to produce an excess of fare revenue over variable cost and that we wish to accomplish this with the least possible loss in efficiency. As in Figure 2, the loss in efficiency due to an increase in the fare on one service is measured as consumers' willingness to pay for the rides forgone due to the fare increase minus the value of the inputs released when these rides are no longer produced. Thus, if the fare for service A is raised from OX to OC, the loss of efficiency is equal to the area NEG, which is area $NEJH$, the willingness to pay for the rides forgone, minus area $EJHG$, the value of the inputs released. The increase in transit fare revenue net of costs due to this same rise in fare would be area $XGNC$.

It is evident from the geometry that the marginal loss in efficiency per dollar of extra net revenue due to a fare increase on either service increases as the fare on that service is increased above marginal cost. The second-best-efficient pricing rule would be to raise the two fares in such a way that the marginal efficiency loss per dollar of extra net revenue on the two services remains equal until the deficit constraint is satisfied.

In Figure 3, the application of this pricing rule implies that the fare for service A should be raised more than the fare for service B, because at any given fare above marginal cost the marginal loss in efficiency per dollar of extra net revenue is lower for service A. Because of the specific assumptions made in this example, it happens that the fare increases above marginal cost should be inversely proportional to the slopes of the demand curves; such a change in fares would leave output levels equal for the two services. For example, if the transit system was constrained to produce net revenues above variable costs equal to the sum of the areas *XGNC* and *XGKZ*, the second-best-efficient fare structure would be to charge *OC* on service A and *OZ* on service B, in contrast to the first-best-efficient fares of *OX* on both services. The net efficiency loss would be the sum of the areas *KEG* and *NEG*. This second-best fare structure would be more efficient than setting equal fares for the two services at the level between *OC* and *OZ* at which the deficit constraint would be satisfied.

A little geometry shows that the second-best-efficient pricing result in Figure 3 is consistent with each of the four alternative pricing rules stated by Baumol and Bradford (1970). The simplest of these four pricing rules, which holds only when cross-price elasticities of demand between different transit services are zero, is that the percentage deviation of each fare from marginal social cost must be inversely proportional to the fare-elasticity of demand for that service.[22]

From a practical point of view, the results presented here provide an argument (in addition to the argument based on differences in marginal congestion costs) for charging higher transit fares during peak periods than during off-peak periods. There is considerable empirical evidence that the demand for transit rides is less elastic with respect to the fare during rush hours than at other times.[23] Consequently, if a transit firm is subject to a binding budget constraint there is a second-best-efficiency argument for raising fares in peak periods proportionally more above marginal congestion costs than fares in off-peak periods.

---

22 Baumol and Bradford (1970, 268). It is the income-compensated fare-elasticity of demand which is relevant. For further discussion and technical analysis, see the references in the preceding footnote.

23 Bly (1976), Glaister and Lewis (1978, 348-9), Kraft and Domencich (1972), Tebb (1978, 15), Toronto Transit Commission (1977, 109), Wabe and Coles (1975), Webster (1977, 23). However, the differences in fare elasticities are observed in situations where the same fares are charged during peak and off-peak periods. It does not necessarily follow that the fare elasticities would be different at fare levels equal to marginal congestion costs.

Fare discrimination

Suppose that a transit firm which faces a binding deficit constraint is able to charge different fares for a given service for different groups in the population, e.g. different age groups. The preceding discussion could easily be extended to demonstrate that the second-best-efficient fare structure for such a firm would involve a higher fare for population groups with lower fare-elasticities of demand.

According to a Joint Metro/TTC Transit Policy Committee report (1979a, 18-19), there is evidence from New York, Los Angeles, London (England), and Montreal that the fare-elasticity of demand is greater for senior citizens than for other adults. However, the report states that TTC ridership data do not support that hypothesis.

According to a study of Montreal (Gaudry 1978a), the fare-elasticity of demand for transit is greater for school children than for adults.

It should be noted that even if the fare-elasticity of demand for *all* transit rides is greater for senior citizens or school children than for adults, one could not necessarily conclude that this would be true at a given time of day. The differences in elasticities could reflect differences in time of travel.

Implications of unpriced automobile congestion

So far we have assumed that use of automobiles was priced at marginal social cost. If there is unpriced automobile congestion, as there is in the real world, then the analysis must be modified.

The basic principle of deficit-constrained second-best pricing remains unchanged when automobile congestion is unpriced, i.e. if there are two transit services the fares should be raised above the otherwise efficient levels in such a way that the marginal efficiency loss per dollar of extra net revenue on the two services remains equal. However, the efficiency loss in question must be measured differently when automobile congestion is unpriced.

As we have seen, when the use of automobiles is priced at its marginal social cost, the loss of efficiency due to an increase in the fare on one transit service is measured as consumers' willingness to pay for the rides forgone due to the fare increase minus the value of the inputs released when these rides are no longer produced. When automobile congestion is unpriced, the loss of efficiency due to an increase in the fare also includes the marginal congestion costs imposed by any additional automobile trips caused by the fare increase.

Suppose that transit fares on different services are initially set at the levels which would be second-best-efficient when automobile congestion is unpriced and there is no deficit constraint on the transit system. Suppose that a deficit constraint is then imposed on the transit system so that transit fares must be increased. In this case, other things equal, the fare should be increased less on a transit service if the cross-elasticity of demand for automobile use under congested circumstances with respect to that fare is high, and the fare should be increased more if the fare-elasticity of demand for that transit service is low. The same reasoning can be applied to fares for different groups in the population as well as for different services.

In practical terms this analysis suggests that if a transit firm must satisfy a budget constraint it should do so somewhat differently if automobile congestion is unpriced than if automobile use is priced at marginal social cost. When automobile use is unpriced, the ratio between the increases in peak-hour fares and off-peak period fares should probably be less than would be indicated by a comparison of the fare-elasticities of demand for these two kinds of trips alone. However, if the empirical findings in the study by Glaister and Lewis are correct, it is probably safe to conclude that the efficient peak-hour fare would still be substantially higher than the efficient off-peak fare.

THE WELFARE GAIN FROM EFFICIENT FARE POLICIES

How large are the efficiency losses involved in current fare policies compared to the alternative fare policies analysed above? Estimates of the current losses would enable us to compare the gains from more complex fare systems with the higher collection costs of such systems, and thus get a better idea of the most efficient fare policies.

Unfortunately, very little is known about the costs incurred through the current inefficient fare policies. Only one study deals directly with this subject. Glaister (1979) estimates the efficiency loss in London, England, which resulted from the fact that bus and rail fares were each set at a single level regardless of time of day rather than differentiated efficiently between peak and off-peak periods. He estimates the real welfare loss at 3 per cent of total expenditure on all goods and services in the urban area or 109 per cent of the (optimal) fare revenue on the transit and rail systems.[24] This estimate is much higher than most people would probably expect. However, this estimate was intended to be only an illustration of Glaister's proposals for the measurement of welfare losses, not as

24 Glaister (1979) compares existing fares, which did not vary with time of day, with the efficient peak and off-peak fares calculated in Glaister and Lewis (1978), who estimated that the efficient peak fares were 2.25 and 11.3 times the efficient off-peak fares for bus and rail respectively. These fares are actually the ones which would be second-best efficient if automobile congestion was unpriced, but Glaister (1979) treats them as the first-best fares.

Figure 4
Gains from charging the efficient fare

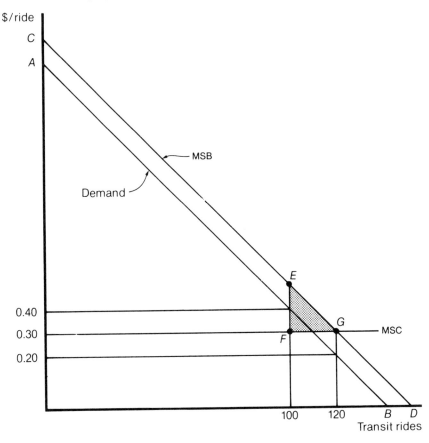

an accurate measure of the welfare loss due to non-optimal pricing in public transport.

To obtain a very rough idea we shall consider a very simple hypothetical example (Figure 4). Suppose that a transit system provides only one type of service and charges a uniform fare. The marginal social cost (MSC) of producing a transit ride equals the marginal private cost for the transit firm and is constant at 30 cents. The demand for transit rides depends only on the fare, and the demand curve is given by the line *AB*. Because road users are not charged for their marginal congestion costs, each transit ride has an external benefit in terms of reduced road congestions of 10 cents, so that the marginal social benefit (MSB) curve for transit rides *CD* is parallel to, and 10 cents above, the demand curve. Initially the fare is 40 cents and the number of rides is 100. At the initial equilibrium, the fare-elasticity of demand is -0.4.

The efficient level of transit use is determined where MSC and MSB intersect, i.e. at 120 rides. In order to induce transit users to take 120 rides, the fare would have to be 20 cents, which is the second-best-efficient fare when automobile users are not charged for their congestion costs.

If the transit fare was reduced from 40 to 20 cents, the efficiency gain would be the area *EFG*, which equals $2. This is approximately 6 per cent of the value of the inputs used by the transit system to produce the efficient number of rides. It should be noted that 6 per cent of the inputs used by public transit systems in Ontario would be over $20 million a year. Of course, this hypothetical calculation cannot bear too much weight.

The principal conclusion is that further empirical research on the magnitude of the gains from more efficient fare policies is required as a basis for rational decisions on fare policies.

THE ECONOMIC COST OF FARE COLLECTION

Collection costs are borne in part by the transit authority, such as the personnel and equipment costs required for the sale, collection, and inspection of tickets and (if the number of vehicle *miles* of service is held constant) the operating costs for vehicles which are stopped while the driver is involved in selling and collecting tickets. Collection costs are also borne by transit riders, such as the time spent buying tickets outside transit vehicles, the increased time spent boarding transit vehicles, the reduced average speed of travel due to slower boarding of other passengers, and (if the number of vehicle *hours* of service is held constant) the increased waiting time because of the reduction in the frequency of transit service. Finally, some collection costs are borne by road users who are caught behind stopped transit vehicles while drivers collect fares.

Fare collection costs depend on the structure of fares, such as whether the transit system charges a uniform fare for all rides, charges differential fares which depend on time of day, distance travelled, and age of rider, or offers multi-ride tickets or monthly passes. Consequently collection costs are one determinant of the optimal fare structure. Obviously, consideration of collection costs works in favour of simplifications in fare structures.

Fare collection costs depend not only on the structure of fares but also on the method of fare collection. The basic alternative methods of fare collection on surface transit vehicles are as follows: Method 1: a conductor who rides on the vehicle sells and cancels tickets and checks transfers and passes; Method 2:

passengers entering the vehicle pass the driver, who collects or supervises pay-ment of fares, sells and collects tickets, and checks transfers and passes; Method 3: passengers are responsible for purchasing tickets before they enter the vehicle or from a machine on the vehicle and for validating (cancelling) their own tickets, and inspectors check passengers at random to make sure they have valid tickets. Generally speaking, surface transport systems in North America rely on Method 2 while surface transport systems in northwestern Europe have been converting from Method 1 to variations of Method 3 during the past fifteen years. Method 3 involves a combination of what is called 'automatic fare collection,' that is, the use of ticket issuing and/or validating machines installed either on or off the vehicle, and 'honour fare collection,' that is, the checking of a random sample of passengers rather than all passengers to make sure they have valid tickets, with fines for those who do not.

Finally, fare collection costs depend on the design of the transit vehicles and their rights-of-way. For example, in the case of Method 2, fare collection costs depend on whether passengers entering the vehicle must go single file or have room to move in a double stream, e.g., one for people buying tickets and the other for people with valid transfers and passes. Similarly, with Method 3, fare collection costs depend on the total number of doors available for use in boarding; on the standard buses used in Canada, for instance, there are only two doorways, each designed for single-file movement, whereas on the articulated buses used in many European cities there are three sets of double doors, so that with an automatic/honour fare system boarding would still take much longer on a standard Canadian bus than on a European articulated bus. Fare collection costs would also depend on the design of rights-of-way, which might employ bus bays for instance, so that cars can pass buses while passengers are boarding.

Thus, fare collection costs depend on the structure of fares, the method of fare collection, and the design of transit vehicles and rights-of-way. Furthermore, the *increase* in fare collection costs involved in moving from a uniform fare structure to a fare structure involving different fares at different times of day or for trips of different length will depend upon the method of fare collection and the design of transit vehicles. Similarly, the *change* in fare collection costs involved in going from Method 2 to Method 3 depends heavily on whether one uses standard buses or articulated buses. This last point is fairly obvious, because Method 2 requires that passengers enter past the driver, while Method 3 allows passengers to enter any door, and articulated buses have more doors.

In the long run any transit system faces a rather complex problem of simul-taneously determining the optimal fare structure, fare collection method, and right-of-way and vehicle specifications. The problem is further complicated by the fact that the optimal solution will vary, depending upon city size, transit passenger densities, and the extent of road congestion. For example, the use of articulated buses is efficient only in large cities with high passenger densities, so that only there are the benefits of Method 3 likely to outweigh the extra costs compared to Method 2.

The important issue is to determine empirically how the costs of fare collection depend upon the fare structure, assuming that fare collection methods and right-of-way and vehicle specifications are simultaneously determined in an optimal manner. There has, again, been very little quantitative research on this subject, so that all we can do is get an idea of some of the magnitudes involved.

We will begin by considering the effect of alternative fare structures, fare collection methods, and related vehicle designs on average passenger boarding times and on the average speed of surface transit vehicles. The most detailed available study of this issue was carried out by Cundhill and Watts (1973) using data for eleven different bus systems in the UK in 1970-71. They calculated the marginal boarding time per passenger for a bus that was already stopped during both peak and off-peak periods. The observations covered five different fare collection methods, cases where the driver or conductor gave change and cases where exact fares were required, three fare structures (flat fares, fares by distance, and passes), and bus designs which permitted either one or two streams of passengers to board at a time. Table 3 summarizes the results, except on the effect of passes. None of the systems studied used the automatic/honour fare systems described above or buses which could be boarded through more than one doorway. Cundhill and Watts reached several interesting conclusions. First, systems 3 to 11 in Table 3, which involved payment of a fare upon boarding, required about one to three seconds more to board a marginal passenger than did systems 1 and 2, which involved collection of the fare by a conductor while the vehicle was in motion. The costs of fare collection for Method 2 are therefore not trivial. Second, among systems 3 to 11, marginal boarding times were generally lowest for the systems which used a fare box supervised by the driver (systems 5 to 8), particularly in cases where the driver did not give change (systems 7 and 8). In systems 9 to 11 there was no fare box, just a ticket vending machine (with the passenger having the option of paying the driver). On average it took drivers three seconds to give change, and where change was available about one-sixth of the riders asked for it; consequently, the marginal boarding time per passenger is reduced by about 0.5 seconds by requiring exact fares. Third, it was found that the use of a pass reduced the marginal boarding time per passenger by 1.5 seconds in peak periods and 2.0 seconds in off-peak periods.

Watts (1974) reports data on marginal boarding times for Copenhagen and The Hague. In both cases, passengers entered in two streams: one stream passed the driver, who gave change; the other stream was served by a token-accepting

TABLE 3

Marginal boarding time per passenger in the U.K.

System	Fare collection method					Exact fare[a]	Fare by distance[b]	Number of streams boarding bus[c]	Marginal boarding time per passenger (seconds)[d]	
	Pay conductor	Pay driver	Fare box supervised by driver	Pay driver or machine	Pay machine				Peak	Off-peak
1	X					No	Yes	2	1.15	1.35
2	X					No	Yes	2	1.50	1.75
3		X				No	Yes	1	3.90	3.50
4		X				No	Yes	1	4.75	6.60
5			X			No	No	1	2.60	2.70
6			X			No	No	1	3.00	3.30
7			X			Yes	Yes	1	2.25	2.45
8			X			Yes	Yes	1	2.45	2.60
9				X		No	Yes	2	4.00	4.85
10					X	No	Yes	2	2.70	3.20
11					X	No	No	2	3.30	5.00

a 'No' means the driver or conductor gives change.
b 'No' means fare is not dependent on length of trip.
c 1 means passengers enter single file.
d Observations exclude infirm passengers, passengers with luggage, passengers using passes, and 'unusual' occurrences.
SOURCE: Cundhill and Watts (1973, Tables 1 to 3)

machine in Copenhagen and a ticket-canceller in The Hague. In both cities the fare was independent of the distance travelled. The peak-hour marginal boarding time per passenger was 1.85 seconds, substantially lower than the time achieved by any of the UK systems in Table 3 without conductors or passes. Watts attributed the lower boarding times to a high level of prepayment, including tokens, multi-ride tickets cancelled by the passengers themselves, and passes, and the fact that fares were independent of distance.

A study of alternative fare structures in Ottawa reports that the simultaneous introduction of exact fares and transit passes led to a reduction of 25 per cent in the average boarding time per passenger (Bureau of Management Consulting 1977).

Werz (1973) reports that European transit systems that changed from Method 1, where a conductor collects fares, to Method 2, where the driver collects fares, found that this change reduced the speed of surface transit vehicles on average by 10 per cent because of the longer time the vehicles spent standing at stops while passengers boarded. Also according to Werz, European transit systems which changed from Method 2 to Method 3, with automatic/honour fare collection, found that on average this increased the average speed of transit vehicles by about 11 per cent.

One would expect that with Method 3 it would take a group of passengers as much as four times as long to board the standard bus using a single door as to board an articulated bus using two double doors.

Some information is available on how the equipment costs of the transit system might depend upon the fare structure and the fare collection method. According to a Toronto study (Joint Metro/TTC Transit Policy Committee 1979a, 10), the introduction of peak/off-peak fare differentials in that city would involve a one-time capital cost of $0.7 million. However, according to the same report, the introduction of fares based on distance during peak periods would require the Toronto transit system to adopt a variation of Method 3, which would involve a one-time capital cost of $9 million to $12 million and an increase in annual operating costs by $5 million to $8 million because of the need for fare inspectors. (Of course the adoption of Method 3 would bring other benefits besides the ability to implement fares based on distance and other fare structures.)

The introduction of automatic fare collection would require the installation of ticket automats (vending machines), unless tickets were sold across the counter at commissioned sales outlets, and ticket cancellers (validators) at stops or on vehicles. Ticket automats cost about $10 000-$12 000 each and cancellers cost about $1000-$2000 each.

Changes in fare structures, fare collection methods, and related vehicle designs can thus have significant effects on fare collection costs, including average boarding times and hence the average speed of transit vehicles and the amount of congestion imposed by transit vehicles on other road users.[25] Consideration of fare collection costs could therefore modify our conclusions on efficient fare structures. Much more information is needed to determine how fare collection costs would affect the efficient fare structure and what the efficient fare collection method would be. Government-subsidized demonstration projects in this area would be justified, provided they are accompanied by carefully designed monitoring programs.

Demonstration projects could test fares that vary by time of day or by distance and direction at rush hour and semi-automatic fare collection on surface vehicles. The latter would allow passengers to enter past the driver and buy tickets for exact cash fares or to enter another door and use cancelling machines on the vehicle to validate pre-purchased multi-ride tickets. Passengers with valid transfers and passes could also enter this other door. The multi-ride tickets could be issued through sales outlets and could be priced at a discount which would lead to an appropriate balance between passengers using cash and multi-ride tickets. This system would have to be combined with an honour fare system and could also be combined with a test of articulated buses.

If such demonstrations were accompanied by proper research they would generate valuable information that could also be used by other transit systems. Provincially subsidized demonstration projects would probably be most appropriate for medium-to-large urban areas such as London, Hamilton, or Ottawa. The latter is already being considered for a demonstration project on semi-automatic fare collection (DeLeuw Cather 1978). It is more difficult to justify provincially subsidized demonstration projects in Toronto, because the information generated would not necessarily be useful to other Ontario cities. However, the gains from changes in the fare structure and from introduction of automatic fare collection on subways could be large enough that Toronto might opt for such changes on the basis of careful research.[26]

Since there are already several transit systems in Ontario which use monthly transit passes, demonstration projects involving passes would not seem to be necessary. However, careful economic analysis of the data for these systems would be useful as a way of determining the effects of passes on fare collection costs. This issue is considered in the following chapter.

25 In addition, fare collection methods affect the ability of buses to adhere to schedules and the extent of bus platooning.

26 Automatic fare collection is recommended in a consulting report by J.W. Leas and Associates for the TTC (see Joint Metro / Toronto Transit Commission Transit Policy Committee 1979a).

4

Transit fare policies: additional issues

This chapter considers three additional issues involved in setting transit fares. The efficiency of monthly transit passes is evaluated. The second section considers how transit fares might be modified if one wished to use fare policies to promote a more equal distribution of income. Against the tendency of transit companies to prefer the fare policy which maximizes transit ridership, the third section demonstrates that an efficient allocation of resources could require a significantly different fare policy from that which maximizes transit ridership. Finally, a number of conclusions reached on the basis of Chapters 3 and 4 are presented, along with comments on existing fare policies in Ontario and possible alternatives.

TRANSIT PASSES

In recent years, a large number of transit systems have introduced monthly transit passes, which enable the buyer to take any number of transit trips during the month for a fixed fee.[1] They have continued to offer rides at a fixed fare per ride to people without passes.

When considering the economic efficiency of this pricing option, the two critical issues are whether passes should be valid for peak hour trips only, for off-peak trips only, or for all trips and how passes should be priced.

---

1 Cities and years of introduction are: Edmonton 1962, Saskatoon 1967, Regina and Thunder Bay 1970, Calgary 1975, Montreal, Ottawa, and Whitehorse 1976, Brandon, Hamilton, Laval, Moose Jaw, Quebec, and Sarnia 1977, Hull, Red Deer, and Winnipeg 1978, London and Toronto 1980. In addition, monthly passes are used on the GO Transit commuter rail/bus system in Toronto. Passes offered in Canada are not transferable among riders, and our analysis is restricted to non-transferable passes.

Model of the decision to buy a pass

Let us begin with a simple model of how a person might decide whether to purchase a monthly pass, assuming that the introduction of the pass does not affect the regular fare or transit service.

Assume that individual A has a fixed number of hours T, which he is free to allocate between work and travelling by transit. He earns w dollars per hour worked. Each transit trip requires t hours of time and F dollars for the fare. All money not spent on transit fares is used to buy a composite consumption good C at the fixed price $P_C = 1$. Thus, the individual faces the following budget constraint:

$$(F + wt)R + C = wT,$$

where R is number of transit rides. The term $(F + wt)$ is the price or 'generalized cost' of a transit ride in terms of money plus value of travel time.[2] We assume that, subject to this budget constraint, the individual chooses C and R to maximize a utility function $U^A(C, R)$. Finally, we assume that a second individual B faces an identical budget constraint but has a different utility function $U^B(C, R)$.

Figure 5a illustrates this model. The way the indifference curves of individuals A and B have been drawn, individual B takes more transit rides than does individual A.

We now suppose that the transit system offers to sell a transit pass, which allows travel without payment of the fare, at a price of P. We assume that the fare F and travel time t per trip are unchanged. This introduces an alternative budget constraint for both individuals:

$$wtR + C = wT - P.$$

Each individual now simultaneously chooses C and R *and* decides whether to buy a pass (i.e. chooses between constraints) so as to maximize utility.

Figure 5b reproduces Figure 5a with this additional constraint. For the level of P which we have assumed, individual A does not buy the pass, continues to buy the same number of transit rides, and receives no benefit from the pass.

---

2 Of course, this simple model is inconsistent with the empirical evidence that the value of travel time is less than the wage rate. See Frankena (1979, 16-18). However this is not a serious problem, because with a slightly more complex model one could arrive at a 'generalized cost' of a transit ride equal to $(F + vt)$ where v, the value of travel time, is not equal to w.

Figure 5
The decision to buy a pass

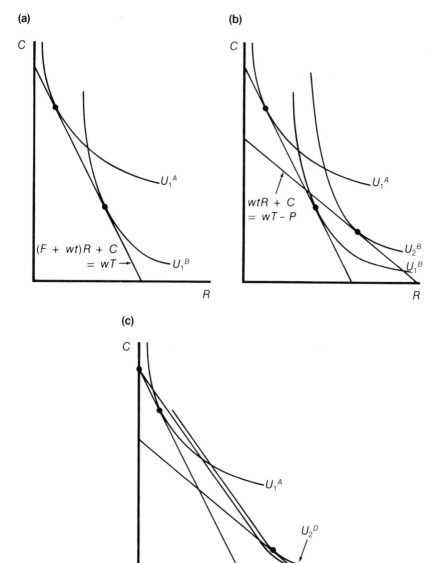

(a)

C

U_1^A

$(F + wt)R + C$
$= wT \rightarrow$

U_1^B

R

(b)

C

U_1^A

$wtR + C$
$= wT - P$

U_2^B

U_1^B

R

(c)

C

U_1^A

U_2^D

U_1^D

R

Individual B on the other hand buys the pass, takes more transit rides, and is better off.

This corresponds to what one would expect to be the 'typical' situation: people who were relatively heavy users of transit before the introduction of the pass would buy the pass and then take even more trips.

However, this result does depend on the assumptions made in Figure 5b about the nature of the indifference curves, in particular the fact that B's indifference curve through any point is steeper than A's. Figure 5c reproduces the two constraints and individual A's indifference curve from Figure 5b, but individual B has now been replaced by individual D. Individual D takes no transit rides at all in the absence of the pass option while, as before, A is a light user of transit. However, D would buy a pass while A would not. This might be like the case where D would switch from automobile to transit when the pass is introduced.

We have thus considered three different types of individuals: Individual A is a light user of transit whether or not passes are available and does not buy a pass. Individual B is a heavy user of transit whether or not passes are available and does buy a pass. In the real world, B might correspond to a person who commutes to work by transit even when no pass is available. When the pass is offered, he takes more non-work trips by transit, probably mainly during off-peak periods. Individual D does not use transit without a pass, but if a pass was offered D would buy it and take a large number of transit rides. In the real world, D might correspond to a person who would switch from automobile to transit for a large number of trips, principally for rush-hour work trips.

The interesting point here is that, in principle at least, two substantially different types of users, B and D, may buy passes. Most important of all, the *extra* transit trips they take because of the introduction of the pass are quite different; for B the extra trips are chiefly non-rush-hour trips while for D they are mainly rush-hour trips.

The price of a pass
It should be evident from the model that, for a given level of the fare F, the decision whether or not to buy a pass would depend critically on the price of the pass P. Thus the level of P will affect the number and the types of individuals who buy passes and the number and the types of extra transit rides taken if a pass option is introduced.

On average, allowing for holidays, there are about twenty-one working days a month for a person who works a five-day week, so that on average a person who commutes to work by transit would take at least forty-two trips a month by transit. Consequently, if P was set so that P/F was less than 42, all people who would commute regularly by transit would find it cheaper to use passes. All the Canadian urban transit systems which offered passes in 1977 set P/F at less than 42. The P/F ration was 32.5 for the Ottawa system and 40 for several of the other systems. By contrast, in 1980 monthly passes were introduced in Toronto at a P/F ratio of 52.

Information on purchasers of passes and additional transit rides
In order to evaluate the transit pass option, it is important to know what share of passes are sold to each of the types of people described above and what share of additional transit trips each is responsible for. Information on this issue is available from two sources: a survey conducted in Ottawa after transit passes were introduced (Bureau of Management Consulting 1977) and a survey conducted in Toronto in connection with an experimental sale of passes (Toronto Transit Commission 1978).

Ottawa
In March 1976 the Ottawa transit system began selling monthly passes for $12 (the price of thirty-six single-ride tickets). In May 1976 a voluntary-response survey asked riders about the number of transit rides taken per day in February (before passes were introduced) and in May.

The survey found that among respondents who purchased a pass in May, 84 per cent took two rush-hour transit trips per day in May and 86 per cent took two rush-hour trips per day in February; thus transit passes were purchased predominantly by people who were regular peak-hour transit commuters regardless of whether passes were available. Thus, most of the purchasers were people like B.

The survey also found that 48 per cent of the respondents who purchased passes in May took one or more off-peak weekday trips by transit during May, compared to only 34 per cent of the same group who did so in February, so that passes appear to have led to an increase in off-peak weekday transit travel.[3]

Finally, according to the Ottawa survey 44 per cent of the new transit trips generated by the passes were trips that would not otherwise have been taken; 28

---

3 However, these figures are not seasonally adjusted, and there is no test for statistical significance. Also, May has more days than February. It could be that people would have taken more off-peak weekday transit trips in May than in February even without the pass. Moreover, the increase in off-peak weekday transit trips was almost exactly offset by declines in peak and weekend trips, presumably due to seasonal or purely random factors. In any event, the average total number of transit rides by respondents who purchased passes in May was fifty-six in both February and May.

per cent would have been made by automobile or taxi; and 23 per cent would have been made by bicycle or by walking.

Toronto

In 1978 the Toronto Transit Commission carried out a test sale of monthly passes, which were offered to a randomly selected group of about one thousand adult riders who took at least four transit trips a week. The passes were valid only for the month of April and were priced at $22 (the price of fifty-one single-ride tokens).

Surveys conducted before and during the period that the passes were in effect led to the conclusion that on average people who purchased passes increased the number of transit rides they took by 20 per cent as a result of the pass. It was also concluded that 'almost all' of the extra rides occurred in off-peak periods.

It was found that 46 per cent of the pass buyers did not own a car, and that 'for pass-buyers who did use an auto, their auto trips declined by 23 per cent after buying a pass' (Toronto Transit Commission 1978, v). Assuming that the groups who 'owned' and 'used' automobiles were identical, these findings imply that on average all pass buyers combined reduced their use of automobiles by 12 per cent as a result of the passes.

Conclusions

The empirical findings correspond to expectations. In Ottawa, P was set so that all regular transit commuters benefited from the pass. Consequently virtually everyone who would have commuted regularly by transit in the absence of the pass option bought a pass. In Toronto, P was set so that many but not all regular transit users benefited from the pass. In both cases, for a person who did buy a pass there was a large percentage decline in the price of *extra* (typically off-peak) trips.[4]

On the other hand, for people who would not have used transit without a pass, its introduction in Ottawa and Toronto represented a relatively small percentage reduction in the total cost of using transit regularly for commuting as well as for other purposes. Consequently, based on other evidence about price-elasticities of modal choice, one would have expected only a very small percentage of these people to buy a pass (Frankena 1978a; 1979, 19-22).

---

4 In addition to this substitution effect, there would be an income effect, but we ignore the income effect on the ground that it would be relatively small because the equivalent cash grant is a small share of income and the income elasticity of demand for transit is low (see Frankena 1979, 21).

Of course one would expect the effect of introducing passes on the level of peak vs off-peak use of transit to depend on the price of the pass P relative to the fare F. If P/F is high, one would expect additional transit trips to be heavily concentrated during off-peak periods, since sale of passes would be concentrated among people who would have commuted regularly by transit (mainly during peak periods) even without passes. If P/F is low, a broader range of people would buy passes, and there would be a greater effect on peak-hour use of transit.

At the risk of oversimplification, therefore, it is useful to assume that at the typical P/F ratios passes have only a minor effect on the number of *peak*-hour trips by either public transit or automobile and that they lead to a significant increase in the number of *off-peak* transit rides. Because of the first assumption, second-best arguments relating to unpriced automobile congestion during rush hour do not have an important bearing on the evaluation of transit passes offered at the typical P/F ratios. Consequently, for the sake of simplicity our analysis of the efficiency of transit passes will assume that use of automobiles is priced at marginal social cost.

Efficiency of passes
We turn now to an analysis of the efficiency effects of transit passes. The transit system must decide whether to introduce a pass, whether to limit its validity (e.g. to rush-hour trips), and what price to charge for it. Thus, the basic problem is to determine simultaneously the categories of trips for which passes will be valid and the prices of passes in order to maximize the efficiency of resource allocation. This problem is complicated by the fact that the efficiency effects of a pass will depend upon whether or not regular fares are equal to the marginal congestion costs of transit trips.

No deficit constraint
Consider a transit system not subject to a deficit constraint[5] and so not forced to raise the regular fare to offset the decline in revenue which typically occurs when a pass is introduced.[6] In this case the efficiency effects of introducing a pass result from eliminating fares for the people who buy passes.

---

5 This discussion would also apply if the transit system receives a subsidy, conditional on introduction of passes, to cover the reduction in net revenue due to the introduction of the pass option.
6 The introduction of passes would reduce the average boarding time and hence improve service for all riders.

If the regular fare is equal to the marginal congestion cost imposed by a rider who pays the regular fare, the elimination of fares for people who buy passes would have two significant effects on the efficiency of resource allocation. First, as we saw in the previous chapter it would reduce the social costs of fare collection associated with the trips taken by passholders. This is the principal efficiency benefit of passes. Second, for people who buy passes the marginal private cost of transit rides would be reduced below the marginal social cost, so that the number of transit rides would increase above the efficient level. The excess of marginal social costs over marginal social benefits for these additional trips would be the principal efficiency cost of passes.

However, if the regular fare is greater than the marginal congestion cost imposed by a rider who pays the regular fare, elimination of fares for people who buy passes would have an additional social benefit: passholders would be induced to take some extra trips for which the marginal social benefits exceed the marginal social costs.

The price of a pass plays an important role in determining the groups in the population for which fares would be eliminated. At one extreme, if the price of a pass were set so high that none were bought, the situation would be the same as when no pass was offered: fares would not be eliminated for anyone. At the other extreme, if the price of the pass were zero, fares would be eliminated for everyone: there would be 'free' transit. Between these extremes, in 1977 five Canadian transit systems which offered passes valid for all trips at P/F ratios between 32.5 and 40 sold passes to 24 to 34 per cent of riders (Toronto Transit Commission 1978, 10), and the Toronto Transit Commission estimated at that time that if it offered passes valid for all trips at a P/F ratio of 51, then 8 to 12 per cent of adult riders would buy the passes (ibid. iv). An important issue here is what price per pass would maximize the economic efficiency of passes valid for any particular category of trips.

Elimination of fares for passholders: peak vs. off-peak passes. Because there are important differences in the effects of passes betwen rush and non-rush periods, we will distinguish between the efficiency implications of passes during these two periods.

The reduced fare collection costs resulting from use of a pass would probably be greater during a peak period than during an off-peak period. This is because the social benefit of reducing the delay caused by fare collection for a crowded bus on a congested road would be much greater than the social benefit of reducing the delay for an empty bus on an uncongested road.[7]

---

7 This would probably be true even though the evidence reported in Chapter 3 indicates that the effect of passes on boarding time is greater in off-peak periods than in peak periods. The efficiency benefit per ride would probably also be greater for buses than for subways. Of course the benefit would also depend on the method of fare collection.

By contrast, it is difficult to compare the efficiency cost of passes during peak and off-peak periods. Assuming regular peak and off-peak fares are equal to the marginal congestion costs of a transit ride at those times, elimination of the fare would induce passholders to take some inefficient trips. On the one hand this inefficiency would tend to be greater during peak periods than off-peak periods because the regular peak fare is higher than the regular off-peak fare. On the other hand this inefficiency would tend to be greater during off-peak periods than during peak periods because the fare-elasticity of demand for transit rides on the part of people who would buy passes is greater during off-peak periods than during peak periods. On balance, it seems reasonable to reach the tentative conclusion that the average efficiency cost per trip taken by passholders would be lower during peak than off-peak periods.

Thus, it seems reasonable to expect that if regular fares were equal to marginal congestion costs, the efficiency benefits would be greater and the efficiency costs lower per trip taken by passholders in the case of passes valid only at rush hour than in the case of passes valid only during non-rush periods. Tentatively, therefore, if regular fares were equal to marginal congestion costs, passes valid only at rush hour would more likely be efficient than passes valid only during off-peak periods.

However, virtually all transit systems in Ontario now charge the same regular fare at rush hour and during off-peak periods. Since the marginal congestion cost imposed by an extra transit trip is greater in peak than in off-peak periods, current off-peak fares probably exceed marginal congestion costs while peak fares do not. The elimination of off-peak fares for people who buy passes would thus have an additional social benefit, though there would probably be no corresponding benefit during peak periods; off-peak passholders would be induced to take some extra off-peak trips for which the marginal social benefits would exceed the marginal social costs.

Because of this final complication we cannot tell without further research whether passes valid only in peak periods would be more efficient than passes valid only in off-peak periods when the regular fare is the same during both periods.

Elimination of fares for all riders. The next issue is whether efficiency would be improved if people who bought passes were charged different fares from those who did not. Any such justification would have to rest on differences between these two groups in either the fare-elasticity of demand for transit or, in the absence of efficient road pricing, the cross-elasticity of demand for automobile use under congested conditions with respect to transit fares. We shall confine our attention to the case in which passes are valid for all categories of trips and are priced at roughly forty times the regular fare.

The empirical evidence suggests that the fare-elasticity of demand for peak hour transit rides is substantially lower for passholders than for non-passholders, because the former tend to commute regularly by transit during rush hour in any case. This provides an efficiency argument for making *peak-hour* fares lower for those who buy passes.

However, there is no evidence that the fare-elasticity of demand for off-peak transit rides is significantly different for passholders and non-passholders. Nor is there information on differences in cross-elasticities of demand for automobile use under congested conditions. Thus, there does not appear to be any efficiency argument for charging lower *off-peak* fares for passholders.

Passes valid only during peak periods. From available information we cannot be sure whether a pass restricted to peak-hour trips would be more efficient than a pass valid for all trips. The issue hinges in part on how much greater (if any) the existing off-peak fare is than the efficient off-peak fare. Nevertheless, transit systems should consider the alternative of a pass valid only for peak-hour trips. Such a pass should be offered at a price (relative to the peak-hour fare) at which they would be purchased only by regular transit commuters. All transit riders would pay the same fare for rides during off-peak periods.

Deficit constraint

Transit systems tend to operate under deficit constraints. If the introduction of passes changed the system's net revenues, it would force a change in the regular fare or service level, and the efficiency effects of these changes would have to be evaluated.

It is possible that a pass system could increase gross revenues and reduce operating costs (because of reduced boarding times) so that net revenue would increase. In practice, however, they have reduced both gross and net revenues. This is not surprising, because the price of a pass P is almost always set below the total cost of two regular fares F for each working day in the average month, i.e. $P/F < 42$. Moreover, an experiment conducted by the Toronto Transit Commission (1978) indicated that even with a P/F ratio of 51 the introduction of passes would reduce revenue.

Given the budget constraint and the way P is chosen, the introduction of passes would entail an increase in the regular fare or a reduction in service or both. Such changes would probably weaken any efficiency argument that might be made for transit passes.

Benefit-cost analysis of passes in Toronto

This section summarizes the benefits and costs of introducing a pass in Toronto, assuming the pass would be valid for all trips and $P/F = 51$, based on the analysis carried out by the Toronto Transit Commission (TTC) in 1978. The present discussion will focus on the issue of economic efficiency, while the TTC analysis was carried out from a different perspective.

Benefits

According to the TTC, introduction of the pass option described above would reduce the fare collection costs borne by the TTC itself by $70000 to $110000 annually after the first year. (During the first year these savings would be offset by the start-up costs involved in issuing passes.) These savings are primarily a result of the lower TTC labour costs involved in selling passes rather than tokens. Presumably there would also be some reduction in the time costs borne by transit users in acquiring passes rather than tokens, and this should be added to the $70000-$110000 figure.

Surprisingly, the TTC concluded that the use of passes would not lead to a change in operating schedules and hence would not lead to a reduction in the TTC's cost per vehicle mile of service or to a reduction in average travel time for riders. This contrasts with the apparent results of introducing passes in Ottawa. If the TTC's conclusion is correct, the apparently most important benefits from introduction of passes would not exist. Because of the importance of this issue, the TTC statement on this is quoted in full:

It has been suggested that the use of passes results in improved loading times for surface vehicles. On a system where tickets are sold on the vehicles, this is almost certainly the case, since pass users no longer buy tickets. However, with an exact fare system such as the TTC has, the savings would be less.

OC Transpo in Ottawa claims an average reduction in boarding times of 22 per cent after passes were implemented. The committee investigating the operational impacts of passes on the TTC felt that the savings on the TTC would be considerably lower, due to the many free body transfer points on the TTC, and the occasional delays caused by attempts to use a pass fraudulently.

In fact, the committee concluded that there would not be sufficient time savings with passes to permit schedule improvements that would reduce costs. Overall, the system would operate roughly as it does now, including both surface routes and the subway. (Toronto Transit Commission 1978)

Costs

According to the TTC, passholders would increase their number of rides by 20 per cent. To the extent that the marginal private cost of riding transit was less than the marginal social cost after elimination of fares, these extra transit rides would be inefficient, that is, their value to the people taking them would be less than the social costs of producing them. On the other hand, to the extent that existing fares exceeded marginal congestion costs for transit trips during off-peak periods, these extra rides would be efficient. Unfortunately, without a careful study of the efficient off-peak fare, it is not possible to determine whether, on balance, production of the additional trips would be efficient or not.

According to the TTC, introducing passes would lead to a decline in revenues from riders and hence require either an increase in subsidies ($2 to $4 million annually) or an increase in regular fares (3 to 4 per cent) for non-passholders. Either of these would involve a distortion which would reduce the efficiency of resource allocation. In the absence of lump-sum taxation, any attempt to raise revenues to finance additional subsidies (e.g. by increasing property taxes, sales taxes, income taxes, etc.) would distort resource allocation to some extent in the economy. Also, unless regular fares were at present below the efficient level, an increase in fares would deter efficient transit travel by non-passholders.

Another category of costs involved in introducing passes is that the TTC would lose information on number of riders, since there would be no record of the number of trips by passholders. To acquire such information, the TTC would have to conduct an annual ridership survey at a cost of about $10 000 per year.[8]

Finally, the TTC anticipated that, like any significant policy change, the introduction of passes would involve some disruption during its initial phases.

Conclusions
If the TTC was correct about the effects of introducing passes, it is difficult to imagine that the efficiency benefits would exceed the efficiency costs. Moreover, if they did, it would almost certainly be because the regular off-peak fare exceeded the marginal congestion cost of off-peak transit rides. In that case the appropriate step for the TTC would be to reduce off-peak fares, not to introduce passes.

On the other hand, if the TTC underestimated the effect on operating schedules of introducing passes, a careful analysis might predict an increase in the efficiency of resource allocation. Thus, the effect of introduction of passes on operating schedules should receive careful study.

INCOME DISTRIBUTION AND TRANSIT FARES

Thus far our analysis of transit fare policies has focused on achieving an economically efficient allocation of resources. We shall now consider how transit fares might be modified if there is also an objective to promote a more equal distribution of income.

If lump-sum redistribution of income is not possible and the social marginal utility of income varies with the level of family income, the distributional effects should be considered in setting public transit fares. However, the use of public transit fare policies to redistribute income is limited by two considerations: first,

8 Optical/electronic counting devices mounted at bus doorways are being developed.

even in a 'closed' city there would be an efficiency loss associated with the distortion in consumption patterns which would result from a departure from the efficient fare; secondly, in an 'open' city an attempt to redistribute income at the local level would encourage inefficient migration, and this migration could limit the feasible redistribution.[9]

We shall assume that the social marginal utility of income is inversely related to family income, i.e. a lump-sum transfer of income from rich to poor would increase social welfare. Of course, this is an ethical judgment, with which the reader may disagree.

Unless otherwise specified, we shall also assume that the public transit firm is subject to a binding deficit constraint, so that the question is how consideration of income redistributional effects would affect optimal fares given the level of subsidies.

We shall consider in turn how distributional considerations might change our evaluation of: differential peak / off-peak fares, fares based on distance travelled and number of transfers, two-part tariffs, different fares for different services, fare discrimination, and monthly passes.

Peak / off-peak fare differentials

We have reviewed the efficiency arguments for charging higher fares at peak travel times than during off-peak periods, regardless of whether one considers the first-best situation, the second-best situation where automobile congestion is unpriced, or the second-best situation where the transit firm is subject to a deficit constraint. We now consider the distributional effects of increasing the fare at peak periods and reducing the fare at off-peak periods, compared to charging the same fare at all times.

Unfortunately, there are no data available for Ontario on the income distributions of transit riders at different times of day. The only data we have found are for daytime, weekday, central-business-district-oriented bus riders in Minneapolis in the early 1970s (see Table 4). These data show that the mean family income of off-peak riders ($9463) is slightly less than the mean family income ($9661 in the morning and $9583 in the evening) of peak riders. However, more detailed data show that people with annual family incomes under $8000 and over $20000 accounted for a larger share of off-peak trips than of peak trips, while people with annual family incomes between $8000 and $20000 accounted for a smaller share of off-peak trips than of peak trips.

9 In a 'closed' city, the decision to live in the city is not influenced by transit fare policies. In an 'open' city, the decision to live in the city would depend among other things on transit fare policies.

TABLE 4

Income distribution of CBD-oriented bus riders in Minneapolis (percentages)

Family income ($000)	Morning peak	Evening peak	Daytime off-peak
<3	11.0	14.3	17.8
3-8	29.4	23.3	27.9
8-12	27.0	32.2	23.6
12-20	29.8	28.0	23.7
>20	2.5	2.2	7.0
Mean income	$9661	$9583	$9463

SOURCE: Allen (1975, 104)

For the categories of trips covered by the data, therefore, an increase in peak hour fares and a reduction in off-peak fares would transfer income from middle-income families to low-income families and (to a lesser extent) to high-income families.[10]

How these results would modify one's recommendations about peak / off-peak fare differentials depends on how one weights the well-being of these different income groups.

Fare-by-distance and charging for transfers

Because there are few data on the average length of transit trips and the average number of transfers by people in different income groups, we shall consider the matter generally before examining the limited empirical evidence.

One might be tempted to argue that the average length of transit trips would increase with family income level because, on average, the distance of residences from the centre of a city increases with family income level, and most transit systems are oriented toward providing service between residential areas and the city centre.

However, high-income people, who have a high value of travel time, would be more likely to use conventional transit (excluding commuter railways) for short trips than for long trips because conventional transit is faster than automobile for short trips to the city centre. For example, Dewees (1977) reports that in Metropolitan Toronto door-to-door travel times are lower for transit than for

10 This ignores the distribution of gains and losses resulting from changes in resource allocation, e.g. changes in patterns of road congestion.

automobiles for short trips to the central business district but not for other categories of trips.

Thus, in spite of the conventional wisdom that the average length of trips would increase with family income because of residential location patterns, it is not clear that average length of transit trips (excluding express commuter rail/bus systems such as GO Transit) would be significantly related to income.

Similar considerations apply in the relation between average number of transfers and income. On the one hand, one might expect that, on average, trips originating in higher-income suburbs would involve more transfers than trips originating in lower-income central areas. However, because of their higher valuation of travel time, higher-income people would be less likely than lower-income people to use transit for trips requiring a high number of transfers.

One source of evidence on the relation between family income and the average length of transit trips is a simulation study carried out for Metropolitan Toronto, which produced the result that average simulated transit work trip length would increase slightly with family income level. This model took account of differences in residential locations, employment locations, and modal choice behaviour for different income groups. However, the data and model used were crude, and the range of average simulated work trip lengths was not large, from 5.3 miles for households in the bottom quartile of the income distribution to 5.8 miles for housholds in the top quartile of the income distributions (Frankena 1974, 62-3; 1973).

The only empirical data that could be found on these matters concern estimated trip *times* for different income groups on the Toronto transit system (not including the GO Transit commuter rail/bus system) in 1976. The data reflect not only differences in distance travelled and number of transfers but also in frequency of service and speed of travel. Consequently, one must be careful about relating fares to distances or number of transfers, particularly since the data combine both bus/streetcar and subway trips.

Another problem is that the data cover only 'heavy' transit users (people who take ten or more transit trips a week) and only the 'most frequent trip' taken by the respondent, so that disproportionate weight is given to work trips. However, this is not entirely unfortunate, because if fares were related to distance only at rush hour (as suggested in Chapter 3), these are the trips that would be most affected.

Table 5 shows the distribution of estimated trip times for the most frequent trip for heavy transit users by household income in Toronto in 1976. If one looks only at people with household incomes under $7000 and over $20000 annually, one would conclude that, on average, trip time is shorter for low-income heavy

TABLE 5

Distribution of estimated times for the most frequent transit trip for heavy transit users
in Toronto, by household income, 1976

Annual household	Percentage		
income ($000)	0-20 min.	21-45 min.	46 min. or more
<5	31.5	46.2	22.3
5-7	26.3	47.3	26.3
7-10	20.0	57.0	23.0
10-15	23.2	56.3	20.3
15-20	28.9	51.7	19.5
>20	21.8	49.3	28.9

SOURCE: Toronto Transit Commission (1977, 119)

transit users than for high-income heavy transit users. However, the difference in
average trip length is probably not very large, and the picture is considerably
more complex if one looks at all income groups, because there is no simple
relation between trip time distributions and household incomes.

In conclusion, there is some weak evidence in support of the hypothesis that
average transit trip length is greater for high-income households than for low-
income households, at least at rush hour. However, no simple or strong relationship can be established between trip length and income. Changing from uniform
transit fares to fares by distance would thus probably not have an important
effect on the extent of income inequality in Toronto.

Two-part tariffs

As we have seen, a two-part tariff with the 'fare' set somewhat above the
marginal congestion cost imposed by a transit passenger trip may be a second-
best efficient pricing scheme for a transit system operating with a budget
constraint that makes simple marginal-cost pricing not feasible. We now consider how distributional considerations might affect the optimal two-part tariff
for a public transit system. For simplicity, we shall assume that the transit system
offers a single service and that the 'permit' charge and fare are uniform for all
customers.

Feldstein (1972b) analyses this issue for the case in which every household
chooses to buy a permit. But that case does not apply without modification to
public transit. With transit, individuals rather than households would presumably be required to buy permits. Secondly, the level of the permit charge would
certainly affect some individuals' decisions on whether to use transit at all.

In Feldstein's case a permit charge is equivalent to a lump-sum tax on families and is regressive. Feldstein demonstrates that if distributional considerations are relevant, and if the demand for the good in question has a positive income elasticity,[11] the permit charge should be below the second-best-efficient level and the fare above the second-best-efficient level. This is because a higher fare would make higher-income families pay a larger share of total costs. On the other hand, for an inferior good (which has a negative income elasticity of demand), the permit charge should be above the second-best-efficient level and the fare below the second-best-efficient level.

The lower the absolute value of the income-elasticity of demand, the larger the deviation from the second-best-efficient two-part tariff required to bring about a given redistribution. Also, the lower the absolute value of the price-elasticity of demand, the smaller the efficiency loss involved in any given deviation from the second-best-efficient two-part tariff. Thus, the practical relevance of Feldstein's discussion is greatest if the absolute value of the income-elasticity is large while the absolute value of the price-elasticity is small.[12]

To apply Feldstein's analysis to public transit, two modifications are required. First, a public transit permit charge would be required for each individual, not each family. If the marginal social utility of income depends on family income level, one must consider how the number of individuals per family as well as the use of transit by all family members combined varies with family income. Thus, assuming that all individuals buy permits, the relevant issue is whether the family income-elasticity of demand for transit rides exceeds the family income-elasticity of family size.

Second, not all individuals would choose to buy permits, and the decision to buy a permit would depend on the structure of the two-part tariff in a complex way. Thus, the permit charge-fare combination chosen by the transit firm would affect not only the total number of individuals buying permits but also the type of individuals, including the family income distribution.

It is impossible to draw a firm empirical conclusion on how distributional considerations would affect the optimal two-part tariff for public transit because not all the necessary information is available. For example, we do not know whether the income-elasticity of demand for the number of transit rides (which affects the expenditure on fares) exceeds the income-elasticity of the number of transit users per family (which affects the expenditure on permits).

11 The income elasticity must be positive at the two-part tariff, that is optimal when distributional effects are relevant.

12 See Feldstein (1972b) for a numerical example of the welfare gain involved in taking distributional considerations into account in setting a two-part tariff for electricity.

The information available suggests at most a rather limited scope for socially optimal redistributions of income through departures from the second-best-efficient two-part tariff for public transit. Although the evidence is somewhat mixed (Frankena 1979), the absolute value of the income elasticity of demand for transit rides seems not to be large. It appears to be low relative even to the absolute value of the fare elasticity of demand for transit.[13] Evidently the total number of intra-urban trips per family by all modes increases with family income, largely because the number of people tends to be higher in higher-income families. At the same time, people in higher-income families take a smaller *share* of all intra-urban trips by transit, partly because of the higher value of their travel time and their higher automobile ownership and partly because the standard of transit service is usually lower in high-income, low-density suburbs than in low-income central areas. Consequently, total number of transit rides per family does not seem to vary much with family income.[14]

Of course one might still be able to affect the income distribution through the structure of a two-part tariff for public transit if the number of transit riders per family varied with family income. Although Statistics Canada data show that family size tends to increase with family income, there are no data on how the number of transit riders per family varies with family income.

Thus, based on available information, one must conclude that there is no evidence that, with a given budget constraint, changes in the sizes of the permit charge and fare portions of a two-part tariff for public transit would have an important effect on income distribution. Consequently, distributional considerations cannot justify a departure from the second-best-efficient levels for the permit charge and fare.

The structure of fares for different services
We have considered Ramsey-Boiteux second-best-efficient pricing for a public transit system operating subject to an overall deficit constraint and offering more than one type of service. Feldstein (1972a) has analysed how these pricing rules would be modified if distributional effects were relevant. Based on assumptions about demand common to much of this literature,[15] Feldstein reaches the reasonable conclusion that the more the consumption of a good or service is concentrated in lower-income families the lower its price should be.

13 The demand elasticities estimated in Chapter 10 are not typical in this respect.
14 See the family expenditure data in Chapter 5 for support for this conclusion.
15 Zero income effects and zero cross-price elasticities of demand among transit services and between transit services and goods which are taxed.

Thus, compared to the transit fare structure that would be second-best-efficient according to the Ramsey-Boiteux literature, if distributional considerations are relevant one should reduce fares for services used heavily by low-income groups and raise the fares for services used heavily by high-income groups.

Fare discrimination
In Chapter 3 we considered second-best-efficient price discrimination for a public transit system operating subject to a deficit constraint which sells rides to different population groups with different fare elasticities of demand. That analysis suggested charging higher fares for population groups with more inelastic demands.

If distributional considerations are relevant, that analysis should be modified. Fares for population groups with relatively high concentrations of low-income members should be reduced below the second-best-efficient level, and fares for population groups with relatively high concentrations of high-income members should be increased.

In practical terms, this would justify lower fares for senior citizens, at least if one bases social marginal utility of income on current income. It might also justify lower fares for welfare recipients or other identifiable low-income people.

Passes
If a transit firm operates subject to a deficit constraint, introduction of transit passes would probably be accompanied by an increase in the regular fare. Thus, the introduction of passes would involve an income transfer from non-passholders (lighter users of transit) to pass-holders (heavier users of transit). In order to determine which income groups would benefit from such a transfer, one must know the distribution of transit riders broken down by number of rides a week or month and by family income. The only available data of this type come from the 1978 ridership survey carried out in Toronto.

To evaluate the income distributional effects of introducing in Toronto a monthly transit pass valid for all trips, we assume that the loss of revenue caused by introduction of the pass is made up by a fare increase, and that the pass would be sold at a price of fifty-two times the new fare. We also assume that the number of trips taken by each rider is not changed by the introduction of the pass or the fare increase, and that there is no charge in transit service or in the time costs of travel by transit. In short, we assume that there is no change in the allocation of resources, so that income distributional effects are found simply by examining income transfers due to price changes. The implications of this rather extreme assumption are discussed later. Finally, we assume that all riders who take more than fifty-two trips a month purchase a pass while other riders do not.

In this highly simplified case, the gross benefits of the pass will be distributed between individuals in proportion to the number of trips they take a month over fifty-two. The gross costs of the pass will be distributed between individuals in proportion to the number of trips they take a month up to and including the fifty-second trip. From ridership data for Toronto, individuals were grouped by family income and the percentage of gross benefits and gross costs for each income group computed.

Table 6 shows that under the assumptions made here individuals with annual family incomes under $7000 and between $10000 and $20000 would on average receive net benefits from the introduction of the pass, while individuals with annual family incomes between $7000 and $10000 and over $20000 would on average be made worse off. However, the total loss for all individuals with family incomes between $7000 and $10000 is only 6 per cent of the total gain by all individuals with family incomes below $7000, so that if one aggregated the three lowest income groups one would find that on average members of those three groups would be better off.

Thus, on the assumptions made here, it appears that introduction of a monthly transit pass in Toronto would reduce income inequality. However, this conclusion should be carefully qualified. First, even if the introduction of transit passes would reduce income inequality, the redistribution would be quite small and would not alone provide a sensible justification for passes. Second, it should be noted that on the assumptions used in constructing Table 5, within every income group a majority of transit riders would be worse off as a result of the pass, since the large majority of riders do not take enough trips to benefit from a monthly pass priced at fifty-two times the regular fare. Thus, the introduction of the pass would raise important questions of horizontal equity.

The calculations above were made under the unrealistic assumption that the introduction of passes would not lead to any change in the allocation of resources. In fact, of course, there would be a number of changes in resource allocation which could have important distributional implications. For example, people who bought passes would benefit not only from the lower money cost of trips they would have taken anyway but also because they would take more trips. With a given number of vehicle hours of service, all transit users would benefit from the lower travel time per trip that would result from reduced average boarding times, but they would also bear the cost of the higher travel time per trip that would result from increased transit ridership. One would expect a change in travel time per trip to affect members of different income groups in quite different ways because of differences not only in their levels of transit usage but also in their values of travel time.

TABLE 6

Distribution of benefits and costs of a transit pass among income groups in Toronto

Annual household income ($000)	Percentage of total gross costs	Percentage of total gross benefits
<5	5.2	3.9
5-7	14.4	4.8
7-10	8.6	9.2
10-15	26.2	21.5
15-20	19.3	16.7
>20	26.2	43.9
Total	100.0	100.0

SOURCE: Based on unpublished data provided by the Toronto Transit Commission

Conclusions

The preceding sections indicate that distributional considerations might justify modifications in public transit fares from second-best-efficient levels given any particular deficit constraint for the transit system, i.e. taking the level of subsidies as given. In all these cases, the redistribution in question is *among transit users.* In Chapter 5 we shall consider the distinct issue of distributional justifications for transit subsidies where redistribution is *between taxpayers and transit users.*

The reader should keep in mind that all such methods of redistributing income are relevant only because lump-sum transfers of income are impossible. In principle at least, it would be more efficient to use lump-sum transfers than departures from efficient pricing in order to redistribute income.

COMPARISON OF RIDERSHIP MAXIMIZATION AND ECONOMIC EFFICIENCY

I have proposed that the objective of the urban transit firm should be to increase economic efficiency and, perhaps, to reduce income inequality. However, there is an incipient trend among urban transit systems to adopt an objective of maximizing ridership, measured by either the number of rides or the number of passenger miles.

The London, England, transit system adopted maximization of passenger miles as an objective in 1975. A task force report prepared by the Joint Metro / Toronto Transit Commission Transit Policy Committee (1979b) recommended that the Toronto transit system should adopt maximization of ridership as an objective, and consulting studies on the transit industry routinely take it for granted that the benefits and costs of various policy options should be measured in terms of effects on ridership.

There is an important difference between the economic efficiency objective and the ridership maximization objective, and they would lead to different fare structures and service levels (for a related discussion see Appendix C). To the extent that these two objectives differ, ridership maximization will lead to a waste of scarce resources; hence ridership maximization should be rejected as an objective of transit policy.

The basic argument here is independent of how ridership is measured (by rides or passenger miles), although there are some important practical differences between these two ways of measuring ridership when trips vary in length. Since the current discussion in Ontario emphasizes the number of rides, I shall deal explicitly with this case.

In comparing economic efficiency and ridership maximization, we shall assume that the transit firm is subject to a deficit constraint and automobile use is priced at marginal social cost.

The appeal of ridership maximization
Ridership maximization is an appealing objective for transit companies. It is convenient, easily understood, and fairly easy to implement. Ridership changes can readily be measured and used to demonstrate to the public and to various levels of government what has been done with their subsidy dollars.

Furthermore, the maximization of ridership subject to a budget constraint appears on the surface to be a reasonable objective. It seems (incorrectly) to be identical to maximization of output for a given level of inputs, which is a reasonable objective. The problem is that maximization of number of rides subject to a given deficit constraint is not the same as maximization of number of rides produced with a given amount of scarce resources.

Consider a simple example. Suppose a transit system is required to break even, and that initially it does so by charging a low fare, offering a low level of service, and producing a low level of rides. Suppose that it could also break even, i.e. satisfy the same budget constraint, by charging a high fare, offering a high level of service, and producing the same low number of rides. In this case, the system's output in terms of rides is the same in the two situations, and the system is satisfying the same budget constraint. Thus, if one were maximizing ridership subject to a break-even constraint, one would be indifferent between the two situations.

However, there are important differences in the amounts of scarce resources used to produce trips in the two cases. First, in order to achieve the new, higher service level, the transit firm itself must use more scarce labour, capital, fuel, and so on. Second, because of the new, higher service level, transit riders will use less of their scarce time to travel. Which of these two cases (low fare/low service or high fare/high service) represents the superior allocation of resources (ignoring income distributional effects) depends upon how the value of the extra resources used by the transit system to produce the higher level of service compares with the value of the travel time saved by transit riders as a result of the higher level of service. This is precisely the comparison called for by an analysis of economic efficiency. Ridership maximization ignores this issue.

The criterion of extra subsidy cost per additional ride

A transit firm which maximizes the number of rides given its deficit constraint will, of course, respond to an additional (lump-sum) subsidy by reducing those fares and/or expanding those services for which the marginal subsidy cost per additional ride is lowest. It is important to understand that the practice of ranking alternative marginal changes in operating policy in terms of the criterion of marginal subsidy cost per additional ride shares all the weaknesses of the ridership maximization objective.

It is easy to see that a ranking of changes in operating policy based on marginal subsidy cost per ride does not make much sense from society's point of view. Consider two alternative policies: a fare reduction that (assuming demand is perfectly inelastic with respect to the fare) would involve no increase in ridership and a reduction of $1 million in fare revenue, combined with a $1 million increase in subsidies; and an expansion of service at a cost of $1.05 million, which we assume would lead to an increase in rides by 100000, combined with a $1 million increase in subsidies. In the first case the marginal subsidy cost per ride is infinite, while in the second the marginal subsidy cost per ride is $10.00, so that on the basis of the criterion of marginal subsidy cost per ride the latter seems vastly superior.

Unfortunately, the criterion of marginal subsidy cost per ride measures both the costs and the benefits of policy changes in a nonsensical way. The first option has no real resource cost and no aggregate benefit at all, since there is no change in resource allocation. There is a $1 million transfer payment from taxpayers to transit riders, but no additional real resources (labour, capital, etc.) are used to produce transit service. By contrast, the second option has a real resource cost of $1.05 million, since $1.05 million worth of additional labour, capital, and energy are used to produce additional transit service; it also has two aggregate benefits: people already travelling will spend less time per trip because of increased service, and people will take additional transit rides for which they would be willing to pay more than the marginal private cost. The important issue is whether these two categories of benefits are worth more than $1.05 million or not. This issue is not considered by the objective of ridership maximization or the criterion of marginal subsidy cost per rider. It is precisely the issue eveluated by an analysis of economic efficiency.

Fare structures implied by ridership maximization vs economic efficiency
To illustrate the differences between ridership maximization and economic efficiency, we shall consider the different fare structures that could be implied by these objectives in some specific cases. We begin by considering a highly simplified case: The transit system may offer two categories of rides. The demand for each category of rides depends only on the fare for that category and is independent of income, the fare for the other category, and travel times. The total cost borne by the transit authority is proportional to the total number of rides in the two categories combined and is identical to the total social cost. The transit firm must break even. Consistent with these assumptions, suppose that the demand and cost functions for the two categories of rides are as shown in Figure 6. Note that in Figure 6b the demand curve lies below the marginal cost curve.

To maximize total ridership subject to the break-even constraint, the transit firm would set the fare in market A at F_a, which would entail a ridership level of R_a and a profit level equal to the cross-hatched area $F_aMNF_a^*$. The transit firm would set the fare in market B at F_b, which would entail a ridership level of R_b and a loss equal to the cross-hatched area F_bEGH. The basic conditions for equilibrium are $F_aMNF_a^* = F_bEGH$, i.e. zero profits, and $MC_a - MR_a = MC_b - MR_b$, i.e. equality of the marginal loss per passenger in the two markets.

By contrast, efficiency would involve setting the fare in market A at F_a^*, which would entail ridership of R_a^* and zero profits in market A. The fare in market B would be set above J, the level at which ridership would be zero, and hence no trips would be produced in market B.

Using consumer surplus, one can measure the aggregate welfare loss involved in maximization of ridership rather than efficiency. Maximization of ridership involves a forgone consumer surplus equal to the area MNK in Figure 6a due to limited production of trips for market A and a waste of resources equal to the area $JEGH$ in Figure 6b due to the production of trips for which consumers are willing to pay less than the opportunity cost.

Generalizing from this example, and drawing on results demonstrated in Glaister and Collings (1978) and Nash (1978), one can reach several conclusions about the objective of ridership maximization in the case where a transit system may offer two or more categories of service.

With a given budget constraint, ridership maximization and efficiency imply different fare and service structures. At one extreme the operating policies implied by these two objectives will converge as the required profit level is

Figure 6
Ridership maximization vs efficiency

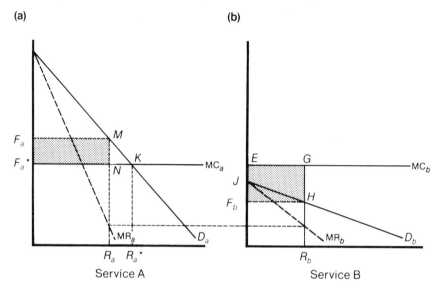

(a)

(b)

Service A

Service B

increased to the profit level that would be achieved under profit maximization, since the feasible set of operating policies would then converge to a single point. At the other extreme, if the transit system receives large lump-sum subsidies the operating policies implied by these two objectives may become very different.

If demand elasticities and/or marginal costs vary among categories of trips, then under a ridership maximization policy the fares for some services might be above efficient levels while the fares for other services might be below efficient levels. In order to maximize ridership, the transit firm might raise the fare for a trip category with a less elastic demand and use the profit earned on that category to subsidize a loss on a category with a more elastic demand, as in Figure 6.

In the absence of externalities, efficiency would not entail fares below marginal costs. When the profit constraint is not binding, efficiency would entail fares equal to marginal costs. As the profit constraint is raised, all fares would be raised above marginal cost (as discussed in Chapter 3). By contrast, maximization of ridership may entail setting some fares below marginal cost, as in Figure 6b.

Some categories of service which would not be offered under efficiency might be offered under ridership maximization. This could occur where the demand curve for a service was below the marginal cost curve, as in Figure 6b.

Welfare loss due to ridership maximization
It is difficult to generalize about the magnitude of the aggregate welfare loss that would result from choosing transit operating policies to maximize ridership rather than to achieve the most efficient allocation of resources given the budget constraint. The loss depends on how unequal own-price elasticities of demand for different categories of trips are, on how unequal marginal costs are, on the magnitude of cross-price elasticities, on the size of the required profit level or subsidy, and so on. Glaister and Collings present calculations for London, England, in which the aggregate welfare loss due to maximization of passenger miles is in the range of 30 per cent of total money expenditures on public transit. Nash calculates that the corresponding welfare loss for break-even operation was 8 to 12 per cent of total money expenditures on public transit.[16] Thus, the welfare loss probably would not be trivial.

CONCLUSIONS AND COMMENTS ON FARE POLICY OPTIONS IN ONTARIO

Transit fares should be set so as to promote economic efficiency and perhaps reduce income inequality. Maximization of ridership is not an appropriate objective for urban transit systems. This conclusion is in conflict with the thrust of the recommendations made in 1979 by the Joint Metro/Toronto Transit Commission Transit Policy Committee.

Considerations of economic efficiency indicate that transit rides should be priced below marginal social cost because the use of automobiles is priced below marginal social cost; hence transit fares should be set below the marginal congestion costs imposed by additional transit riders. However, recognition of the real resource costs of raising tax revenues to finance transit deficits decreases the extent to which it is efficient to reduce transit fares in order to induce automobile users to ride transit.

Ignoring fare collection costs, we have seen that it would be economically efficient to charge higher fares during peak periods than during off-peak periods, to charge for transfers, and on certain types of routes to base fares in part on distance travelled during peak periods. The proposed changes represent a significant departure from current fare structures in Ontario. At present only one urban area (Oakville) charges different fares in peak and off-peak periods; fares are not based on distance except crudely in a few minor cases where there are zone fares; and transfers are free.

16 Glaister and Collings (1978, 317-19) and Nash (1978, 80). See the former for a discussion of the conditions under which maximization of weighted passenger miles is equivalent to maximization of net social surplus or economic efficiency.

Attempts to implement some of the suggested changes in fare structure without others would lead to some undesirable consequences. For example, charging for transfers without a reduction in the basic fare for off-peak trips would lead to serious overpricing of off-peak trips involving transfers.

However, some of the economic efficiency gains from more complex fare structures might be offset by higher fare collection costs. This would be particularly true in smaller cities where automobile and transit congestion are limited. Nevertheless, there are a number of innovations in fare collection methods which might yield substantial reductions in fare collection costs. Additional research on the economics of fare collection is necessary, and provincially subsidized demonstrations of options such as semi-automatic fare collection and honour fare collection should be considered for medium-to-large urban areas in Ontario.

One method of reducing fare collection costs is to introduce monthly passes. More research on the efficiency of monthly passes should be undertaken. Until such studies are done, other transit systems in Ontario should not introduce monthly passes, unless this is part of a carefully designed demonstration project.

5
The justification for transit subsidies

The problems of financing and subsidizing public transit are among the most pressing urban transportation issues in Ontario. The remainder of this study is devoted to an economic analysis of urban transit subsidies. The present chapter explains the economic justifications for transit subsidies based on considerations of efficiency of resource allocation and income redistribution. Chapter 6 describes urban transit subsidy policies in Ontario, and Chapters 7 to 10 analyse their effects.

There are four arguments for subsidizing public transit to increase the efficiency of resource allocation:

- for public transit the marginal cost is below the average cost because of increasing returns to scale;
- private automobile trips are priced below their marginal social cost;
- there are external benefits associated with the form of urban development promoted by the existence of high-quality, low-fare public transit; and
- the knowledge gained from transit research and demonstration projects in one urban area benefits other areas.

After examining these justifications for transit subsidies, we shall consider the justification based on income distributional effects.

Finally, we shall consider the implications of efficiency and income redistribution arguments for two important issues in transit subsidies: how the level of subsidies should vary among cities of different sizes and how the burden of subsidies should be allocated among local, provincial, and federal governments.

SUBSIDIES BASED ON INCREASING RETURNS TO SCALE

In Chapter 2 we saw that if the production of trips is subject to constant returns to scale (or constant long-run average social cost) and the capacity of the transportation facility is at the efficient level, the revenues from efficient user charges will be equal to the costs borne by the transportation authority, provided there are no pollution externalities. This argument ignores the second-best, externality, and public-goods justifications for subsidies analysed below.

It follows that if the production of public transit trips were subject to constant returns to scale, if there were no relevant second-best, externality, or public goods considerations, and if the transit authority provided the efficient level of service, the first-best-efficient transit fares of the type discussed in Chapter 3 would raise just enough revenue to cover the costs of providing the transit service.

If any production process (e.g. the production of tractors, telephone calls, or transit trips) is subject to increasing returns to scale, the long-run average cost per unit of output declines as the level of output is increased, and the long-run marginal cost is less than the long-run average cost. If the price of output is set equal to the long-run marginal cost, as first-best-efficient pricing requires when capacity is at the efficient level, the price will be less than the long-run average cost, and the total revenue from the sale of output will be less than the long-run total cost of production. In the absence of a subsidy, it would be necessary to raise the price above the efficient level and reduce output below the efficient level in order to break even. In short, if there were increasing returns to scale a subsidy would be required in order for the allocation of resources to be efficient.

In relation to urban public transit the crucial point in the argument is that the long-run average social cost per passenger trip by transit declines as the number of passenger trips per hour increases because the cost of rights-of-way, the cost of vehicle operation, and the waiting time per passenger trip all decrease as the number of passenger trips per hour increases.[1]

Consider how the efficient level of service and cost per passenger trip would change if the number of people wishing to travel on a given transit route doubled. In the case of commuter railways, rail rapid transit, and other systems which use separate rights of way, a doubling in the number of passenger trips per

---

1 The in-vehicle travel time per passenger trip would increase, because average bus size and hence passenger loading and unloading time per mile would increase. However, this source of decreasing returns to scale would be outweighed by the three sources of increasing returns to scale discussed in the text.

hour normally would not require a doubling of right-of-way investments. Indeed, in many cases it would probably be possible to double the number of vehicle-miles of service without any increase in the scale of rights-of-way. Consequently, as the number of passenger trips per hour increases, the 'overhead' cost per passenger trip of providing rights-of-way decreases.[2]

If the number of passengers travelling per route-mile on the transit system were to double, an efficiently operated transit system would increase the average size of transit vehicles or the average length of vehicle trains (Mohring 1972; 1979). This would lead to a reduction in vehicle operating costs (particularly wages of drivers) per passenger trip.

If the number of passengers travelling per route-mile of the transit system were to double, an efficiently operated transit system would increase the number of vehicle hours and hence the frequency of service. This would reduce the average waiting time per passenger trip for users.[3]

It follows from these three sources of increasing returns to scale that the long-run average social cost curve for public transit trips would be negatively sloped, and the long-run marginal social cost curve would lie below the long-run average social cost curve, as in Figure 7.

An efficient allocation of resources requires that transit trips should be taken by all people who are willing to pay the long-run marginal social cost of their trips and only by these people. The efficient number of trips is therefore determined where the demand and long-run marginal social cost curves for transit trips intersect.[4] With the demand curve for transit trips depicted in Figure 7, to achieve an efficient allocation of resources a total of OQ trips per hour should be taken, and these trips should be taken by the people who are willing to pay the most for them.

If the transit system provides the amount of rights of way and the number of vehicle-hours of service which would minimize the long-run total social cost of producing OQ trips, the short-run marginal social cost curve would intersect the long-run marginal social cost curve where the latter intersects the demand curve.

2 Pozdena and Merewitz (1978) found economies of scale in the production of vehicle-miles of rail rapid transit service using data for Toronto, Montreal, and nine American cities.
3 Mohring (1972; 1979). It might also increase the density of routes and hence reduce the average walking time per passenger trip for users.
4 This assumes that the total social benefits exceed the total social costs of transit service at that number of trips. The complications which arise from differences in the demand for trips during rush and non-rush hours do not affect the fundamental conclusions concerning increasing returns to scale and subsidization (see Mohring 1976, 62-7).

Figure 7
Model of a mass transit system with increasing returns to scale

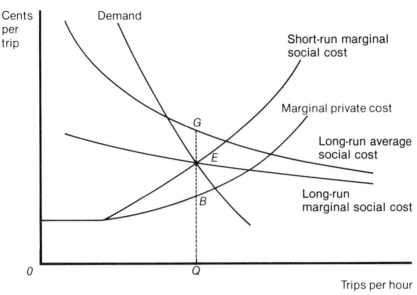

Note: The curve labelled 'marginal private cost' depicts the short-run average
      variable social cost.

The short-run marginal social cost curve in Figure 7 corresponds to the marginal
social cost curve in Figure 1, except that in the former the curve refers to the cost
of person-trips by transit rather than the cost per mile of road-vehicle trips. In
the case of transit, the short-run marginal social cost of an extra transit passenger trip includes both the value of travel time of the person who takes the trip
and the marginal congestion costs imposed by the extra passenger trip on other
transit users.

    If we take the point of view of an individual transit rider and ignore the
marginal congestion costs imposed on others, we can measure the value of time
required to take a trip at each level of transit ridership. This private time cost
(which does not include the transit fare) is represented by the curve labelled
'marginal private cost' in Figure 7.

    From our analysis of user charges we know that in order to achieve efficient
use of the facilities it provides, the transit authority should charge a fare equal to
the marginal congestion costs imposed by the last trip (i.e. the distance between

the 'marginal private cost' and the 'short-run marginal social cost' curves) at the level of travel where the demand curve intersects the short-run marginal social cost curve. In this case the appropriate fare would be BE. If this fare was charged, OQ trips per hour would be taken, and the allocation of resources would be efficient. The revenue raised per hour by a fare of BE collected on OQ trips would be OQ times BE.

We must now compare the transit system's fare revenue with the cost of providing rights of way and vehicles. QG measures the long-run average social cost per trip when OQ trips are produced. QB measures the portion of this cost borne by each of the users in terms of value of travel time. Thus, BG (QG minus QB) measures the cost per trip borne by the transit system, and the total cost per hour to the transit system of providing OQ trips would be OQ times BG. Comparing the transit system's fare revenue with its costs, we find the costs exceed revenues by OQ times EG (EG equals BG minus BE) per hour.

In summary, if there are increasing returns to scale in public transit, an efficient allocation of resources can be achieved in the long run only if the transit system is subsidized. If transit were required to be self-financing, a fare higher than BE would be charged, and fewer than OQ trips would be produced. This would be inefficient because the higher fare would deter some people from taking transit trips even though they would be willing to pay the marginal social cost of these trips.

Mohring (1972) estimated that increasing returns to scale could justify a subsidy of roughly 50 to 60 per cent of the costs borne by the transit authority for a system using standard 55-passenger buses in a large American urban area in order to achieve an efficient allocation of resources between public transit and other uses. Subsequently, Mohring (1981) noted that if a transit system used twelve-passenger minibuses rather than standard buses the extent of increasing returns to scale and hence the subsidies they could justify would be much smaller, in fact less than 10 per cent of those for a standard bus system. This is because a major source of increasing returns to scale in Mohring's study is the reduction in waiting time per passenger that occurs when service frequency increases. When service is provided by smaller buses, service is more frequent and waiting time is less. Consequently, the reduction in waiting time per passenger that results from a given percentage increase in frequency of service is substantially smaller for minibuses than for standard buses. However, unless transit systems actually switch to minibuses, this qualification does not affect the practical argument for subsidies.

In addition, Mohring (1981) points out that if private automobiles were required to pay congestion tolls then public transit buses should also pay congestion tolls.[5] Mohring calculates that in a first-best situation the revenues collected from congestion tolls imposed on standard buses operated by a monopolistic transit firm would offset about 60 per cent of the subsidies paid to the transit firm on account of increasing returns to scale.

SUBSIDIES BASED ON UNDERPRICING OF AUTOMOBILE TRAVEL

We saw in Chapter 3 that when the use of automobiles is priced below marginal social cost there is a second-best-efficiency argument for pricing transit rides below their marginal social cost. Consequently, second-best-efficient fares would be lower than the first-best-efficient fares discussed above, and the level of transit subsidies required to achieve the second-best-efficient allocation of resources would be even greater than the level justified by increasing returns to scale alone.

Glaister and Lewis show for London, England, that because of the failure to charge peak-period automobile users for their marginal congestion costs, second-best considerations alone would justify a subsidy to the bus system of about 27 per cent of total capital and operating costs.[6]

Glaister and Lewis consider only one of the ways in which automobile users now pay less than the marginal social cost of their trips in Ontario. In addition to not being charged for their marginal congestion costs, automobile users do not pay pollution and road maintenance costs,[7] and many automobile users pay less than the marginal social cost of their use of parking spaces.[8]

Moreover, in measuring the gain from second-best-efficient transit fares, Glaister and Lewis use demand elasticities that in effect take urban land use as

5 Mohring (1981) estimates that efficient road congestion tolls would amount to $1.12 to $1.20 (in 1975 dollars) per bus mile. Keeler, Cluff, and Small (1974, 111) estimate road congestion costs at $1.31 to $2.61 (in 1972 dollars) per bus mile for peak periods in the central business district.

6 Glaister and Lewis (1978). These figures assume that buses do not pay road congestion tolls. Thus, failure to charge private automobiles for the marginal social cost of using roads provides an efficiency justification not only for exempting transit vehicles from congestion tolls but also for increasing transit subsidies above the level justified by increasing returns to scale.

7 Automobile users do pay taxes on motor fuel, but for the purposes of this paragraph these taxes are treated as part of the price paid for fuel.

8 Also, given the way automobile and health insurance premiums are determined and the way health care costs are financed, automobile users do not pay all the marginal accident costs of their trips.

given. Consequently they ignore the benefits from second-best fares that would arise from changes in land use.

However, when the use of automobiles is priced below marginal social cost, the pricing of transit rides below their marginal social cost is not the only second-best policy. An alternative is to give buses preferential access over private automobiles to the road system, for example by providing them with reserved lanes on streets. Mohring (1979) concludes that the benefits related to diversion of trips from automobiles to buses that arise when subsidies enable transit firms to set fares below marginal social cost can also be achieved without such explicit subsidies if a sufficient share of road capacity is reserved for buses. In fact, Mohring presents an example in which a system with reserved bus lanes is more efficient than a system with second-best transit subsidies.

SUBSIDIES BASED ON LAND USE EFFECTS

It is frequently argued, particularly by urban planners, that the existence of a high-quality, low-fare public transit system would encourage a more desirable urban spatial structure than would occur with a lower-quality, higher-fare transit system. For example, it is often argued that better public transit, particularly massive investments in rail rapid transit, would encourage higher density urban development. It has been argued that a light rail transit line between Toronto and Scarborough would encourage commercial development in Scarborough Town Centre.

It is important to distinguish two issues. The failure to price automobile use at marginal social cost contributes to an inefficient pattern of urban land use, as we have seen. Then again there may be external benefits associated with certain forms of urban development that transportation policy can promote. For example, although they do not express the matter in economic terms, some urban planners seem to believe that many people would be willing to pay to live in an urban area with a rather different spatial structure than would be produced by market forces even if all transportation modes were priced at marginal social cost. If high-quality, low-fare urban transit would contribute to a spatial structure with such external benefits, there would be a reason for subsidizing it.

In practice, however, nothing whatsoever is known about the latter question. Very little is known about the effect of transit service or fares on urban location decisions for either households or firms. And there is no empirical evidence about how much, if anything, people would be willing to pay for any changes in urban spatial structure that would be brought about by increased transit service. Consequently, it is impossible to do even the most rudimentary cost-benefit analysis for public transit investments aimed at producing changes in land use.

In light of current ignorance of the relevant issues, it would appear to be unwise to provide large subsidies for multimillion dollar mass transit investments whose principal purpose is to reshape urban areas to satisfy the tastes of professional planners.

SUBSIDIES FOR RESEARCH AND DEMONSTRATION PROJECTS

There is a straightforward economic efficiency justification for subsidies for competent research on engineering, economic, and other aspects of urban transit and for relevant demonstration projects by urban transit systems. Competent research (e.g. on a topic such as the effect of transit passes on ridership) would produce information for which many transit systems would be willing to pay. However, the value of the expected information from such a study to any one transit system would sometimes be less than the total cost of the study, so that in some cases no individual transit system would undertake to finance the study. Provided the total willingness to pay on the part of all transit systems combined would exceed the total cost of the study, there would be an economic efficiency argument for government funding of the study. A similar argument could be made concerning relevant demonstration projects (e.g. on automatic fare collection methods in medium-sized cities).

SUBSIDIES BASED ON INCOME DISTRIBUTIONAL EFFECTS

Apart from the case for subsidizing urban transit on efficiency grounds, transit subsidies might be supported because of their effects on income distribution. However, to redistribute income it would be more efficient to rely on cash grants to deserving individuals than on policies which distort transit fares and service levels.

First we shall assume that subsidies are used to reduce fares but have no effect on the allocation of resources. Second, we shall consider the complications that arise when we allow for those effects on the prices of other goods and services.

Ignoring effects on resource allocation and other prices
On average, the percentage of family income spent on urban public transit decreases as family income increases (Table 7). Consequently, if all transit fares were reduced from their existing levels by the same percentage as a result of a government subsidy, the direct benefit of the subsidy as a percentage of income would be greater for low-income people than for high-income people. Provided the subsidy was financed by a proportional or progressive tax, so that the percentage of family income paid to finance the subsidy program would be

TABLE 7

Average expenditure on public transit by households and individuals, fourteen
Canadian urban areas, 1974

Annual family income ($000)	Expenditure as a percentage of income
4-5	1.3
5-6	1.2
6-7	1.3
7-8	1.1
8-9	0.8
9-10	0.7
10-12	0.7
12-15	0.5
15-20	0.4
20-25	0.3

NOTE: Computed at midpoints of income interval
SOURCE: Statistics Canada (Cat. 62-544, 1974) 98-9

constant or increase as income increased, the net effect of the subsidy would be to
make low-income people better off.

Of course, under other assumptions the income distributional effects of subsidies could be quite different. For example, if subsidies were used primarily to
reduce fares on services used disproportionately by high-income people, or if
subsidies were financed by a regressive tax, the net effect of the subsidy could be to
make low-income people worse off.

Considering effects on resource allocation and other prices
In the real world, of course, transit subsidies would lead to a variety of changes in
the allocation of resources and in prices of goods, factors, and assets. Consideration of these changes considerably complicates the analysis of distributional
effects.

For example, rather than devote subsidies entirely to fare reductions, a transit
system would probably devote part of the subsidy to covering the costs of a higher
level of service. Because high-income people place a higher value on their travel
time than do low-income people, one would expect the distribution of benefits
from service improvements to be less progressive (i.e. accrue less to low-income
people and more to high-income people) than the distribution of benefits from fare
reductions.

Also, transit fare reductions and service improvements would induce more
people to use transit and hence reduce automobile congestion. Because higher-
income people take a higher share of their trips by automobile and place a higher
value on their travel time than do low-income people, one would again expect

the distribution of benefits from reduced road congestion to be less progressive than the distribution of benefits from fare reductions.

Finally, because of transit fare reductions, transit service improvements, and decongestion of roads, there would be a reduction in the private cost of transportation in the urban area. This would lead to complex changes in the spatial structures of urban property values and rents, and these would have additional income distributional effects.

TRANSIT SUBSIDIES AND CITY SIZE

An important practical problem for the province in determining transit subsidy levels is to decide how subsidies should vary between urban areas of different sizes. At present, both provincial operating subsidies and all operating subsidies combined as a percentage of operating cost are inversely related to city size (Table 8). Consequently, the provincial operating subsidy per vehicle mile (or per passenger trip or per passenger mile) is highest in the smallest cities. In Toronto, which has received massive capital subsidies for the subway system and for the GO Transit commuter rail/bus system, lower operating subsidies are offset by higher capital grants. As a result, in practice the medium-large cities such as Hamilton and London probably receive the lowest average rate of provincial subsidy per vehicle mile, per passenger trip, or per passenger mile.

To determine whether it makes sense to discriminate between urban areas on the basis of size, we shall examine the implications of each of three arguments for transit subsidies: increasing returns to scale, second-best considerations when automobiles are underpriced, and income distributional effects.

In the case of increasing returns to scale, it can be seen in Figure 7 that the ratio of the efficient subsidy to the total costs borne by the transit system at the efficient level of output OQ is equal to EG/BG. The shapes of the LRASC and LRMSC curves in Figure 7 have been drawn consistent with Mohring's (1972) analysis of increasing returns to scale in bus transit. It appears that the ratio of the efficient transit subsidy to the total costs borne by the transit system will be greater on lightly travelled transit routes than on heavily travelled ones. Since transit routes in small urban areas will be less heavily travelled than routes in large urban areas, this indicates that the rate of subsidy justified by increasing returns to scale would be higher in small urban areas than in large urban areas.[9]

---

9 Before subsidizing a transit system on the grounds of efficiency, the government should make sure that the total social benefits exceed the total social costs of transit service. One would expect that the smaller the urban area, the less likely it would be that this condition would be satisfied.

TABLE 8

Provincial operating subsidy rate and average operating deficit as a percentage of operating cost in Ontario, by city size

City population group	Provincial operating subsidy rate 1977-9	Average operating deficit as a percentage of operating costs			
		1975	1976	1977	1978
0-100 000	25.00	52	50	51	50
100 000-200 000	20.00-22.50	49	48	49	49
200 000-1 000 000	17.50	44	41	40	43
Metro Toronto	13.75	34	28	30	31
All		38	34	35	37

NOTE: Provincial operating subsidy rate from Table 18
SOURCE: Ontario Ministry of Transportation and Communications (unpublished data)

In the case of second-best efficiency, one would expect the efficient rate of subsidy to be higher in large urban areas, where the marginal congestion and pollution costs of automobile use are probably higher and where the effect of transit fares on automobile use is probably greater.

In the case of income distribution, one would expect the average incomes of transit riders to be higher in large urban areas than in small areas, principally because transit is probably used more heavily by high-income commuters in large urban areas than in small urban areas. Consequently, the case for subsidizing urban transit on income distributional grounds is probably stronger in small urban areas than in large ones.

Thus the arguments from increasing returns to scale and income distribution suggest that provincial subsidy rates for transit should be greater (per vehicle mile or per passenger mile) in small urban areas, whereas the second-best argument suggests the reverse. On the basis of available information it is impossible to determine on balance how the socially optimal rate of subsidy would vary with city size.

FEDERAL VS PROVINCIAL VS MUNICIPAL TRANSIT SUBSIDIES

Effect on resource allocation in transit
Suppose that a municipal transit system (or a municipal government) makes transit investment and operating policy decisions on the basis of a comparison of total benefits and total costs for municipal residents, while ignoring benefits and costs for non-residents. Suppose also that all benefits from the transit system accrue to municipal residents. In this case, federal or provincial subsidies which

depend on the investment and operating policies of the municipal transit system are likely to induce the transit system to allocate resources inefficiently from the federal or provincial point of view.

Suppose that the province offers to pay 25 per cent of the costs of urban transit service. Suppose also that the transit system is contemplating introduction of transit service which would have a total social cost of $100 million and a total social benefit of $80 million. Obviously it would be inefficient from the provincial point of view to introduce this service. However, from the local point of view the benefits of $80 million would exceed the local costs (after 25 per cent provincial subsidy) of $75 million. Consequently, on the behavioural assumption made above, the transit system would introduce the service.

By contrast, if the same subsidy were provided by the municipal government instead of the provincial government, the transit system would not introduce the service, since the subsidy cost would still be borne by municipal residents. Thus municipal funding would be more efficient than provincial funding under the assumptions made here.

To avoid this problem, while continuing to raise funds for transit subsidies at the provincial level if this was deemed desirable, the provincial government could either make its transit subsidies independent of the behaviour of the transit system or replace the transit subsidies with unconditional grants to the municipal government. Either option would increase the efficiency of resource allocation if the benefits of transit accrue at the local level, and local decisions would be made on the basis of local social benefits and costs. On the other hand if local decisions are not motivated by local efficiency considerations, replacing a provincial cost subsidy for transit by a provincial lump-sum subsidy for transit would not necessarily increase efficiency.[10]

Also, if some of the net benefits of local transit systems accrued to people who did not reside in the urban area, then on the behavioural assumptions made above there would be an efficiency argument for provincial transit subsidies. This would be true if benefits were received by non-resident landowners or non-resident commuters. It would also be true in the case of transit research and demonstration projects, which would produce information of value to other urban areas.

Effect on the cost of raising revenues
To finance transit subsidies a government must levy taxes. These taxes normally lead to a reduction in the efficiency of resource allocation elsewhere in the

10 The implications of alternative transit objective functions and subsidy formulas are analysed in Chapter 8 and Appendix c.

economy, because they raise prices above marginal social costs for other goods and services. The efficiency loss per dollar of revenue raised will presumably vary with the type of tax. Since municipal, provincial, and federal governments rely on different types of taxes, it may be more efficient to raise taxes at one level of government than another. For example, one advantage of raising revenues at the provincial level rather than at the municipal level is that municipal taxes may distort location decisions within the province.[11]

Of course, even if provincial taxes are more efficient than municipal taxes this would simply provide an argument for replacing municipal taxes with provincial-municipal unconditional grants. It would not justify a provincial transit subsidy program.

Effect on income distribution
One should also consider income distributional effects in determining the appropriate level of government to raise revenues. However, this issue really bears on the choice between using municipal taxes or provincial-municipal grants to finance municipal government, not on the question of transit subsidies. Consequently, we will not pursue the issue here.

CONCLUSIONS

The economic efficiency case for subsidizing conventional public transit rests almost entirely on the existence of increasing returns to scale in public transit and the practice of pricing automobile trips below their marginal social cost. Each of these arguments has been carefully evaluated and verified in an empirical study. Mohring estimated that increasing returns to scale alone could justify a subsidy of roughly 50 to 60 per cent of the total costs borne by a bus system in a large American urban area, and Glaister and Lewis estimated that failure to charge automobile users for their marginal congestion costs alone could justify a subsidy of 27 per cent of the total costs borne by the bus system in London, England.

There is a distinct economic efficiency argument for subsidizing competent research and relevant demonstration projects in the field of urban transit if they produce useful information which is a public good.

There is also an income distributional argument for subsidizing urban transit, on the ground that in urban areas low-income people spend a larger share of their income on urban transit than do high-income people.

11 Of course there might be a second-best argument for levying higher taxes on activities in large urban areas because of the failure to charge appropriate congestion and pollution taxes.

Thus on the one hand we conclude that there are strong economic arguments for subsidizing urban transit. On the other hand in practice the efficiency and redistributional gains from transit subsidies may be less than expected. To finance transit subsidies the government must levy taxes. These taxes lead to a reduction in the efficiency of resource allocation elsewhere in the economy, because they raise prices above marginal social costs for other goods and services. This important consideration will reduce the size of socially optimal transit subsidies.

Furthermore, the fact that a case can be made for some form of subsidy for urban transit on both efficiency and income distributional grounds does not imply that *existing* subsidy programs necessarily contribute to efficiency or reduce income inequality. The fact that a transit firm receives a subsidy does not imply that the subsidy will necessarily be used by the transit firm to move toward the optimal set of services and fares. It is possible that the transit firm would choose to use a subsidy to introduce a new route in a high-income suburb where the demand does not justify the cost of providing the service. In this case, the subsidy might bring about a less efficient allocation of resources and a less equal distribution of income. This important problem is considered further in Chapter 7.[12]

12 Actually, there are two separate problems. First, poorly designed transit subsidy policies may provide incentives. Second, transit managers may have perverse objectives. Chapter 8 and Appendix C consider in detail the role of subsidy formulas and transit firm objectives in determining the effect of subsidies.

6

Historical transit subsidies in Ontario

This chapter describes the subsidies given to urban transit in Ontario by municipal, provincial, and federal governments. Cross-subsidies provided for certain urban transit operations by the bodies responsible for transit services are described and comparisons are made with subsidy programs in other provinces, the United States, and Western Europe.

CAPITAL VS OPERATING SUBSIDIES

In describing subsidy programs, we adopt the conventional dichotomy of 'capital' and 'operating' subsidies. Capital subsidies are policies which subsidize the use of capital without subsidizing the use of other resources. In practice, most capital subsidies are grants given explicitly to finance expenditures on capital goods, but capital subsidies also include such things as exemptions from excise, sales, and real property taxes on capital goods and subsidies for interest and debt-servicing charges.

All subsidies which are not exclusively capital subsidies are considered to be operating subsidies. In principle, operating subsidies could include lump-sum subsidies given to a transit system independent of its performance or subsidies related to transit vehicle miles of service, ridership, operating costs, or operating deficits. In practice, the most important provincial operating subsidies in Ontario have been subsidies based on operating costs or operating deficits.

The principal reason for distinguishing between capital and operating subsidies in this way is that capital subsidies are capital-biased; because they entail a higher percentage rate of subsidy for capital than non-capital inputs, they encourage an inefficiently high capital intensity.[1] The implications of capital-biased subsidies are discussed in detail in Chapter 7.

---

1 However, some capital subsidies, such as exemption from real property taxes, might remove a disincentive to use of the efficient capital-intensity.

EXPENDITURE VS COST SUBSIDIES

In the case of capital goods, subsidies for the year are often based on expenditures (or even reserves accumulated to finance future expenditures) rather than costs, i.e. depreciation and interest. Consequently, a portion (even a large proportion) of the subsidy received by a transit system in any given year might actually apply to the firm's operations in future years. As a result, care is required to determine the extent to which transit operations in any particular year have been subsidized by governments during that year and/or previous years.

MUNICIPAL SUBSIDIES FOR TRANSIT IN ONTARIO

Municipal capital subsidies

Toronto subway
The principal case of a municipal government capital subsidy for transit in Ontario is the Metro Toronto subsidy for capital expenditures for the subway system and more recently for light rail transit (LRT) vehicles, the modern streetcars.

Municipal capital subsidies for the Toronto subway (see Tables 9 and 10) were first given in 1959, and in 1964 they were extended retroactively to cover capital expenditures made as early as 1949. In 1964 the municipal government began to receive partial reimbursement for its capital subsidies from the provincial government. Consequently, over time the burden of financing capital expenditures for the Toronto subway system has shifted, with the Toronto Transit Commission's share declining to zero for commitments since 1969 (and hence for expenditures since 1972), the Metro share declining to 25 per cent for commitments since 1972, and the provincial share rising to 75 per cent for commitments since 1972. According to a 1976 TTC report, the overall allocation of the burden of financing capital expenditures for the Toronto subway system between 1949 and the late 1970s is given by Table 11.

In addition to receiving municipal subsidies for capital expenditures on the subway, since 1968 the TTC has been exempt from municipal property taxes on capital used in the subway system, an exemption estimated at $970 000 in 1968.

Apart from the subway system, in 1976 Metro Toronto agreed to give a 25 per cent capital subsidy amounting to approximately $12.3 million (in 1976 dollars) for expenditures by the TTC on 125 modern streetcars to be delivered by the Urban Transportation Development Corporation by 1979.

TABLE 9

Municipal capital subsidies for Metro Toronto subway and final allocation of capital costs

Subway line	Approval	Construction	Municipal capital subsidy	Final allocation of capital costs (millions of current dollars and percentage)			
				TTC	Metro	Province	Federal
1. Yonge St	1946	1949-54	The TTC built the first subway line without subsidy relying partly on surpluses accumulated during 1940-6 and partly on debentures. However, in 1963 the municipal government agreed to give a retroactive capital subsidy and on 1 January 1964 assumed responsibility for 70 per cent of the unmatured debentures issued by the TTC. There was no provincial subsidy.	$32.8 (49%)	$34.2 (51%)	–	–
2. Bloor-Danforth-University	1958	1959-66	100 per cent on right of way and 50 per cent on other construction expenditures. There was no provincial subsidy. The result was a 45-55% split of total costs between the TTC and Metro.	$70.0 (26%)	$167.5 (63%) (includes subway line 3)	$20.6 (8%)	$7.4 (3%)

3. Bloor-Danforth Extensions	1963	1965-8	100 per cent on 'right of way' expenditures for land and subway construction costs, i.e. expenditures which would not be incurred in the case of surface operation on public thoroughfares. Both TTC and Metro shares were subject to partial reimbursement through provincial subsidies (see Table 15).		(included in subway line 2)		
4. North Yonge Extension to Sheppard	1967	1968-74	Same as (3)	$9.2 (9%)	$48.8 (48%)	$43.3 (43%)	–
5. North Yonge Extension to Finch	1969	1973-4	100 per cent on all capital expenditures, including vehicles. Metro share was subject to partial reimbursement through provincial subsidies (see Table 15).	– (47%)	$14.7 (53%)	$16.5	–
6. Spadina	1973	1974-	Same as (5)	–	$58.8[a] (27%)	$160.2[a] (73%)	–
7. Bloor-Danforth Extensions to Kennedy and Kipling	1973	1975	Same as (5)	–	$33.8[a] (25%)	$101.3[a] (75%)	–

a Estimated by the TTC.
SOURCE: Toronto Transit Commission (1976)

TABLE 10

Municipal capital subsidies for the Toronto subway ($ million)

Year	Current dollars	1978 dollars
1959	1.7	4.1
1960	5.8	13.7
1961	8.3	19.4
1962	9.1	21.0
1963	10.1	22.9
1964[a]	81.3	181.1
1965[a]	21.7	47.2
1966	19.6	41.1
1967	15.0	30.4
1968	6.7	13.0
1969	10.1	18.8
1970	12.0	21.6
1971	11.1	19.4
1972	14.5	24.2
1973	8.7	13.5
1974	3.7	5.2
1975	11.1	14.0

a Figure for 1964 includes retroactive adjustments. Data for 1964-5 include a total of $7.4 million in federal capital subsidies.

NOTE: Figures are for municipal capital subsidies net of provincial reimbursement. In addition to these subsidies, land for subway rights of way was purchased and owned by the municipal government and was provided free to the transit system. This omission is apparently the reason that the total of current dollar municipal capital subsidies for the period through 1974 in this table is less than that in Tables 9 and 11.

SOURCE: Toronto Transit Commission (1977, Appendix A)

TABLE 11

Financing for capital expenditures for the Toronto subway ($ million current)

	TTC	Metro	Province	Federal
Expenditures 1949-74	112.0	265.9	81.2	7.4
Expenditures 1974-6 and estimated expenditures for projects under construction in 1976	0.0	110.9	313.5	0.0
Total	112.0	376.8	394.7	7.4

NOTE: Data for government financing cover capital grants only.
SOURCE: Toronto Transit Commission (1976)

Interest subsidies

Long before it was common for municipal governments to give explicit subsidies to their transit systems, some municipal governments such as Toronto and London provided an implicit subsidy by supplying financial capital at favourable interest rates. For example, in cases where the credit ratings of municipal governments were higher than those of their transit systems because of risk differentials, municipal governments have issued debentures and loaned the proceeds to their transit systems at the same interest rate paid by the government. In assuming the risk on the debentures, and in charging the average rather than the marginal cost of funds, the municipal governments effectively subsidized the interest rate for their transit systems.

More recently, some municipal governments have gone further and cancelled interest charges on funds loaned in the past to their transit systems. For example, in 1974 the City of London permanently cancelled interest payments on $457 000 in loans to its transit system.

It is important to keep in mind that these two different types of interest subsidies do not appear in the statistics for subsidy levels presented in the tables in this chapter.

Other municipal capital subsidies

Apart from Metro Toronto subsidies for the subway and streetcar and interest subsidies, municipal capital subsidies (subsidies for the use of capital but not other resources) have been uncommon in Ontario. Indeed, only a few examples have been found. A very small number of transit systems are exempt from municipal property taxes; for example, the Niagara Falls system has been exempt at least since 1962. In 1968 the Kingston municipal government paid $67 288, or 100 per cent of the cost of two new buses for the public transit system. In 1969 the St Catharines municipal government paid $51 000 in capital subsidies to the transit system. Since 1973 the London municipal government has subsidized approved capital expenditures of the London transit system. Otherwise, municipal governments have not explicitly distinguished between capital and other resources in determining transit subsidies, so that the remaining municipal subsidies are considered below as operating subsidies.

Municipal operating subsidies

Transit systems in most of the smaller cities in Ontario have received municipal operating subsidies at least since the early 1960s. By contrast, transit systems in most of the larger cities operated without subsidies until the late 1960s or early 1970s.

TABLE 12

Transit systems with and without municipal operating subsidies during 1960-5

Systems with operating subsidies	Systems without operating subsidies
Barrie	Galt
Belleville	Guelph
Brantford	Hamilton
Chatham	Kitchener
Fort William	London
Kingston	Ottawa
Lindsay	Sudbury
Newmarket	Windsor
Niagara Falls	
Oshawa	
Peterborough	
Port Arthur	
Richmond Hill	
Sarnia	
Sault Ste Marie	
St Catharines	
St Thomas	

NOTE: Toronto did not receive regular municipal operating subsidies. However, it did receive a municipal operating subsidy of $2.5 million in 1963, and it received municipal capital subsidies for the subway.

Tables 12 to 14 list some of the transit systems operating with and without municipal operating subsidies during 1960-5 and 1969. Tables 13 and 14 also detail subsidy formulas and amounts for 1969 broken down by public and private ownership.

The Toronto transit system did not receive regular municipal operating subsidies until 1970; in that year the transit system began to receive municipal subsidies to compensate for fare concessions for elderly and handicapped people, and in 1971 it began to receive municipal subsidies for general operations. However, the Toronto transit system did receive municipal operating subsidies in 1956 and 1963, and it received massive municipal capital subsidies for the subway system beginning in 1959. In 1956 the municipal government gave the Toronto transit system an operating subsidy of $2.3 million to cover losses incurred when services were extended from the City of Toronto to Metro Toronto following creation of the metropolitan government in 1954. In 1963 the municipal government gave the Toronto transit system an operating subsidy of $2.5 million to allow it to rescind a 17 per cent increase in the fare.

TABLE 13

Municipal operating subsidies for publicly owned transit systems, 1969

Subsidy policy	System	Subsidy ($000)	Ratio of subsidy to total non-subsidy revenue
No subsidy	Galt	0	0.00
	Kitchener	0	0.00
	London	0	0.00
Subsidy for senior citizen fare concession	Hamilton	224	0.04
Subsidy for fare stabilization	Ottawa	540	0.07
Subsidy for excess of current expenditure over revenue	Brantford	150	0.29
	St Catharines	164	0.21
Subsidy for excess of expenditure over revenue. Expenditure includes debt principal repayment and/or capital expenditures	Belleville[a]	52	0.30
	Fort William	215	0.40[b]
	Guelph	108	0.20
	Kingston	329	0.64
	Niagara Falls	65	0.25
	Oshawa	265	0.48
	Port Arthur	172	0.40[b]
	Sault Ste Marie	260	0.53
	Stratford	77	0.48
	Woodstock	9	0.29

a Also exempt from municipal business taxes
b For Thunder Bay (Fort William and Port Arthur combined)
SOURCES: Woods, Gordon (1971, Appendices 3 and 15) and City of Woodstock Transportation Service (1970)

TABLE 14

Municipal subsidies for privately owned transit systems, 1969

Subsidy policy	System	Formula	Subsidy ($000)
No subsidy	Burlington		0
	Cornwall		0
	Oakville		0
	Sudbury		0
Operator paid per vehicle mile; municipality receives fare revenue	Chatham	65.6¢ a mile	90
	Mississauga	65¢ a mile in 1971	n.a.
	Newmarket	57.5¢ a mile	5
	North Bay	60¢ a mile	n.a.
	Port Hope	40¢ a mile	4
Operator guaranteed minimum revenue per vehicle mile	Barrie	55¢ a mile plus 50 per cent of fare revenue in excess of 55¢ a mile	22
	Richmond Hill	68¢ a mile plus 50 per cent of fare revenue in excess of 68¢ a mile in 1971	15
Operator guaranteed minimum profit	Peterborough	$15 000 net profit after tax	63
Operator guaranteed gross revenue	Midland	$19 350 gross revenue from fares and subsidy, up to $5 500 subsidy	6
Lump-sum subsidy	Lindsay	$450 a month in 1971	n.a.
	Orillia		9
	Owen Sound		10
	Sarnia	$8 667 a month in 1971	n.a.
	Welland		19
Subsidy per mile and per passenger	Timmins	12¢ a mile plus 10¢ a passenger if total receipts are less than $105 000	32

NOTE: n.a. means not available.
SOURCE: Woods, Gordon (1971, Appendix 16)

Municipal operating subsidies began in Hamilton in 1966 to compensate for fare concessions for special population groups and in 1971 for general operations; in Ottawa they began in 1969, and in London in 1972.

Since 1972, all municipal governments in Ontario have given substantial operating subsidies to their transit systems. Between 1971 and 1976, municipal governments shared their urban transit operating deficits with the provincial government, generally on a 50-50 basis. Consequently, during this period the aggregate amount of municipal operating subsidies can be inferred approximately from the level of provincial operating subsidies.[2] In 1977 Metro Toronto adopted a five-year formula for financing the Toronto transit system. The formula involved a 70-15-15 split in current operating expenditures between fare revenues, Metro subsidies, and provincial subsidies respectively.

Revenue sources for municipal subsidies
In the case of the Metro Toronto subsidy for the subway system, a special two-mill property tax levy was earmarked as a source of revenue between 1959 and 1976. This tax provided an average of $10 million a year in revenue during the period 1962-71. The levy was increased to three mills in 1977 and 1978 and then reduced to zero in 1979. Otherwise, all municipal subsidies in Ontario as well as all the provincial and federal subsidies discussed below have been financed out of general revenues.

PROVINCIAL GOVERNMENT SUBSIDIES FOR TRANSIT IN ONTARIO

Provincial capital subsidies

Sales tax exemptions
Since 1964 the province has exempted purchases of buses and spare parts by urban transit systems from the provincial sales tax, which has varied between 3 and 7 per cent. This subsidy does not appear in any of the tables below listing the amounts of provincial subsidies.

The Toronto subway
The provincial government has subsidized capital expenditures on the Toronto subway system since 1 April 1964. Table 15 shows the rates of subsidy and

---

2 See Table 17 below. Since the province subsidized capital expenditures under a separate capital subsidy program while municipal governments generally subsidized capital expenditures along with other expenditures under what we have called operating subsidy programs, municipal operating subsidies naturally exceeded provincial operating subsidies. An upper limit on this difference between 1972 and 1976 would be one-third of the amount of provincial capital subsidies for surface transit in the province (Table 16, column 6).

TABLE 15

Provincial capital subsidies for the Metro Toronto subway

Dates	Rate of subsidy
1 April 1964- 31 Dec. 1969	33⅓ per cent for roadbed construction. No subsidy for land, construction of stations and yards, or equipment.
1 Jan. 1970- 22 July 1971	50 per cent for roadbed construction. No subsidy for land, construction of stations and yards, or equipment.
23 July 1971- 30 Nov. 1972	50 per cent for virtually all capital expenditures
1 Dec. 1972- present	75 per cent for virtually all capital expenditures

eligible expenditures which have prevailed since 1964. Table 16, column 5, and Table 17, column 1, show the level of provincial capital subsidies in each year. Two points are evident from these tables as well as from Tables 9 and 11. First, provincial capital subsidies for the Toronto subway increased steadily until 1976 both as percentages of capital expenditures and in dollar amounts (even if one deflates for changes in the construction cost index). Second, these capital subsidies represent a substantial share of all provincial subsidies for urban transit in every year.

In addition to these capital grants, the province provided an implicit subsidy for the Toronto subway by extending to the Toronto Transit Commission $33.6 million in loans at the province's borrowing rate between 1962 and 1965.

Moreover, between 1962 and 1965 the province extended to Metro Toronto another $25.3 million in loans to finance municipal capital subsidies for the subway. Furthermore, since December 1972 Metro Toronto's interest costs on debentures used to finance municipal government capital subsidies for the subway before December 1972 have been eligible for provincial subsidy. These interest costs averaged $9.2 million a year in 1972-3.

Surface transit
During 1965 a number of urban transit systems received small construction labour subsidies under the Municipal Winter Works Incentive Program funded jointly by the federal and provincial governments. For example, the Kingston system received $22 120 and the London system $46 990.

Since 1 December 1972 the provincial government has provided a subsidy of 75 per cent for approved capital expenditures for surface transportation by all municipal transit systems in Ontario. The eligible items of expenditure are: new

TABLE 16

Provincial capital subsidies for municipal transit by city size group ($ million)

	City population (000)			Metro Toronto		Total	
	0-45	45-200	200-1000				
	(1)	(2)	(3)	(4)	(5)	(6)	(7)
Type of system	Surface	Surface	Surface	Surface	Subway	Surface	Surface and subway
1964	–	–	–	–	5.8	–	5.8
1965	–	–	–	–	3.5	–	3.5
1966	–	–	–	–	5.8	–	5.8
1967	–	–	–	–	2.0	–	2.0
1968	–	–	–	–	1.6	–	1.6
1969	–	–	–	–	4.2	–	4.2
1970	–	–	–	–	8.6	–	8.6
1971	–	–	–	–	16.7	–	16.7
1972	–	–	–	–	17.5	–	17.5
1973	1.0	4.3	6.6	5.3	14.4	17.2	31.6
1974	0.9	5.2	6.6	4.9	24.6	17.6	42.2
1975	2.2	5.9	8.6	10.9	54.7	27.6	82.3
1976	1.9	7.7	11.0	2.9	74.5	23.5	98.0
1977		8.3	10.4	8.1[b]	67.1	26.8[b]	93.9
1978		7.5	9.6	19.0[b]	36.5	36.1[b]	72.6
Number of systems subsidized[a]	13 to 17	17 to 20	4	1		35 to 42	

a Data cover 1964-76 only.
b These data include subsidies for the seventy-five modern streetcars subsidized under the demonstration projects subsidy program.
SOURCE: Data from Ontario, Ministry of Transportation and Communications

TABLE 17

Provincial subsidies for urban transit in Ontario ($ million)

Year	(1) Capital subsidies Toronto subway	(2) Intra-urban surface transit	(3) GO Transit	(4) Demon-stration projects	(5) Operating subsidies Intra-urban transit	(6) GO Transit	(7) Demon-stration projects	(8) Other Local transit planning studies	(9) Municipal transit program administration
1964	5.8	0.0	0.0		0.0	0.0			
1965	3.5	0.0	0.0		0.0	0.0			
1966	5.8	0.0	0.0		0.0	0.0			
1967	2.0	0.0			0.0				
1968	1.6	0.0	10.1		0.0	2.7			
1969	4.2	0.0	0.5		0.0	2.0			
1970	8.6	0.0	2.3		0.0	2.5			
1971	16.7	0.0	0.5		6.8	3.3		0.4	
1972	17.5	0.0	3.4		11.3	2.8			
1973	14.4	17.2	14.7		18.3	4.1		0.4	0.1
1974	24.6	17.6	6.5		36.2	7.8			
1975	54.7	27.6	14.4	5.1	45.4	9.5	0.8		0.2
1976	74.5	23.5	24.5	3.1	45.7	10.9	0.4		0.2
1977	67.1	26.8[a]	42.3	7.5[b]	51.2[b]	14.6	0.1	0.3	0.9
1978	36.5	36.1[a]	28.6	7.9[b]	56.3	22.3	0.0	0.1	0.9

a Includes 125 streetcars
b Includes subsidies for streetcars
NOTE: Data are generally for fiscal years, e.g. 1968=1968/9.
SOURCE: Ontario, Ministry of Transportation and Communications (1971-2 to 1976-7); Ontario, Ministry of Transportation and Communications (1978, 2); Ontario, Ministry of Treasury and Economics (annual) Public Accounts; Toronto Transit Commission (1976, 30-3); Johnston and McMillan (1978, 43)

motor buses, trolley coaches, and streetcars; major rebuilding of trolley coaches and streetcars; land and buildings for maintenance and terminal facilities; roadside shelters, signs, and benches; and parking lots operated as a part of a public transit system. The annual subsidy has been subject in principle but not in practice to a ceiling of $1.50 per capita for the first 150 000 people in the municipality plus $2.25 per capita for the remaining people. In addition to the above assets, for which the subsidy is in principle limited on the basis of population, the province will give subsidies of 75 per cent of expenditures on other assets, subject to prior approval.

The levels of provincial subsidies in each year under this program both in total and broken down by city-size group are shown in Table 16, columns 1-4 and 6.

In addition to this regular program of subsidies for surface transit capital expenditures, the provincial government has given subsidies at a higher rate for modern streetcars produced by the provincial government's Urban Transportation Development Corporation (UTDC) for the Toronto Transit Commission. In 1976 the TTC ordered two hundred modern streetcars and spares from the UTDC. As of 1977 the vehicles were to be delivered by 1980 at an approximate selling price in 1977 dollars of $89.7 million. The province agreed to pay the regular 75 percent subsidy on 125 of them and to purchase the other seventy-five and lease them to the TTC for five years at a nominal annual charge of $1 per vehicle. In other words the province agreed to a 100 per cent subsidy for five years. The higher 100 per cent subsidy on the seventy-five streetcars was given as part of the province's program of subsidies for demonstration projects, discussed below.

Demonstration projects
Since 1972 the provincial government has paid a subsidy of 75 per cent (and in some cases 100 per cent) of capital expenditures for approved transit demonstration projects. In cases where the subsidy rate is 100 per cent, the province retains ownership of the capital assets, and at the conclusion of the demonstration the transit system has the option to purchase the assets, subject to the usual 75 per cent provincial capital subsidy.

Provincially subsidized demonstration projects have included such things as experiments with dial-a-ride transit services in a number of urban areas, a transit marketing project, and experiments with articulated buses and transit services for the physically disabled. The purchase of modern streetcars by the TTC was by far the largest demonstration project subsidized by the province. In 1975-8, demonstration project capital subsidies averaged $5.9 million a year (Table 17, column 4).

Services for the physically disabled
In the 1977 throne speech, the provincial government announced proposals for a new subsidy program for the provision of transit services for the physically disabled.

Provincial operating subsidies

Income tax exemptions
Like other municipally owned corporations, publicly owned urban transit systems are exempt from the provincial corporation income tax. This was of considerable importance before 1970 when transit system revenues often exceeded operating costs, because funds which would otherwise have been paid in tax were left as retained earnings.

It should be noted that this subsidy and the equivalent federal subsidy apply only to publicly owned transit systems. Consequently, these subsidies encouraged municipal acquisition of transit systems as tax rates, and hence the importance of these subsidies, increased.

Intraurban transit operating grants
The provincial government has provided operating subsidies for urban transit since 1971. The subsidy formulas, ceilings, and eligibility requirements for each year are listed in Table 18, and the aggregate amounts of subsidies are listed in Table 17, column 5. Table 19 provides a breakdown of these subsidies by city-size group.

Four points should be noted in Table 18. First, the provincial government has had trouble deciding on an appropriate subsidy formula. The province paid 50 per cent of operating *deficits* during 1971-6, a certain percentage of operating *costs* during 1977-9, and then a certain percentage of operating costs plus an amount based on the operating deficit in 1980.

Second, the subsidy ceilings which existed in 1972 and 1973 were not always binding because municipal governments often were not willing to provide a matching subsidy large enough to qualify for the maximum provincial subsidy.[3]

---

3 For example, in budgeting for 1973 the London Transportation Commission calculated that the ceiling on its provincial operating subsidy would be $702500, based on the expected number of revenue passengers. However, London City Council approved municipal payments of only $312120 toward the operating deficit eligible for provincial subsidy, so that the London Transit Commission budgeted for only $312120 in provincial operating subsidies. In the end, the London transit system received only $290850 in provincial operating subsidies for 1973 because the deficit was less than expected.

Third, between April 1974 and March 1975 there was a freeze on transit fares. Otherwise, the province has not intervened directly in transit operating policies.

Fourth, beginning in 1977 the operating subsidy for new transit services with exclusive rights of way was higher than the operating subsidy for other new services. This provided an inefficient incentive to opt for new services with exclusive rights of way, for reasons that will be discussed in Chapter 7. The principal recipient of these special grants was the Toronto transit system. One effect of these grants was to raise the average provincial operating subsidy for the TTC in 1977-9 to about 15 per cent of operating costs from the basic rate of 13.75 (see Table 18) (Joint Metro/Toronto Transit Commission Transit Policy Committee 1979b, 15).

GO Transit[4]

In 1976 the provincial government established a surburban commuter railway system in Toronto known as GO Transit. The system was expanded in 1970 to include suburban commuter buses, and in 1974 day-to-day operation was turned over to the Toronto Area Transit Operating Authority (TATOA).

Since the inception of GO Transit, the provincial government has paid 100 per cent of the capital expenditures of the system (Table 17, column 3). By the end of fiscal 1978-9, the cumulative total of these capital subsidies amounted to around $150 million (in current dollars).

The province also pays 100 per cent of the operating deficit for GO Transit (Table 17, column 6). Nominally, there is a provincial policy that fare revenues should cover 65 per cent of operating costs (excluding capital costs) for GO Transit, but in the late 1970s the reality was quite different. For example, in fiscal 1978/9 GO Transit fare revenues were $19.8 million, while GO Transit expenses (excluding capital costs) were $48.0 million, including $34.3 attributed to 'train and bus operations,' $10.4 million to 'terminals and plant,' and $3.4 million to 'general and administration' (Toronto Area Transit Operating Authority 1979).

---

4 Because the province has also paid 100 per cent of the GO Transit operating deficit since 1967 (Table 17, column 6), the capital subsidies do not provide an inefficient bias to opt for an excessive capital intensity within the GO Transit system. For this reason, all subsidies for GO Transit are treated as operating subsidies here, even though separate figures are provided for capital and operating subsidies in Table 17. In fact there is no clear distinction between capital and operating subsidies for GO Transit. For example, in 1977 and 1978, $10.9 million of the so-called capital subsidy was actually used to finance the excess of the operating loss over the operating subsidy. Of course it is still possible that differences in subsidies between GO Transit and other less capital-intensive forms of municipal transit may be a source of inefficiency.

TABLE 18

Provincial operating subsidies for urban transit, 1971-8

Year	Subsidy formula		Ceiling on annual subsidies	Conditions
1971[a]	50 per cent of eligible operating deficit[b]		None	Municipal government must pay the other 50 per cent of eligible operating deficit
1972	Same as 1971		$0.50 per capita for first 10000 population plus $1.50 per capita for remaining population, plus $0.01 per revenue passenger[c]	Same as 1971
1973	Same as 1971		Same as 1972 except raised to $0.025 per revenue passenger	Same as 1971
1974	Same as 1971		Same as 1973 until 9 April, then removed retroactive to 1 January	Same as 1971. Also, freeze on transit fares beginning 9 April
1975	Same as 1971		None	Same as 1971. Freeze on transit fares removed 3 March
1976	Same as 1971		105 per cent of operating subsidy received in 1975	Same as 1971
1977	'Basic' subsidy for operating costs at per-centage rates dependent on population:		75 per cent of operating deficit. (The 1977 operating subsidy was also subject to a floor equal to the 1976 operating subsidy.)	None
	City population	Percentage		
	over 1 000 000	13.75		
	200 001-1 000 000	17.50		
	150 001- 200 000	20.00		
	100 001- 150 000	22.50		
	0- 100 000	25.00		

	The subsidy for operating costs was increased by 1½ per cent above the basic rate for each 1 per cent growth in population above 4 per cent during the preceding year. New transit facilities with exclusive rights of way received a special 50 per cent subsidy for start up costs plus a special 50 per cent subsidy for the operating deficit (revenue computed at half the system average marginal cost) for the *first* year in lieu of the subsidy of operating costs.		
1978	Same as 1977, except special 50 per cent subsidy for operating deficit of new transit facilities with exclusive rights of way was extended to the first *three* years	Same ceiling as 1977 (Floor equal to 'basic' operating subsidy in preceding year.)	None
1979	Same as 1978	Same as 1978	None
1980	Same as 1979, except a supplementary subsidy was provided if the operating deficit of the transit system exceeded twice the basic subsidy computed using the table above for 1977. The supplementary subsidy was 25 per cent of the excess of the operating deficit over twice the basic subsidy.	Supplementary subsidy limited to 12.5 per cent of the basic subsidy.	None

a Nominally the subsidy began 1 June 1971, but the province actually paid 50 per cent of the entire year's operating deficit.

b Certain items of expenditure (e.g. interest paid to the municipal government) were not eligible for subsidy. However, interest and repayment of principal on other debts, and contributions to reserve funds, were subsidized.

c Judging from the statistics on amounts of subsidies, in practice the ceiling was the greater of this amount and the actual operating subsidy received in the previous year. In 1972, thirteen of the forty-four transit systems receiving subsidies had deficits larger than the amount eligible for the 50 per cent provincial subsidy.

TABLE 19

Provincial operating subsidies for municipal transit by city size group ($ million)

City population (000)	0-45 (1)	45-200 (2)	200-1000 (3)	Metro Toronto (4)	Total (5)
1971	0.3	1.9	1.5	3.0	6.8
1972	0.4	2.4	2.0	6.6	11.3
1973	0.6	2.9	3.4	11.4	18.3
1974	0.9	5.5	6.2	23.6	36.2
1975	1.5	7.6	10.3	26.0	45.4
1976	1.6	8.0	11.5	24.5	45.7
1977	2.4	9.6	12.0	27.2	51.2
1978	12.4		13.4	30.4	56.2
Number of systems subsidized[a]	17 to 29	19 to 21	4	1	41 to 55

a Data are for 1971-7 only.
SOURCE: Data from Ontario, Ministry of Transportation and Communications

During the period 1976-8 capital and operating subsidies for GO Transit accounted for 25 per cent of all provincial subsidies for urban transit in Ontario.

Demonstration projects
The province pays up to 100 per cent of the operating deficit of demonstration projects such as dial-a-ride experiments. During 1975-8, these subsidies averaged $0.3 million a year (Table 17, column 7).

Other provincial transit subsidies
The province pays 75 per cent of the cost of local transit planning studies. In 1977-8 these subsidies averaged $0.2 million a year (Table 17, column 8).

Another cost to the province of its activities to subsidize and otherwise promote public transit in the province is the administration of the various programs. According to the Ontario *Public Accounts*, the annual costs of administration for the municipal transit program were $0.9 million in 1977-8 (Table 17, column 9). However, this is presumably an underestimate of total administrative costs; for example, the government does not include an imputed rent on government-owned buildings in calculating costs, and the Ministry of Transportation and Communications had $27 million in administrative overhead costs which were not assigned to specific programs in 1977.

Large provincial subsidies are provided for research and development in transit technology carried out by the provincially owned Urban Transportation Development Corporation. For example, during 1975-7 the annual losses of the

UTDC averaged $9.7 million. The true provincial subsidy was larger than this, since it also includes the forgone normal income on the provincial investment in the UTDC. However, since the UTDC is involved in the research and development and production of vehicles used by the transit industry rather than in the provision of transit services, this study does not consider subsidies to the UTDC to be subsidies for urban transit.[5] Of course it is possible that some of these subsidies will be passed on to the transit industry in the form of cheaper or better vehicles.

New directions in provincial subsidies
During 1979 the provincial government was developing a new subsidy program for transit investments designed to bring about changes in the spatial structure of urban areas. The immediate motivation behind this new program was to design a mechanism to provide greater provincial support than would be available under the regular formulas for a Toronto transit system light rapid transit line to the Scarborough Town Centre. As of 1979 the province appeared to be leaning in the direction of a subsidy formula based both on costs and on ridership.

FEDERAL SUBSIDIES FOR TRANSIT IN ONTARIO

Federal capital subsidies

Capital grants
During 1964-5, under the federal government's Municipal Development and Loan Program, the Toronto transit system received grants totalling $7.4 million and loans totalling $22.1 million at subsidized interest rates, with grants at $16^2/_3$ per cent and loans at 50 per cent of subway construction expenditures excluding rolling stock. During the same period a number of other urban transit systems in Ontario received much smaller subsidies for expenditures on construction labour under the Municipal Winter Works Incentive Program funded jointly by the federal and provincial governments.

In 1975 the federal government announced the Capital Assistance Program for Urban Commuter Services under which it would provide $100 million nationally over five years beginning in 1977 for capital expenditures on new public transit systems for suburban commuters in major metropolitan areas, particularly commuter rail vehicles and stations and express buses on reserved

---

5 Details of provincial subsidies for the UTDC are available in Ontario, Ministry of Treasury and Economics (annual).

lanes. In 1977 the federal government announced the 'Urban Transportation Assistance Program under which it would provide $230 million nationally over five years beginning in 1978 for urban transit capital expenditures, for construction of railway/highway grade separations, and for research studies and demonstration projects. The funds were to be allocated to the provinces in proportion to population (i.e. $10 per capita). The program announced in 1977 was to replace the Capital Assistance Program for Urban Commuter Services of 1975 and also the Railway Relocation and Crossing program introduced in 1974.

In reality, the federal government provided little assistance for capital expenditures on urban transit either nationally or in Ontario during the 1970s. The announced programs simply were not implemented on the scales or schedules indicated. Apparently the only federal capital grant for urban transit in Ontario during the 1970s was $9.7 million in 1975 for expenditures on rolling stock for a new peak-period GO Transit commuter rail service between Toronto and Richmond Hill.

Sales tax exemption
In 1974 the federal government removed its sales tax on urban transit vehicles as well as certain other transportation equipment (railway cars, large trucks and buses, and commercial aircraft). The basic sales tax rate was 12 per cent between 1974 and late 1978 and has been 9 per cent since late 1978.

Federal operating subsidies

Income tax exemption
As noted in the discussion of the provincial subsidies, municipal corporations including publicly owned urban transit systems are exempt from income taxes.

Gasoline excise tax
When the federal government imposed an excise tax of 10 cents a gallon on gasoline in 1975, it exempted municipal transit systems as well as most other commercial users. The excise tax was reduced to 7 cents a gallon in 1978. However, this exemption is not important for municipal transit systems in Ontario, which use very few gasoline-powered buses. More important is the fact that the excise tax was not applied to diesel fuel.[6]

---

6 Municipal transit systems in Ontario use about fifty gallons of diesel fuel for every gallon of gasoline (Statistics Canada, Cat. 53-003).

VIA Rail commuter services
The federal government subsidizes interurban railway passenger services provided by VIA Rail (previously CN and CP Rail). Some of these services are in fact used by commuters.

Demonstration projects
During the 1970s the federal government subsidized research and demonstration projects in urban transit, principally through Transport Canada's Urban Transportation Research Branch (formerly the Transportation Development Agency). However, the UTRB was abolished in 1979 along with the federal Ministry of State for Urban Affairs.

CROSS-SUBSIDIES FOR URBAN TRANSIT

Apart from government subsidies for public transit, an important aspect of transit financing is cross-subsidization. Even in the absence of government subsidies transit systems have often provided certain operations at a loss, or operated during certain periods at a loss, and covered those losses from profits earned on other activities or at other times.

Transit systems have often earned a profit for several years in a row and then used this profit to subsidize their operations in later years. For example, the Toronto transit system had an operating surplus every year from 1940 to 1949, with large surpluses during the second world war. These surpluses were used to finance construction of part of the Yonge Street subway. Thus people who used the Toronto transit system in the 1940s subsidized the operation of the system during the 1950s. Similarly, users of the London transit system in the early 1950s subsidized later users.

In a few cases the organizations which have provided urban transit services have also provided other services, such as interurban bus passenger and freight services or electric power. In some of these cases the organization has earned a profit on the interurban service or on electric power and used it to subsidize losses on the urban transit service.[7] For example, in the past the profits earned by Gray Coach lines and Canada Coach Lines on interurban bus services were used to subsidize intra-urban and suburban commuter bus services in Toronto and Hamilton, and the profits earned by the Cornwall Street Railway, Light and Power Company on electric power were used to subsidize urban transit services.

7 However, public utility commissions in Ontario are prevented by law from engaging in such cross-subsidization.

Although transit systems sometimes discriminate between riders on the basis of age (see below), they generally charge a uniform fare for all trips regardless of day, time, route, length, and number of transfers. The only significant departures from this are premium fares for express and dial-a-ride service and fares which increase with distance for GO Transit. In the past a number of urban systems charged zone fares, but these have now been abandoned except in a few cases where routes extend beyond the city limits. Only one transit system in the province (Oakville) charges different fares at peak and off-peak hours, and only one charges different fares on different days of the week (Toronto for Sunday and holiday passes). The result of the uniform fare system prior to government subsidies was that transit systems earned profits on some services and used these to subsidize losses on other services. For example, in 1966 the London transit system earned a profit on inner-city weekday services and used this to subsidize losses on suburban, Sunday, and holiday services. At present the result of uniform fares is that different services within a given city receive widely different rates of government subsidy.

While transit systems generally charge uniform fares for different types of trips by a given rider, they often discriminate between riders on the basis of age and, in a few cases, on the basis of frequency of use. In some cases fare concessions for certain age groups are financed by special government subsidies earmarked for that purpose; for instance the Hamilton and London systems receive subsidies specifically to finance lower fares for senior citizens. In other cases, however, the fare discrimination has not been subsidized; for example the London transit system charged lower fares for children as early as 1948 (three years before it became publicly owned). Since fare-elasticities of demand are evidently less than unity for all population groups, there was effectively a cross-subsidy from adults to children. Several transit systems in the province disciminate between riders on the basis of frequency of use by offering monthly passes for an unlimited number of rides at a fixed price; for the most part only people who commute regularly by transit can take advantage of the resulting lower average fare (and zero marginal fare) per ride.

TRANSIT SUBSIDIES OUTSIDE ONTARIO

There is substantial variation between Canadian provinces and between countries in the share of transit costs financed by governments, in the subsidy formulas used, and in the sources of revenues used to subsidize transit. This section illustrates some of this variety.

TABLE 20

Provincial subsidies for urban transit, 1977

Province	Capital subsidies	Operating subsidies
British Columbia	100 per cent for vehicles. Vehicles leased to Vancouver and Victoria without charge	100 per cent of operating deficit for Vancouver and Victoria; 50 per cent of operating deficit for other municipalities
Alberta	100 per cent, with a ceiling of $7.5 million a year each for Calgary and Edmonton	50 per cent of operating deficit up to a maximum of $3.33 per capita.
Saskatchewan	50 per cent for vehicles; 75 per cent for other facilities	3 cents per passenger carried
Manitoba	50 per cent for vehicles made in Manitoba	50 per cent of operating deficit or 40 per cent of revenue in previous year, whichever is less
Ontario	75 per cent for intra-urban transit; 100 per cent for GO Transit Computer System	Subsidies of intra-urban transit operating costs ranging from 13.75 per cent for cities with populations over 1 million up to 25 per cent for cities with populations under 100,00[a]; 100 per cent of operating deficit for GO Transit
Quebec	30 per cent for vehicles made in Quebec; 10 per cent for vehicles made elsewhere; $33^1/_3$ per cent for public acquisition of previously private systems; 60 per cent of capital servicing costs for Montreal subway	45 per cent of operating deficit, with 1 per cent extra for each 1 per cent increase in ridership, up to an extra 10 per cent[b]
New Brunswick	None	Provincial grants to municipalities based on net cost of local services, including municipal transit subsidies
Prince Edward Island	None	None
Nova Scotia	50 per cent	$3 per capita in urban area
Newfoundland	None	$4 per capita in urban area[c]

a Operating costs excludes depreciation on the non-subsidized portion of subsidized capital goods.

b Operating deficit includes depreciation on the non-subsidized portion of subsidized capital goods.

c St John's had the only urban transit system in Newfoundland. The provincial operating subsidies were $385 000 in 1976 and $1.4 million in 1977.

NOTE: In 1978 the Yukon government gave $49 000 to the Whitehouse transit system.

Other Canadian provinces
The above discussion of federal subsidies applies to other Canadian provinces as well as to Ontario and will not be repeated here.

Table 20 shows the formulas used for provincial capital and operating subsidies for urban transit across Canada in 1977. While some of these formulas have now been revised, three important points can be seen. It is common in other provinces as well as in Ontario for capital costs to be subsidized more heavily than other costs. Moreover, unlike Ontario, Manitoba and Quebec discriminate in capital subsidy rates between vehicles produced within the province and vehicles produced outside, in effect using part of the subsidy to protect their local bus manufacturing industries rather than to promote urban transit. Finally, subsidy formulas vary substantially between provinces; in 1977, for instance, one province offered no operating subsidies, while in other cases provincial operating subsidies were based on municipal operating subsidies, operating deficits, operating costs, passengers carried, and/or population.

Data on municipal subsidies outside Ontario are not readily available. But one general observation is possible. In the case of urban areas in Alberta, Saskatchewan, and Manitoba, transit services have for many years been provided directly by departments of municipal governments with substantial municipal subsidies. By contrast, until recently in several urban areas in Quebec (excluding Montreal) and New Brunswick, transit services were provided by private companies without government subsidies.

A variety of tax exemptions are available for urban transit in other provinces. Transit systems in several provinces are exempt from provincial fuel taxes, and transit systems in a number of cities in other provinces are exempt from municipal property and business taxes.

There are a few urban areas outside Ontario where there were substantial cross-subsidies for transit services provided by power companies, particularly prior to the 1970s; in Halifax, Vancouver, and Victoria transit services were subsidized from profits on electricity during the 1960s.

United States
The American states receive a substantially smaller share of total government revenue than do the provinces in Canada, and the U.S. federal government receives a larger share. Because of this, the U.S. federal government plays a much larger role in subsidization of urban transit than does the Canadian federal government and the states a much smaller role than the Canadian provinces.

After introducing a relatively limited program of subsidies for transit demonstration projects in 1961, the U.S. federal government introduced capital grants for urban transit in 1965. The grants initially covered two thirds of 'net' capital expenditures (that portion which could not be financed out of transit revenues), but the rate was raised to 80 per cent in 1974. In 1974 Congress authorized capital grants averaging $1.2 billion a year for 1975-80. These federal capital grants are conditional upon state and municipal capital grants to pay the balance of net capital expenditures.

Federal operating subsidies were introduced in 1975. In 1978 Congress authorized an average of $1.6 billion a year for transit operating subsidies for 1979-82, to be allocated to urban areas on the basis of population and population density, with a ceiling of 50 per cent of the transit system's operating deficit. Transit systems are also exempt from federal excise taxes on fuel, vehicles, and parts. The net effect of U.S. federal programs has been to subsidize capital costs at a significantly higher rate than non-capital costs.

Most of the American states have capital subsidy programs (usually for 15 per cent of net capital expenditures, based on the matching requirement for federal capital grants) and operating subsidy programs (usually based on operating deficits or costs). A few states provide operating subsidies partly on the basis of vehicle miles of service and/or number of passengers.

The most notable feature of state and municipal subsidies for urban transit in the United States is the variety of specific revenue sources earmarked for transit. Thus, in one or more states or municipalities earmarked funds include part of the revenues from gasoline taxes, motor vehicle excise taxes, motor vehicle registration fees, bridge and tunnel tolls, sales taxes, cigarette taxes, public utility excise taxes, property taxes, mortgage transfer taxes, and payroll taxes. The only thing comparable in Canada is the property tax levy in Toronto, which is earmarked for subway capital expenditures.

Western Europe, Australia, and New Zealand
Table 21 compares average rates of operating subsidy for transit systems in Canada and the United States with ten Western European countries, Australia, and New Zealand in 1975. The average subsidy rate in Canada was roughly the median for this set of fourteen countries but was below the American rate.

SUMMARY

The discussion in this chapter has revealed a complex array of municipal, provincial, and federal subsidies for urban transit in Ontario, involving a variety of grants, subsidized loans, and tax exemptions. At the risk of some oversimplification, it may be useful to pick out a few salient features of these programs in Ontario:

TABLE 21

Urban transit operating subsidies in fourteen countries, 1975

Country	Operating subsidy as a percentage of operating costs
Netherlands	70
Belgium	69
France	56
United States	46
Australia	45
Sweden	45
Canada	38
Switzerland	35
New Zealand	34
United Kingdom	29
Spain	20
Eire	15
Finland	11
Greece	11

SOURCE: Bly, Webster, and Pounds (1980, Table 3)

The level of government subsidies for urban transit has increased continually over the past two decades, whether measured in nominal or real dollars, by a total dollar amount, amount per vehicle mile or per passenger, or as a percentage of total costs. The percentage rate of increase in government subsidies was greatest during the first half of the 1970s. However, in the late 1970s growth of subsidies may have stopped, at least in real terms.

In descending order of importance, the sources of subsidies are the provincial, municipal, and federal governments.

Capital costs are subsidized at a higher percentage rate than non-capital costs, in two ways. First, capital costs are generally subsidized at a higher percentage rate than non-capital costs for a given public transit mode (e.g. bus transit) in a given urban area. Second, in Toronto, where there are several public transit modes, both municipal and provincial subsidies for the more capital-intensive subways and commuter railways have been at higher percentage rates than for the less capital-intensive buses.

In every year a substantial majority of all transit subsidies in Ontario have gone to intra-urban and regional commuter services for Metro Toronto. For example, in the case of provincial government subsidies, Metro Toronto has received about half of all intra-urban transit operating subsidies and a substantial majority of all intra-urban capital subsidies; in addition the GO Transit

TABLE 22

Provincial and municipal grants for urban transit in Ontario in 1976

	$ million
Provincial grants	
Capital grants	
Intra-urban surface transit	23.5
Metro subway	74.5
Demonstration projects	3.1
Operating grants	
Intra-urban transit	45.7
GO Transit[a]	35.4
Demonstration projects	0.4
Municipal grants	
Capital grants	
Metro subway	24.8[b]
Operating grants	
Intra-urban transit[a]	53.5[b]
Grand total	260.9

a Includes grants for capital expenditures
b Estimated from provincial levels
SOURCE: Table 17

system has been heavily subsidized. Of course, Toronto also accounts for almost two-thirds of the intra-urban transit passenger trips in the province.

Table 22 gives a reasonably accurate measure of the amounts of provincial and municipal *grants* for urban transit, which amounted to about $261 million in 1976. However, it must be kept in mind that these figures do not include the subsidy value of subsidized loans or tax exemptions given by federal, provincial, and municipal governments.

7
Effects of transit subsidies

Chapters 7 to 10 analyse the effects of urban transit subsidies. Chapters 8 to 10, on how subsidies affect the aggregate city-wide levels of transit fares, service, and ridership, amplify the first section of this chapter. This chapter also considers a number of other effects of urban transit subsidies: on the *structure* of fares and services, on capital-intensity, on labour contract terms and equipment prices, on technical efficiency, and on income distribution, as well as the effects of provincial subsidy policies on the level of municipal subsidies.

EFFECTS ON FARES, SERVICE, AND RIDERSHIP

This section briefly summarizes the findings of Chapters 8 to 10.

Chapter 8 analyses the effects of different transit subsidy formulas on fares, service, and ridership in the context of an explicit theoretical model of a transit system under alternative assumptions about the objectives of the transit firm. In general, for a given cost to the taxpayer, the effect of a transit subsidy is found to depend on both the objectives of the transit firm and the subsidy formula. However, with some transit objectives different subsidy formulas would lead to the same results.

The three alternative subsidy formulas are a lump-sum subsidy, a given amount of money not dependent upon the transit firm's operating performance; a cost subsidy, a given percentage of the transit firm's costs; and a passenger subsidy, a given amount of money per passenger carried.

One finding is that if the objective of the transit firm is to maximize the number of vehicle miles of service, then lump-sum and cost subsidies with the same cost to the taxpayer will have the same effects on the fare, service, and ridership. By contrast, a passenger subsidy with the same cost to taxpayers would lead to a lower fare, a lower level of service, and a higher level of ridership than either a lump-sum or a cost subsidy.

If the objective of the transit firm is to maximize ridership, then lump-sum and passenger subsidies will have the same effects, but a cost subsidy with the same cost to taxpayers would lead to a higher fare, a higher level of service, and a lower level of ridership than either the lump-sum or ridership subsidy.

In contrast to the analysis in Chapter 8, which is entirely theoretical, Chapters 9 and 10 provide empirical studies of the effects of transit subsidies on fares, service, and ridership. The empirical analysis is carried out at two levels using different sets of data. Chapter 9 uses data from nine urban areas in Ontario for the period 1950-78 for a casual graphical analysis of the effects of subsidies. Chapter 10 uses data from London, Ontario, for a statistical analysis of the effects of subsidies using an explicit econometric model.

These analyses suggest that provincial and municipal government transit subsidies led to a significant increase in the number of transit vehicle miles of service, a significant reduction in the real fare, and a significant increase in transit ridership compared to what would have occurred in the absence of subsidies in urban areas in Ontario during the 1970s.

EFFECTS ON THE STRUCTURE OF FARES AND SERVICES

The analyses summarized in the preceding section assume that transit operations can be described by a single fare (average revenue per passenger) and a single service variable (number of vehicle miles) and hence ignore the *structure* of fares and services. When a transit system offers more than one type of service and charges more than one fare level, aggregate fare and service indexes may hide important changes over time in the structure of fares and services. For example, many different changes in the structure of fares, which may have significantly different effects on the efficiency of resource allocation and the distribution of income, may produce the same change in average revenue per passenger.

In fact, there have been a number of important changes in the structure of transit fares and services in urban areas in Ontario since subsidies were introduced on a large scale, but there are difficulties in determining whether these changes in structure are a result of the subsidies. For example, suppose that a transit system is observed to eliminate zone fares and use an increase in subsidy funds to finance the resulting increase in its deficit. Should one conclude that the additional subsidy funds led to the elimination of zone fares (on the assumption that zone fares would not otherwise have been eliminated) or that the additional subsidy funds prevented an increase in the basic fare level (on the assumption that zone fares would have been eliminated anyway)? Without a detailed behavioural model of the urban transit firm, one cannot be sure which inference would be correct. Because of this problem, we can only review some of the changes in fare and service structures which took place during the periods when subsidies changed substantially and propose some hypotheses about the effects of subsidies.

The major changes in the structure of urban transit fares which have occured in Ontario since the introduction of large municipal and provincial subsidies are the introduction of lower fares for elderly people and students, the elimination of zone fares, and the introduction of monthly passes. In each case one can find statements by transit firms linking these changes to increases in subsidies. For example, according to the Toronto Transit Commission (1977, 35) 'it is doubtful that the fare zones would have been eliminated in 1973 without the provincial subsidy being available.'

The most important change in the structure of urban transit service that has occurred in Ontario since the introduction of large municipal and provincial subsidies has been the expansion of suburban and commuter services, which has been larger in percentage terms than the expansion of inner-city services. This has been true of bus services in most urban areas, but it is most evident in the case of express bus service in Ottawa and subway and GO Transit rail/bus service in Toronto. The implciation is that a large share of subsidies appears to have been used to provide transit service to suburban residents and commuters at the same fare levels that are charged in the inner city.

It is beyond the scope of this study to evaluate the efficiency of the expansions in suburban and commuter services that have taken place in the past decade, although this important issue clearly deserves careful study. We raise the issue of efficiency here because the expansion of these services is one of the principal explanations for the increase in urban transit deficits during the 1970s. Put simply, the question is whether transit systems have used subsidies to expand suburban and commuter services which would not have been justified on the basis of benefit-cost analysis, perhaps at a time when they could instead have expanded service or reduced real fares on inner-city routes in a manner which would have increased the efficiency of resource allocation.[1]

EFFECTS ON CAPITAL-INTENSITY

The cost subsidies discussed above applied at the same percentage rate to all of the transit firm's costs. As explained in Chapter 6, however, many of the transit subsidies available in Ontario, particularly provincial government subsidies, have been *capital* cost subsidies; they have applied only to the costs of capital

1 For former city of Toronto alderman and mayor John Sewell's views on these matters, see Sewell (1978a; b).

inputs and not to the costs of non-capital inputs. Other transit subsidies have applied to non-capital costs or to all (capital and non-capital) costs, but the net effect of all subsidies combined has been to subsidize capital costs substantially more than non-capital costs. In total, therefore, transit cost subsidies have been *capital-biased*.

For example, since December 1972 the province has paid 75 per cent of the cost of purchasing new buses. However, if a transit system opted to maintain existing buses instead of buying new ones to provide the same level of service, since 1977 it would have received provincial subsidies for only 13.75 to 25 per cent of its increased maintenance costs.

Capital-biased subsidy policies can be expected to induce transit firms to use an inefficiently high capital intensity in production and so to lead to a waste of resources compared to 'neutral' subsidy policies providing the same percentage subsidy for all input costs.

Suppose that a transit firm could produce a given level of service using either input combination A, which would involve capital costs of $1 million a year and non-capital costs of $10 million a year, or input combination B, involving capital costs of $4 million a year and non-capital costs of $8 million a year. If the input prices reflect the opportunity costs of the inputs, then the *social* cost of A is $11 million a year while the social cost of B is $12 million a year. Obviously, to use A would be more efficient than to use B.

Suppose now that the government introduced a capital-biased subsidy policy that would provide a 75 per cent subsidy for capital costs and a 20 per cent subsidy for non-capital costs. In this case, the after-subsidy costs to the transit firm of input combinations A and B would be $8.25 million and $7.4 million a year respectively. The transit firm would naturally choose B in order to minimize its private cost, in spite of the fact that A has a lower social cost. This distortion in resource allocation caused by the capital-biased nature of the subsidy would lead to a waste of $1 million a year in real resources, i.e. the excess of the social cost of B over the social cost of A.

Furthermore, a capital-biased subsidy is not worth as much to a transit firm as a neutral subsidy with the same cost to the taxpayer. For example, in the example above, the amount of the subsidy on B would be $4.6 million a year. However, the transit firm receives a benefit of only $3.6 million a year, while $1 million is wasted buying the inefficient input combination. Thus, 22 per cent of the subsidy is actually wasted compared to what would be achieved with a neutral subsidy.

There are several ways that capital-biased subsidies could induce a transit firm to adopt an inefficiently high capital intensity: A capital-biased subsidy would encourage a transit firm to substitute depreciation for maintenance by reducing vehicle maintenance below the economically efficient level and by scrapping vehicles early, to opt for a subway or light-rail transit system even when a bus system would have a lower social cost, or to select more optional equipment for transit vehicles. These three possibilities are discussed below.

Substitution of depreciation and interest for maintenance
If the purchase of new buses is subsidized at a higher percentage rate than maintenance expenditures, transit firms will have an incentive to substitute depreciation and interest for maintenance in order to reduce the private cost per vehicle mile of service. This substitution would raise the social cost per vehicle mile above the minimum attainable and hence would involve a waste of resources.

Maintenance cost per vehicle mile increases as buses become older.[2] Consequently, a transit firm can substitute depreciation and interest for maintenance not only by reducing the standard of maintenance so that vehicles deteriorate more rapidly but also by reducing the number of miles that older buses are driven and by scrapping vehicles earlier. Simultaneously, the transit firm would increase purchases of new buses. From society's point of view the result would be a reduction in average maintenance costs per vehicle mile and an increase in average depreciation and interest costs per vehicle mile.

Tye (1969) simulated the effect of the capital-biased subsidies which existed in the United States in the late 1960s, when the U.S. federal government provided a $66^2/_3$ percent subsidy for the purchase of new transit vehicles but no subsidy for their operation or maintenance. Tye estimated that this subsidy would induce a transit firm which was minimizing private cost per vehicle mile to replace buses at half the efficient age. He also estimated that the resulting waste in resources would equal 27 per cent of the amount of the federal subsidy.

Armour (1980) analysed the effect of an 80 per cent federal subsidy for the purchase of new transit equipment, combined with no subsidy for operation or maintenance, on the age at which buses should be replaced in Seattle in order to minimize local costs. He concluded:

For Seattle Metro, which operates a bus an average of 40 500 miles per year, the economic replacement age is between 20.5 and 26 years at full capital costs, depending on utilization. The same utilization would place the economic replacement age between 8.5 and 10 years if the 20 per cent local share ... is perceived as the only capital cost.

---

2 For a large transit system in 1976, Puccini (1979, Figure 11) reported that bus maintenance costs were higher by 0.69 cents per kilometer for each year of vehicle age.

Obviously UMTA [U.S. Federal Urban Mass Transportation Administration] capital grant program can influence a premature retirement of vehicles. It reduces by about 60 per cent the years a vehicle need be utilized at given outputs in order to minimize local costs. (Ibid., 53)

In order to test the hypothesis that capital-biased subsidies lead to the substitution of depreciation and interest for maintenance, one should develop an economic model of vehicle maintenance, utilization, and scrapping. Such a model would allow not only for the effects of changes in subsidy policies but also for the effects of changes in wage rates, vehicle prices, interest rates, and other variables.

Because of the limitations of data, I was unable to test empirically for the effects of capital-biased subsidies on vehicle maintenance and utilization. Consequently, attention was restricted to the hypothesis that capital-biased subsidies will induce transit firms to scrap buses earlier, or more precisely that capital-biased subsidies will increase the probability that a bus which is still being used at the beginning of any given time period will be scrapped during that time period.

In order to test this hypothesis, data were collected on bus fleets in four urban areas (London, Ottawa, Sault Ste Marie, and St Catharines) between 1962 and 1977. Estimates were made of the probability that a bus of type i ($i = 1, 2, 3$, where 1 is gasoline, 2 is General Motors Canada diesel, 3 is other diesel) and age j would be scrapped in a one-year interval during 1963-72 (before introduction of provincial capital-biased subsidies for buses in December 1972) and in a one-year interval during 1973-7 (after introduction of provincial capital-biased subsidies). Relative frequencies were used as estimates of probabilities. In estimating these probabilities, no allowance was made for changes in vehicle characteristics, wage rates, vehicle prices, interest rates, or other variables besides capital-biased subsidies which may have affected these probabilities.

The estimates of these probabilities are presented in Table 23. In the case of both gasoline buses and other (non-GMC) diesel buses, the estimates suggest that capital-biased subsidies affected the probability of scrapping. The data suggest that for gasoline and 'other diesel' buses thirteen years old and older the introduction of provincial capital-biased subsidies did lead to earlier scrapping and hence a waste of resources.

However, it is also important to observe that the extent to which scrapping decisions were distorted, and hence the waste in resources caused by the capital-biased nature of the subsidies, appears to have been a good deal less than is suggested by the simulations carried out by Tye and Armour, even allowing for

TABLE 23

Estimated scrapping probabilities for buses

Age	1963-72		1973-7	
	Probability[a]	Sample size[b]	Probability	Sample size
Gasoline buses				
10-12	0.000	48	0.066	15
13-15	0.038	185	0.125	8
16-18	0.193	348	0.267	15
19-21	0.171	205	0.400	15
22-24	0.405	79	0.571	14
General Motors Canada diesel buses				
10-12	0.000	418	0.000	307
13-15	0.000	277	0.005	221
16-17[c]	0.000	42	0.004	254
Other diesel buses				
12[d]	0.010	100	0.000	10
13-15	0.114	215	0.268	56
16-18	0.131	90	0.226	31
19[e]	0.000	10	0.444	9

a Number of buses scrapped divided by sample size
b Number of bus-years (or parts thereof) observed
c There were no buses over 17 years old in the sample during 1963-72.
d There were no buses under 12 years old in the sample during 1973-7.
e There were no buses over 19 years old in the sample during 1963-72.
SOURCE: Compiled from unpublished data in Canadian Urban Transit Association files

the fact that the capital-bias in the Ontario program was probably somewhat less than in the U.S. programs they considered.[3] First, virtually no buses of any type were scrapped at an age of less than thirteen years during 1973-7. Second,

3 Actually, it is hard to be sure just how much capital bias there was in provincial subsidies in 1973-6. The province paid 75 per cent of the cost of new buses and 50 per cent of operating losses. Municipalities paid the other 50 per cent of operating losses. If the municipal operating subsidy was a lump-sum grant, then the provincial operating subsidy was a matching lump-sum grant, and hence there was no provincial subsidy of non-capital costs. However, if the municipal subsidy was a cost subsidy, then the province also effectively gave a 50 per cent cost subsidy for non-capital inputs, and the capital-bias was less. In 1977 and in subsequent years, there was clearly a large capital bias because the province paid 75 per cent of the cost of new buses and 17.5 to 22.5 per cent of the cost of non-capital inputs.

virtually no General Motors diesel buses (currently the principal type of vehicle in use) were scrapped at an age of less than eighteen years during 1973-7.

There are several possible explanations for the limited effect of the province's capital-biased subsidies on scrapping age in 1973-7. First, it is possible that Tye and Armour overestimated the extent to which changes in the relative prices of capital and non-capital inputs will change the age at which a bus should be scrapped in order to minimize the private cost of vehicle miles of bus service. If this is true, then capital-biased subsidies will not lead to as large a waste of resources as their work suggests. Second, the minimum age at which buses were scrapped may have been constrained by the bureaucrats who administered the province's transit subsidy program; in fact, they claimed to have imposed such a constraint. If this constraint does exist, and if the result is that transit firms continue to *use* the older buses rather than buy newer ones, this practice will reduce the waste of resources that would otherwise be caused by the capital-biased subsidies. However, if the result is that transit firms merely retain the older buses unused and still buy and use replacements, this practice could actually compound the problem. Third, the long-run effects of capital-biased subsidies may exceed those recorded in the initial five years, because in the long run firms may reduce the level of maintenance throughout a bus's life below the level that prevailed through 1972. Fourth, because of limitations on the total amount of funds available from the province to subsidize the purchase of new buses, during the period 1973-7 transit firms may not have been able to secure approval for purchase of enough new buses to permit them to scrap all the buses they would actually have wished to retire. If so, any increase in the funding of the program in future years could lead to an increase in the incidence of scrapping for 'young' buses.

The reader should keep in mind that the data in Table 23 pertain only to scrapping ages. The effect of capital-biased subsidies on vehicle maintenance or utilization has not been considered. Careful study of these effects could reveal that capital-biased subsidies caused a much larger waste of resources than Table 23 alone suggests. Moreover, in the long term the waste of resources would almost certainly be larger than in the initial five years. Finally, the reader should keep in mind that the test based on the data in Table 23 is rather crude. The number of cities and observations involved is limited, and the test could be biased because no allowance has been made for a number of variables which might have affected scrapping decisions.

Subways instead of buses
Subway and light rail transit systems use a higher ratio of capital to non-capital inputs than do bus systems, so that capital-biased subsidies (including the

special subsidies for subways offered by the province since 1964) will encourage transit systems to opt for rail transportation when bus systems would be more economically efficient. In practical terms, the danger in Ontario is that capital-biased subsidies, particularly those offered by the province, have encouraged the Toronto Transit Commission and the Metro Toronto government to extend and build new subway and streetcar lines even when they would be less economically efficient than the alternatives of conventional, limited-stop, or express buses.

There appear to have been no careful cost-benefit comparisons of subway and bus systems for the recent extensions of the Toronto subway system, so that firm conclusions are not possible. However, economists have compared subway and express bus systems in a number of other large urban areas. These studies provide very strong evidence that express bus systems would be more efficient than subways for travel between suburbs and the central business district in urban areas like Toronto.[4] Consequently, at least some of the recent extensions of the Toronto subway system are probably inefficient. No further extensions of the Toronto subway system should be undertaken unless they can be justified when compared to buses on economic efficiency grounds.

Optional vehicle equipment
Approximately two hundred equipment options are available for standard diesel buses (Puccini 1979, 26). Some of them increase the durability of the bus and hence reduce maintenance costs. Others reduce the workload of the driver and hence may reduce labour costs. Still others, such as air conditioning, increase passenger comfort and hence enable the transit system to attract a given number of riders with fewer vehicle miles of service. Thus, capital-biased subsidies probably encourage transit firms to substitute optional equipment for less capital-intensive maintenance, operating labour, and vehicle miles of service.

In a study of the capital-biased transit subsidies provided in the United States, Hilton (1974, 56) concluded that 'since the program reduced the capital costs of the equipment to a third of what it would otherwise have been, transit operators frequently opted for more capital-intensive buses than they would otherwise have ordered. In a limited number of cases this meant buying standard transit buses in preference to vehicles of the school-bus or microbus type. More often it meant that the transit enterprise opted for air-conditioned equipment to replace non-air-conditioned in hopes of attracting passengers through the higher quality of service.'

Constraints on capital-intensity
The extent of economically inefficient substitution of capital for non-capital inputs, and thus the extent of the waste of resources resulting from the capital-

4 For a summary of this literature, see Frankena (1979, 93-7).

bias of transit subsidies in Ontario, may be limited by the province in three ways (Puccini 1979, 38-9). First, the province has specifically excluded from the capital subsidy program certain bus options such as air-conditioning and power steering. Second, justification on need is required before provincial capital subsidies are approved. In principle, the province could restrict approval to economically efficient capital expenditures. While there is no evidence that the province uses the criterion of economic efficiency, this approval process might restrict the early replacement of buses.[5] Third, provincial capital subsidies are limited by the availability of subsidy funds. In the short run, at least, this may have limited the extent to which transit systems in Ontario could substitute capital for labour.

Conclusions
On balance, the existence of constraints on capital intensity does not provide reason for complacency about the capital bias of transit subsidies in Ontario. The capital bias of the province's transit subsidy program and the deliberate policy of subsidizing subways and commuter rail systems at a higher rate than conventional bus systems represent a serious potential source of inefficiency and unjustified waste of resources. One of the principal recommendations of this study is that the province should modify its subsidy policies to remove the capital bias.

EFFECTS ON LABOUR CONTRACT TERMS AND EQUIPMENT
PRICES

It is often suggested that transit subsidies may lead to higher wages and fringe benefits for transit workers because provincial subsidies will make the transit management and municipal government willing to pay a higher price to avoid or end a strike.

Table 24 shows that in Ontario the wages of transit workers did not rise compared to those of workers in manufacturing during the first half of the 1970s when transit subsidies were expanding.[6] However, fringe benefits are excluded. Moreover, we do not know what would have happened to the relative wages of transit workers in the absence of transit subsidies. It is conceivable that subsidies

---

5 Hilton (1974, 59) reports that the u.s. federal government claimed to require that buses to be replaced be at least fifteen years old. Representatives of the Ontario Ministry of Transportation and Communications Transit Office, which administers provincial transit subsidies, say they would not approve subsidies for premature replacement of buses.
6 Both transit and manufacturing wages were subject to federal Anti-Inflation Board guidelines beginning in 1975.

TABLE 24

Ratio of transit to average manufacturing wage rates

City	1968	1969	1970	1971	1972	1973	1974	1975	1976	1977	1978	1979
Brantford	1.10	1.11	1.13	1.13	1.08	1.08	1.01	1.01	0.99	0.98	0.95	0.92
Cambridge	1.07	1.09	1.12	1.10	1.09	1.08	1.13	1.06	1.04	1.02	1.00	0.99
Guelph	1.12	1.13	1.16	1.12	1.16	1.15	1.11	1.05	1.07	1.05	1.03	1.07
Hamilton	1.05	1.06	1.01	0.99	1.05	1.05	1.03	1.08	1.02	1.01	0.98	0.94
Kingston	0.97	0.98	1.00	0.99	1.00	0.99	0.94	0.96	0.96	0.96	0.94	0.94
Kitchener	1.13	1.16	1.18	1.17	1.17	1.18	1.19	1.17	1.17	1.15	1.12	1.13
London	1.10	1.12	1.10	1.11	1.10	1.10	1.05	1.04	1.06	1.06	1.03	1.01
Niagara Falls	1.06	1.04	1.05	1.06	1.06	1.05	1.06	1.04	1.04	1.04	1.04	1.00
Oshawa	0.90	0.98	0.99	0.97	0.97	0.95	0.96	0.99	1.02	0.99	0.97	0.95
Ottawa	1.05	1.07	1.14	1.10	1.13	1.14	1.12	1.15	1.15	1.10	1.07	1.05
St Catharines	0.95	0.91	0.90	0.86	0.88	0.86	0.85	0.84	0.82	0.82	0.81	0.77
Sarnia	0.77	0.78	0.78	0.77	0.76	0.75	0.74	0.75	0.72	0.69	0.70	0.68
Stratford	1.28	1.17	1.31	1.23	1.21	1.19	1.16	1.10	1.10	1.08	1.11	1.08
Thunder Bay	0.97	0.95	0.98	0.96	0.95	1.01	0.96	0.98	0.87	0.85	0.86	0.86
Toronto	1.21	1.21	1.21	1.22	1.21	1.23	1.23	1.24	1.24	1.22	1.22	1.18
Windsor	0.82	0.90	0.94	0.88	0.85	0.85	0.82	0.87	0.86	0.84	0.82	0.85

SOURCE: Unpublished data from Canadian Urban Transit Association and London Transit Commission, and Statistics Canada (Cat. 72-002)

prevented or moderated a decline in the relative wages of transit workers during the 1970s.

In an early study, Lurie (1960) concluded that as of the 1950s the Boston transit union had raised the wages of its members by about 20 per cent above what they would have been in the absence of the union. Lurie argued that part of this wage premium was a result of the policy of subsidizing the transit system's operating deficit from local tax revenues.

There is some evidence that the conversion of transit systems from private to public ownership leads to increases in wage rates. According to Hilton, 'Pashigian found that in twelve systems converted to public ownership between 1960 and 1965, wages were 1.8 per cent higher than in comparable private systems in 1966, and 4.2 per cent higher in 1970.'[7] Hamermesh (1975) studied the ratio of transit wages to manufacturing wages in American cities between 1963 and 1971 and found a wage premium of about 5 to 9 per cent attributable to public ownership. Anderson (1979, 202) studied the ratio of transit wages to manufacturing wages in a large number of American cities between 1960 and 1975 and found a wage premium of about 5 to 14 per cent attributable to public ownership. By contrast, Barnum (1972) found that wages were about the same for public and private transit firms in the United States.

Anderson (1979, 202) concluded that subsidies led to a significant increase in transit wages, estimating the combined effects of conversion to public ownership and subsidization on wages at 11 to 22 per cent, compared to 5 to 14 per cent for the effect of public ownership alone. However, according to an American study which used data from thirty-two transit systems, 'analysis of the data for the properties in our sample does not confirm the hypothesis that higher operating subsidies in public systems lead to increases in transit wages.'[8]

One cannot conclude that transit subsidies boost transit wages; in fact, the data for Ontario suggest they do not.

It has also been argued that transit subsidies may lead to higher equipment costs, particularly in the case of diesel buses, because of the alleged monopoly power of GM Diesel in the Ontario market. According to Puccini (1979, 25): 'GM supplies about 95 per cent of the Ontario fleet, and competitive tenders for small orders are hard to obtain ... Bus costs have escalated wildly due to general economic trends and perhaps as a result of the availability of government

---

7 Pashigian, B.P. (1973) 'Public versus private ownership: consequences and determinants of public ownership of local transit systems,' unpublished, University of Chicago, cited by Hilton (1974, 55).
8 Miller, Olson, and Stern (1978, 143). However, they do not publish their evidence to support this statement.

subsidy. In 1973 the base price (without options) was $40 000 and in 1976 it had increased to $60 000.' Thus, a central issue is whether GM Diesel does have significant monopoly power in Ontario.

EFFECTS ON TECHNICAL EFFICIENCY

It is often said that transit managements in the United States have been technically inefficient, that they have not achieved the maximum output that could have been produced with the inputs they have used, or that they have not minimized the private cost of production.

Some observers have argued that availability of subsidies may reduce the pressure to minimize costs, and hence may reduce technical efficiency. Some subsidy formulas, such as deficit subsidies, have been claimed to be more harmful in this respect than others, such as passenger subsidies. There is no sound reason for such differences between subsidy formulas, but information has not been gathered on the question.

EFFECTS ON INCOME DISTRIBUTION

In Chapter 5 we saw that if a transit subsidy led to a reduction in all transit fares by a uniform percentage amount, the ratio of benefits from reduced fares to household income would be higher on average for low-income households than for high-income households. We have since seen that transit subsidies led to a reduction in real transit fares during the 1970s. However, it cannot be inferred from this that the ratio of benefits from transit subsidies to household income was in fact higher on average for low-income households than for high-income households.

First, the reductions in average real fares did not in fact take the form of a reduction in all transit fares by a uniform percentage amount. In practice, some fares were reduced more than others. The elimination of zone fares, the introduction of concession fares for senior citizens, the extension of the hours of validity for concession fares for students, and so on all provided larger benefits for certain trip categories than for others.

Second, a large portion of subsidy funds was used to extend service rather than to reduce fares, particularly to extend suburban and commuter services. The benefits of these service extensions were not uniform for trips of different types.

Third, as discussed in Chapter 5, transit subsidies would lead to changes in automobile congestion, changes in property values and rents, and so on, and each of these changes would have distributional effects.

Of course, one could argue that in the absence of subsidies the structure of fares would still have changed and services would still have been extended to new subdivisions, so that the subsidies did in fact prevent a general increase in fares that would otherwise have been required to finance these changes. As we shall see, during the 1960s many transit systems financed extensions of service to new subdivisions by raising their basic fares faster than the cost per vehicle mile of transit service was rising, and in the absence of subsidies this practice might have continued during the 1970s.

In any event, an important shortcoming of existing transit subsidies from the point of view of income redistribution is that subsidy rates (per trip or as a percentage of costs) are generally highest on transit services used heavily by upper-income groups, including suburban and commuter bus and subway routes into outlying low-density residential areas; Toronto's GO Transit suburban commuter rail/bus system; and dial-a-bus systems in low-density residential areas (Frankena 1973). Moreover, these include the types of services that underwent the greatest expansion in recent years.

EFFECTS OF PROVINCIAL SUBSIDY POLICIES ON MUNICIPAL SUBSIDY LEVELS

One issue of concern to the province in designing a subsidy policy is whether provincial subsidies will lead to an increase or decrease in the level of subsidies provided by the municipal government. In order to encourage municipalities to increase their subsidies, the operating subsidy policy introduced by the province in 1971 operated as a matching grant, i.e. the province paid half the transit system's operating deficit provided the municipal government paid the other half. There seems to be little question that this formula led to a major expansion in subsidies provided by the municipal governments of the larger urban areas in Ontario, where transit systems had previously had little or no operating subsidy, such as Toronto, Ottawa, Hamilton, and London. In all these urban areas municipal transit subsidies were introduced more or less at the same time as the provincial subsidy policy came into effect.

CONCLUSIONS ON TRANSIT SUBSIDIES IN ONTARIO

Our review of transit subsidy policies in Ontario reveals two serious weaknesses. First, existing subsidy programs are heavily capital-biased. Capital-biased subsidies may tend to induce transit firms to substitute heavily subsidized capital for other inputs which are less heavily subsidized and hence to increase the average social cost of supplying transit service. To the extent that such subsitution occurs, any increase in the level of transit service or reduction in fares that would be brought about by a capital-biased subsidy could be achieved at a lower cost to the taxpayer by a neutral subsidy, so that capital-biased subsidies lead to a waste of resources. A principal recommendation of this study is that all levels of government should revise their subsidy policies so that any subsidy given for transit costs should apply to all inputs at a uniform percentage rate.

Moreover, existing subsidies appear to be used to a very large degree for suburban and commuter services, including GO Transit. Both the efficiency of resource allocation and the equality of the income distribution probably could be increased by reducing vehicle miles for some of these services, increasing vehicle miles on more centrally located services, and reducing fares from the levels required at present to satisfy the budget constraint given the level of suburban services.

8

How subsidies can affect service, fares, and ridership

The literature on urban transit subsidies reviewed in Chapter 5 analyses the magnitude of the lump-sum subsidy that would enable a transit firm to set service and fares at efficient levels. There is no systematic analysis of the effect of a subsidy on service, fares, and ridership if the objective of the firm is not efficiency and if the subsidy is not a lump sum.[1] An understanding of these issues is important, because transit firms are beginning to define their objectives in terms of ridership maximization rather than efficiency, and because many subsidies, rather than being lump sums, are based on transit expenditures.[2]

This chapter derives predictions about the effects of alternative transit subsidy formulas under various assumptions about the objective function of the transit firm. Under most of the circumstances considered, the model shows, as expected, that transit subsidies would lead to a reduction in fares, an increase in vehicle miles of service, and an increase in ridership. However, under certain assumptions the model predicts that a transit subsidy would not affect the fare or would lead to an increase in the fare. The model also predicts the comparative effects of different subsidy formulas. For example, if a transit firm maximizes ridership, lump-sum and passenger subsidies will have the same effects but a cost subsidy with the same cost to taxpayers would lead to a higher fare, more service, and lower ridership. The predictions derived in this chapter are amenable to econometric testing, and some preliminary empirical results are presented in Chapter 10.

---

1 Preliminary simulation analyses comparing cost and ridership subsidies were carried out by Nelson (1972) and Peskin (1973).
2 For an evaluation of the efficiency of vehicles-miles maximization, ridership maximization, and alternative subsidy formulas in the context of the model used in this chapter, see Appendix C.

AGGREGATE MODEL OF AN URBAN TRANSIT SYSTEM

Transit operations in a single city are described by a model that determines the aggregate city-wide levels of transit ridership and service and the fare. It does not consider temporal or intra-urban spatial variations in the fare, service, or demand for rides. The latter is determined by the fare and the number of vehicle miles of service. The fare and number of vehicle miles are determined by a publicly owned, non-profit, monopolistic transit firm, which maximizes an objective function subject to a budget constraint.[3] The budget constraint requires that the transit firm's costs must equal its revenues after allowing for subsidies.[4]

The budget constraint
To derive a budget constraint for the transit firm, we assume that total transit costs are proportional to vehicle miles of service[5]; all transit revenues are derived

3 One could argue that the transit system determines vehicle hours rather than vehicle miles of service. Vehicle miles would depend upon vehicle hours, in-vehicle travel speed, which would depend on the level of automobile use and hence on transit fares and service, and vehicle loading time, which would depend on the level of transit ridership and hence transit fares and service. The use of vehicle miles rather than hours of service ignores the impact of transit operating policies on the congestion of roads and on the congestion of the transit system itself. For an econometric model which uses vehicle hours, see Gaudry (1980).

4 Similar models have been used by Nelson (1972), Nash (1978), and Frankena (1978a). A preliminary version of the model used here was presented by the author in a report for TEE Consulting Services, as part of a project sponsored by the Ministry of State for Urban Affairs and Transport Canada (see Frankena 1978b). The model and its predictions concerning subsidies can be adapted to other non-profit organizations such as hospitals, educational institutions, performing arts companies, and museums if number of vehicle miles of service is changed to quality of output and revenue and cost functions are modified to allow for philanthropy and for the dependence of cost on quantity as well as quality of output. The quantity of output demanded depends on price and quality of output, which are chosen by the organization to maximize an objective function in which some combination of quantity of output, quality of output, and price appear as arguments. See Newhouse (1970) for an early attempt to analyse such a model of hospital behaviour.

5 This assumption is consistent with empirical studies for bus firms by Lee and Steedman (1970), Nelson (1972), and Pozdena (1975, Chap. 4). The model would be more appropriate for rail systems if one assumed that the total *variable* costs were proportional to vehicle miles of service and introduced fixed costs into the budget constraint. This first assumption excludes the possibility of changing the cost per vehicle mile by changing the size of vehicles.

from fares and subsidies[6]; the fare per ride is uniform; the demand for rides is a decreasing function of the fare and an increasing function of vehicle miles of service; and the absolute value of the fare-elasticity of demand for rides is less than one at low fare levels, increases with the fare, and exceeds one at high fare levels.[7]

Given these assumptions, in the absence of subsidies the transit system chooses a combination of the fare and vehicle miles of service that satisfies the following budget constraint:

$$FR - CM = 0,$$ (1)

where F is the fare per ride, M is the number of vehicle miles of transit service, C is the cost per vehicle mile, and

$$R = R(F, M)$$ (2)

is the demand function for rides.[8]

Substituting (2) into (1) gives a single equation in two unknowns, so that a range of combinations of F and M will normally be consistent with the transit firm's budget constraint. Under reasonable assumptions, the relevant set of feasible combinations of F and M can be represented by a curve like ZZ' (Figure 8), which I will refer to as the 'feasible locus.'[9] In the absence of subsidies based on the number of passengers, the feasible locus slopes upward in the range of F and M for which the fare-elasticity of demand for rides E_F is less than one in absolute value and bends backward where $-E_F > 1$.

---

6 Exogenously determined non-fare revenues, such as investment income, could easily be introduced.

7 The absolute value of the fare-elasticity of demand is assumed to be less than one at low fare levels because empirical studies normally estimate it to be less than one at prevailing fare levels; the absolute value of the fare-elasticity is assumed to rise above one at high fare levels so that the feasible levels of total transit revenue and vehicle miles of service have upper bounds.

8 Appendix c considers whether the operating policy selected by a transit firm which maximizes vehicle miles of service or ridership would be economically efficient, whether the provision of a subsidy to such a firm would increase efficiency, and which subsidy formula would be most efficient.

9 It is conceivable that there will be no feasible operating policy for which $M > 0$. It is also conceivable that the feasible locus would be roughly circular. However, in the latter case the left half of the circle would consist of combinations of F and M at which the marginal revenue generated by an additional vehicle mile exceeds the marginal cost of an

Objective function
The combination of F and M selected by the transit firm depends not only on the feasible locus but also on the firm's objective function, which is assumed to take the form

$$\text{Maximize } U = U(F, M, R), \tag{3}$$

where $U_F \leq 0$, $U_M \geq 0$, and $U_R \geq 0$ but U_M and U_R are not both zero. Cooter and Topakian (1980) provide a rationale for including vehicle miles and ridership as arguments in the objective function on the grounds that transit managerial rewards may be based on these measures of the size of the enterprise, and it would be consistent with their discussion to rationalize inclusion of the fare as an argument in the objective function on the grounds that it is a determinant of electoral support.

Given the demand function (2), the objective function can be simplified:

$$U(F, M, R) = U(F, M, R(F, M)) = V(F, M). \tag{4}$$

Thus, even if the firm cares about ridership as well as about the fare and vehicle miles, its objective function can be represented by indifference curves in which only F and M appear explicitly as arguments.

The indifference curves for three possible objective functions are depicted in Figure 8.[10] The indifference curves for a firm which maximizes vehicle miles are vertical lines, and the firm chooses the operating policy represented by point A (high fare, high vehicle miles, and low ridership). The indifference curves for a firm that maximizes ridership are 'isorider curves,' each of which gives the solutions to the equation $R(F, M) = R^0$ for a different value of R^0, and the firm chooses the operating policy represented by point B (medium fare, medium vehicle miles, and high ridership). It is important to note that maximum ridership occurs at a lower level of F and M than does maximum vehicle miles. The indifference curves for a firm willing to cut service enough that ridership would

---

additional vehicle mile; these combinations of F and M would be dominated by those on the right half of the circle if the marginal utility of M or R in equation (3) is positive, so that the left half of the feasible locus is ignored here. It follows that on the portion of the feasible locus illustrated in Figure 8, $FR_M < C$, or equivalently that the elasticity of demand for rides with respect to vehicle miles of service is less than one. Also, we assume that the positively sloped portion of the feasible locus in Figure 8 is strictly convex in the relevant range of values of F and M.

10 We assume that $V(F, M)$ is quasi-concave. Quasi-concavity of $U(F, M, R)$ and concavity of $R(F, M)$ are sufficient for quasi-concavity of $V(F, M)$.

Figure 8
Feasible locus for unsubsidized firm and indifference
curves for three alternative objective functions

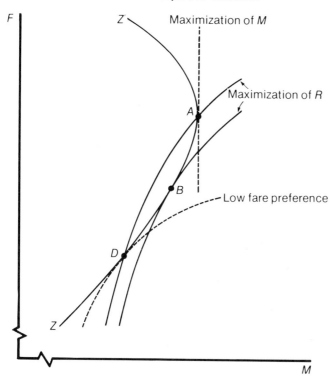

decline in order to reduce the fare would have lower slopes than those corresponding to the objective of maximizing ridership. I will refer to such an objective as 'low fare preference.' A firm with low fare preference chooses an operating policy such as the one represented by point D (low fare, low vehicle miles, and low ridership), southwest of point B.

THE EFFECT OF SUBSIDIES

Alternative subsidy formulas
We will examine three alternative transit subsidy formulas: a lump sum subsidy, an exogenously determined amount of money not dependent upon the transit firm's operating performance; a cost subsidy, an exogenously determined

fraction of costs; and a passenger subsidy, an exogenously determined amount of money per passenger carried.

Given the assumption of constant cost per vehicle mile, a cost subsidy is identical to a service subsidy, an exogenously determined amount of money per vehicle mile. Also, in the absence of lump-sum and passenger subsidies, given the budget constraint, a revenue subsidy, an exogenously determined percentage of the transit firm's revenue, is identical to a cost subsidy at another rate.[11]

In cases where two different levels of government provide subsidies to the same transit firm, it is common for one of the governments to provide a deficit subsidy, an exogenously determined percentage of the transit firm's deficit. Given the budget constraint of the transit firm, the effect of a deficit subsidy from one level of government is to provide a matching grant equal to some percentage of any subsidy provided by the other level of government. Consequently, the present model can be used to analyse the combination of a deficit subsidy from one level of government and a lump-sum, cost, or passenger subsidy from another level of government.

Further assumptions
Two further assumptions must be made to use the model developed here to analyse the effects of subsidies. First, we assume that the subsidies analysed would not change the cost per vehicle mile of transit service. Thus, we rule out the possibility that subsidies would lead to an increase in transit wages.[12] Second, we assume that the provision of government subsidies is not accompanied by government controls over transit operating policies or by organizational changes which would alter the transit firm's objective function.

The effect of subsidies on the constraint
The introduction of subsidies changes the transit firm's budget constraint from (1) to

$$(F + S_3)R + S_1 - (1 - S_2)CM = 0, \tag{5}$$

11 In practice, a common transit subsidy formula is a capital cost subsidy, an exogenously determined percentage of the transit firm's capital costs. If the elasticity of substitution between capital and non-capital inputs were zero, this would be identical to a cost subsidy at some particular rate. However, if the elasticity of substitution were not zero, a capital cost subsidy would lead to an increase in capital-intensity and an increase in the cost of transit service per vehicle mile. Analysis of this case would require introduction of a production function for transit service and is not pursued here.

12 For evidence that subsidies do not lead to higher wages, see Chapter 7.

Figure 9
Feasible loci for no subsidy, lump-sum subsidy, and cost subsidy

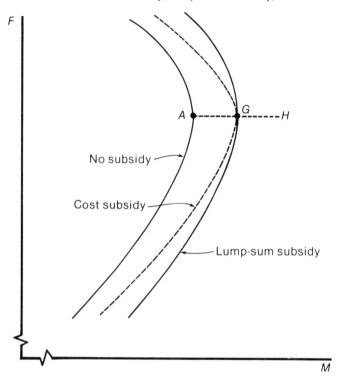

where S_1 is the lump-sum subsidy, S_2 is the fraction of costs covered by the cost subsidy, and S_3 is the passenger subsidy per ride.

To determine how a subsidy would shift the feasible locus, one must make some additional assumptions about the demand function (2). For simplicity, in the figures we may assume that in the relevant range of values for F and M the fare-elasticity of demand E_F is independent of M and the elasticity of demand with respect to vehicle miles of service E_M is independent of F. We also assume that E_M declines as the level of M increases. Some of the geometry and conclusions about the effects of subsidies would be different if we made different assumptions about these elasticities. This point will be illustrated below.

Figure 9 shows the shapes of the feasible loci when there is no subsidy, when there is a lump-sum subsidy, and when there is a cost subsidy. The subsidy rates have been selected so that the feasible loci for the cost and lump-sum subsidies have in common point G, the fare and vehicle miles combination which maximizes vehicle miles. Apart from this common point, the feasible locus for the cost subsidy lies to the left of the feasible locus for the lump-sum subsidy. This is because at point G the total values of the two subsidies are equal. At any lower level of M the total value of the cost subsidy will be lower, while the lump-sum subsidy will be unchanged. Also, given our assumptions about the demand function, the maximum level of M along the feasible loci for the lump-sum and cost subsidies will occur along the horizontal line AGH. This follows from the fact that for either subsidy M is maximized where total revenue and hence passenger revenue is maximized, i.e. where $E_F = -1$, and by assumption E_F is determined by the level of F.

Figure 10 reproduces the feasible loci when there is no subsidy and when there is a lump-sum subsidy from Figure 9 but also includes the feasible locus for a passenger subsidy. The subsidy rates have been selected so that the feasible loci for the passenger and lump-sum subsidies have in common point P, the fare and vehicle miles combination which maximizes ridership. Apart from this common point, the feasible locus for the passenger subsidy lies to the left of the feasible locus for the lump-sum subsidy. This is because at point P the total values of the two subsidies are equal. At any other level of M the level of R and hence the total value of the passenger subsidy will be lower, while the lump-sum subsidy will be unchanged. Also, given our assumptions about the demand function, the maximum level of M along the feasible locus for the passenger subsidy will occur at J, below the horizontal line AG.[13]

The effects of alternative subsidies under the maximum vehicle miles objective
This section analyses the effects of the three subsidy formulas when the objective of the transit firm is to maximize vehicle miles of service.

Lump-sum and cost subsidies
Figure 9 shows that on the assumptions made about the demand function a transit firm which maximizes vehicle miles of service would not change the fare and would simply increase service as much as possible in response to a lump-sum or cost subsidy.

Suppose, however, that we make a different assumption about the demand function, namely that the absolute value of E_F is a decreasing function of M. In

---

13 Maximization of M subject to (2) and (5) yields the condition $|E_F| = (1 + S_3/F)^{-1}$, from which it follows that $|E_F| < 1$, if $S_3 > 0$. Given our assumptions about demand, to reduce $|E_F|$ below 1, F must be reduced below its level along AG.

Figure 10
Feasible loci for no subsidy, lump-sum subsidy, and passenger subsidy

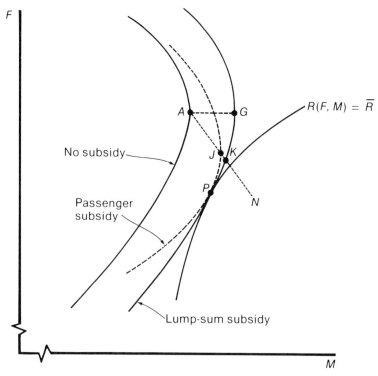

this case a lump-sum or cost subsidy which increases M would reduce the absolute value of E_F. In order to maximize vehicle miles of service, the transit firm would then raise F until $E_F = -1$ again. If Figure 9 were redrawn to be consistent with this assumption about the demand function, the line AGH would slope up to the right. Since the assumption that the absolute value of E_F is a decreasing function of M cannot be ruled out a priori, the strange prediction that a lump-sum or cost subsidy could lead to an increase in the fare is perhaps explained by the fact that transit firms are not expected to maximize vehicle miles of service.

By similar reasoning it is easy to demonstrate that if the absolute value of E_F is an increasing function of M, then a lump-sum or cost subsidy would lead to a reduction in F if the transit firm maximizes M.

In any event, regardless of these assumptions about the demand function, one can conclude that lump-sum and cost subsidies which have the same cost to the taxpayer will have the same effects on F, M, and R if the transit firm maximizes vehicle miles of service.

Passenger subsidy
Figure 10 shows that if the transit firm maximizes vehicle miles of service a passenger subsidy will lead to a reduction in fare and an increase in vehicle miles of service along the path $AJKN$ as the rate of subsidy is increased.

Thus we conclude that if the transit firm maximizes vehicle miles of service, a passenger subsidy will have a distinctly different effect on F and M than either a lump-sum or a cost subsidy which has the same cost to taxpayers. In Figure 10, while a lump-sum or cost subsidy would move the transit system to point G, a passenger subsidy with the same cost to taxpayers would move the transit system to point K. Both F and M would be lower and R would be higher with the passenger subsidy than with the lump-sum or cost subsidy.

The effects of alternative subsidies under the maximum ridership objective

Lump-sum and cost subsidies
On the assumptions about demand in Figure 9, both a lump-sum and a cost subsidy would increase M without affecting F if the transit firm maximized vehicle miles of service. By contrast, lump-sum and cost subsidies would not only increase M but also reduce F if the transit firm maximized ridership. Thus, in Figure 11 a transit firm that maximized ridership would operate at point B in the absence of subsidies. A cost subsidy would lead it to move along the line BTW, and a lump-sum subsidy would lead it to move along the line BXY.

Figure 11 shows that the quantitative effects on F and M of lump-sum and cost subsidies with the same cost to the taxpayer would differ if the transit firm maximizes ridership. Through any point where the feasible locus slopes up to the right, such as point T, the feasible locus corresponding to a cost subsidy would be flatter than the feasible locus corresponding to a lump-sum subsidy, i.e. the opportunity cost to the transit firm of additional vehicle miles in terms of fare increases would be lower under a cost subsidy than under a lump-sum subsidy. Consequently, if the transit firm maximized ridership, a cost subsidy would lead to a larger increase in M and a smaller reduction in F than would a lump-sum subsidy with the same cost to the taxpayer. In Figure 11, the cost subsidy would lead to an equilibrium at point T, while the lump-sum subsidy would lead to an equilibrium at point X, and both subsidy policies would have the same cost to taxpayers since T and X lie on the same lump-sum subsidy locus.

Figure 11
Comparison of lump-sum and cost subsidies

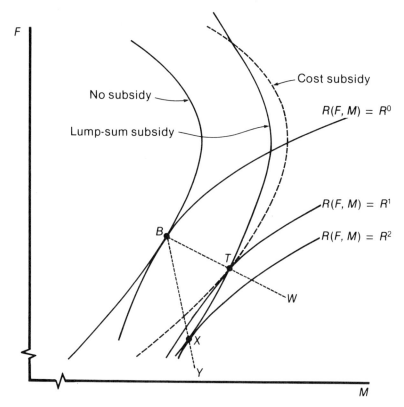

Moreover, if the transit system is maximizing R, a lump-sum subsidy would lead to a larger increase in R than would the cost subsidy with the same cost to taxpayers.

The prediction that a cost subsidy would lead to a reduction in F if the transit firm maximizes ridership depends upon the assumption that E_M decreases as M increases. If E_M is a constant and E_F is independent of M, then a cost subsidy will have no effect on the fare. This follows from the equilibrium condition $-E_F = E_M$.

Lump-sum and passenger subsidies

Figure 10 shows that, if a transit firm maximizes ridership, lump-sum and passenger subsidies with the same cost to taxpayers will have the same effect on F, M, and R. This is because the feasible loci for the two subsidy programs would be tangent to the same isorider curve at the same combination of F and M, as they are at point P.

SUMMARY AND IMPLICATIONS FOR EMPIRICAL RESEARCH

This chapter has demonstrated that the qualitative and quantitative effects of a transit subsidy program with a given cost to taxpayers depend in important ways on the objective function of the transit firm, the subsidy formula, and the form of the demand function. These results should be of interest to government officials responsible for deciding on transit subsidy formulas, because there has been confusion over the differences between them.

Under most of the alternative assumptions considered, the model predicts that transit subsidies would lead to a reduction in fares, an increase in vehicle miles of service, and an increase in ridership.

However, under some assumptions the model predicts, surprisingly, that transit subsidies would not affect the fare or would lead to an increase in the fare. The model predicts that if the transit firm maximizes vehicle miles, lump-sum and cost subsidies will lead to no change in the fare if the fare-elasticity of demand for rides is independent of the level of vehicle miles of service, and that they would lead to an increase in the fare if the absolute value of the fare-elasticity of demand is a decreasing function of the level of vehicle miles of service. The model also predicts that cost subsidies will lead to no change in the fare if the transit firm maximizes ridership, if the elasticity of demand for rides with respect to vehicle miles is constant, and if the fare-elasticity of demand for rides is independent of the level of vehicle miles.

If the transit firm maximizes vehicle miles of service, lump-sum and cost subsidies will have the same effects, but a passenger subsidy with the same cost to taxpayers would lead to a lower fare, a lower level of vehicle miles, and a higher level of ridership than would lump-sum or cost subsidies.

If the transit firm maximizes ridership, lump-sum and passenger subsidies will have the same effects, but a cost subsidy with the same cost to taxpayers would lead to a higher fare, more service, and lower ridership than would lump-sum or passenger subsidies.

A number of points relevant to the specification and testing of econometric models of urban transit have been raised. One should avoid imposing the assumption that the fare and vehicle-mile elasticities of demand are constants, because in the absence of subsidies any fare-elasticity other than -1 is inconsistent with maximization of vehicle miles of service, and any fare-elasticity not equal in absolute value to the vehicle-mile elasticity is inconsistent with maximization of ridership. Moreover, inferences about the objective function of a transit firm can be made both by determining the location of the equilibrium relative to the points of maximum ridership and service along the feasible locus and by testing the predictions concerning the effects of subsidies.[14] Finally, because the fare, service, and ridership are determined simultaneously in the model, demand functions for urban transit rides should generally be estimated using simultaneous equation techniques.

14 For example, the usual conclusion in empirical urban transit demand studies that $E_M >$ $-E_F$ should not be interpreted as a universal property of transit demand at all combinations of F and M. Rather, it suggests that transit firms have objective functions which are characterized by low fare preference. In the model presented in this chapter, a transit firm which has a utility function characterized by $U_F = 0$ would choose a combination of F and M at which $E_M \leq -E_F$, provided it obtained all its revenues from fares and cost subsidies.

9
Subsidies and transit trends in Ontario

This chapter analyses the effect of subsidies on average transit fares, transit service levels, and transit ridership in Ontario. There is first a description of trends in transit ridership, transit service and fares, and transit revenues and costs in Ontario since 1950 and then a non-technical explanation of these trends, emphasizing the effects of subsidies on average fares, service levels, and ridership. Chapter 10 deals with some of the same material but at a more technical level using an econometric model.

DATA ON TRANSIT TRENDS FOR NINE CITIES IN ONTARIO

The only source of published province-wide time-series data on urban transit in Ontario for the period in which we are interested is Statistics Canada. Unfortunately, Statistics Canada data could not be used because the number of transit systems covered by the series varies considerably from year to year, the data do not cover the periods 1950-3 and 1973-4, and the data do not include series on operating expenses (except for 1961-70) or population served by urban transit.

Instead information was collected on nine urban transit systems in Ontario from the Canadian Urban Transit Association: Toronto, Ottawa, Hamilton, London, Windsor, Kitchener, Thunder Bay (formerly Fort William and Port Arthur), Oshawa, and Brantford.[1] These nine cities together accounted for 90 per cent of all revenue passengers in the province in 1976.

The data on Toronto and on Ottawa are presented separately. These cities have the largest transit systems in the province, accounting for 64 and 11 per cent

---

1 The Canadian Urban Transit Association has data only for its members, and many transit systems (particularly smaller ones) were not members continuously during the period 1950-78. Consequently, CUTA data cannot be used to construct complete province-wide data or data on a random sample of systems. Wherever possible, CUTA data were checked

respectively of all passengers in the province in 1976. The next largest system (Hamilton) accounted for only 5 per cent of passengers in 1976. Moreover, while the total number of revenue passengers in the province and in virtually every other city was lower in 1978 than in 1950, Toronto and Ottawa did not fit this pattern.

Since no significant information would be added by treating the other seven cities individually, all data for those cities have been aggregated.[2] The seven cities accounted for 58 per cent of all revenue passengers in Ontario excluding Toronto and Ottawa in 1976. How representative are they of all transit systems in Ontario other than Toronto and Ottawa? Based on revenue passengers, in 1977 these seven systems included five of the six largest systems in the province outside Toronto and Ottawa and none of the thirty-eight smallest systems. This is significant because, among other things, smaller systems generally began to receive municipal subsidies before 1960, while larger systems (apart from the Toronto subway) generally did not receive them until around 1970. Consequently, the operating ratios (operating revenue/operating expenses) for these seven systems remained above unity longer than those of the rest. Furthermore, while the number of revenue passengers in these seven cities declined by 21 per cent between 1954 and 1976, the number of revenue passengers carried by all systems in Ontario excluding Toronto, Ottawa, and these seven cities declined by only about 10 per cent.[3]

In the following discussion, the sample of seven cities (Hamilton, London, Windsor, Kitchener, Thunder Bay, Oshawa, Brantford) will be referred to as 'Seven Cities.'

Transit ridership
Figures 12 and 13 present annual data on the number of revenue passengers carried in Seven Cities, Ottawa, and Toronto. Figure 12 shows the total number of revenue passengers and Figure 13 the number of revenue passengers per capita in the area served.

---

against, and in some cases replaced by, data from the annual reports of the individual transit systems.

The data for Toronto used in this chapter are for the Toronto Transit Commission and not the GO Transit commuter rail/bus system. The 1978 statistics for GO Transit were as follows: passengers 18.15 million, rail train and bus vehicle miles 0.83 million and 6.07 million respectively, average fare $1.09, ratio of passenger revenue to operating expenses 0.41.

2 The data on the seven cities were aggregated before calculating any ratios. For example, to find the number of revenue passengers per capita, the total number of revenue passengers in the seven cities was divided by the total population served by transit.

3 Excluding Windsor, where revenue passengers declined by 59 per cent total revenue passengers declined by 12 per cent in the other six cities.

Figure 12
Number of revenue passengers

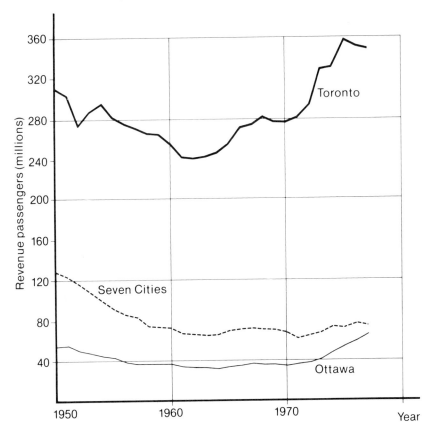

Roughly speaking, all three of the curves in Figure 12 showing the trends in total number of revenue passengers between 1950 and 1978 are U-shaped, with minimum levels reached in the early 1960s. In the seven cities, both as a group and individually, the total number of revenue passengers was substantially lower in 1978 than in 1950. By contrast, in Toronto and in Ottawa the total number of revenue passengers was substantially higher in 1978 than in 1950.

During the period under consideration, the number of people served by public transit increased substantially in the nine cities in our samples. The number of revenue passengers per capita declined substantially between 1950

Figure 13
Number of revenue passengers per capita

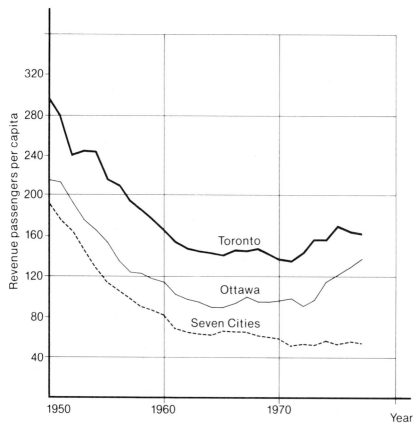

and the early 1970s and then increased during the 1970s (Figure 13).[4] In Seven Cities the increase during the 1970s was insignificant. Although the increases during the 1970s were substantial in Toronto and Ottawa, in both cases the

4 The number of revenue passengers per capita in Toronto is understated between 1950 and 1954 because the population is that within the present boundaries of Metro Toronto, whereas the transit system then served only the City of Toronto. Because of a transit strike in Hamilton in 1971, the figure for revenue passengers per capita in the sample of Seven Cities is abnormally low in that year. There were also strikes in Toronto in 1974 and London in 1975.

number of revenue passengers per capita was considerably lower in 1978 than in 1950.

We shall consider the reasons for these ridership trends later. One naturally expects that they were related to trends in transit service and fares, to which we turn now.

Transit service and fares

Figures 14 and 15 present annual data on the number of vehicle miles of transit service in Seven Cities, Ottawa, and Toronto. Figure 14 shows the total number of vehicle miles of service, Figure 15 the number of vehicle miles per capita, and Figure 16 *real* fares (in 1978 cents).[5]

In Seven Cities, total vehicle miles declined between 1950 and 1960 and then rose again through 1978 to a level substantially higher than in 1950. Vehicle miles per capita declined from 1950 through 1964, then remained roughly constant until 1972, and finally increased between 1973 and 1978. However, the vehicle miles per capita variable was much lower in 1978 than in 1950.

While the trends in Ottawa were qualitatively similar to those in Seven Cities, the magnitudes were quite different. In Ottawa, vehicle miles more than tripled between 1950 and 1978 and more than doubled between 1973 and 1978. In Ottawa, the vehicle miles per capita variable was much higher in 1978 than in 1950.

In Toronto, total vehicle miles declined in the early 1950s before the opening of the subway in 1954, but then more than doubled between 1954 and 1978.[6] As in Ottawa, the level of vehicle miles per capita in Toronto followed a U-shaped trend over the period 1950 through 1978, and it was higher in 1978 than in 1950.

Real fares followed reasonably similar patterns in Seven Cities, Ottawa, and Toronto (Figure 16). They rose considerably between 1950 and about 1970, declined significantly during 1973-5, and then rose to moderately higher levels in 1976-8.[7]

Riders per vehicle mile

Using the data presented above on revenue passengers and vehicle miles of service, we can see (Figure 17) that in Seven Cities revenue passengers per vehicle

---

5 The real fare was found by dividing the passenger revenue by the number of revenue passengers, and then dividing this measure of the nominal fare by the Statistics Canada consumer price index (adjusted so that the CPI for 1978 was 1.00).

6 The figures for vehicle miles per capita in 1950-4 are not comparable to those after 1954, for the reason stated in footnote 4.

7 There were fluctuations around the trend, particularly in Ottawa and Toronto, because (until recently) fares were raised less than once a year.

Figure 14
Number of vehicle miles of service

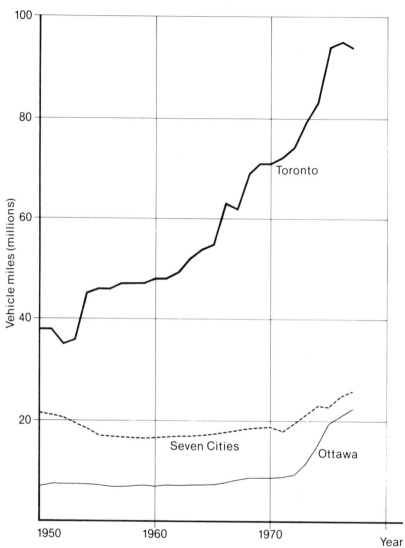

Figure 15
Number of vehicle miles per capita

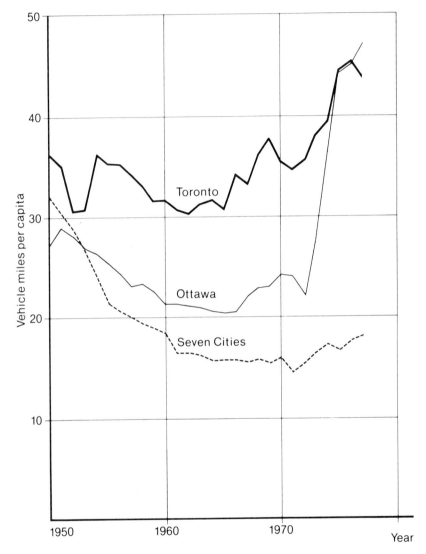

Figure 16
Real fares

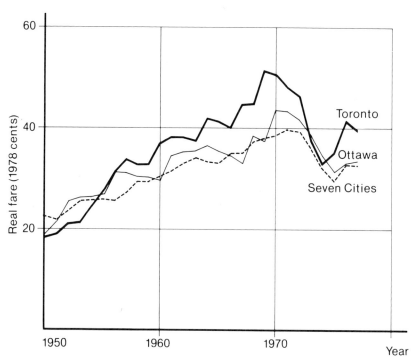

mile fell by half between 1950 and 1978, and the decline was even greater in Ottawa and Toronto.

Operating expenditures

Available data on transit capital costs (depreciation and interest) are not useful for analytical purposes, so that we must confine our attention to data on operating expenditures. Because transit (excluding subways) is labour-intensive, data on operating expenditures provide useful information about the total costs of transit.

In Seven Cities and Toronto, *real* operating expenditures per vehicle mile (in 1978 dollars) increased by about half between 1950 and 1978. The figure for Ottawa was about 20 per cent (Figure 18).

It is also instructive to compare the trends in fares (Figure 16) and operating expenditures per vehicle mile (Figure 18). In Seven Cities, the ratio of the fare to

Figure 17
Revenue passengers per vehicle mile

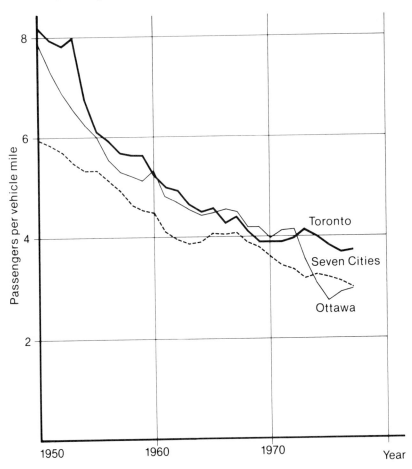

operating expenditures per vehicle mile increased between 1950 and the mid-1960s and then declined again, so that by 1978 it was near the 1950 level. In other words, fares rose faster than operating expenditures per vehicle mile between 1950 and the mid-1960s, and operating expenditures per vehicle mile rose faster than fares after the mid-1960s. The patterns in Ottawa and Toronto were roughly the same.

Figure 18
Real operating expenditure per vehicle mile

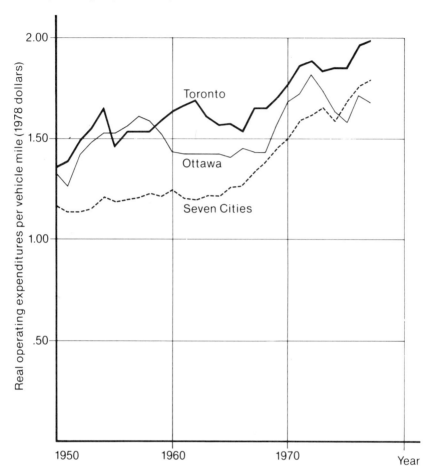

Revenue vs expenditure
We now consider trends in the ratio of passenger revenue to operating expenditure. It should be kept in mind that, since passenger revenue is less than total revenue and operating expenses are less than total costs, a ratio of unity does not mean that a transit system was breaking even.

In Seven Cities the ratio of passenger revenue to operating expenditure ranged between 1.10 and 1.22 during the 1950s, between 0.99 and 1.08 during the

Figure 19
Ratio of passenger revenue to operating expenditures

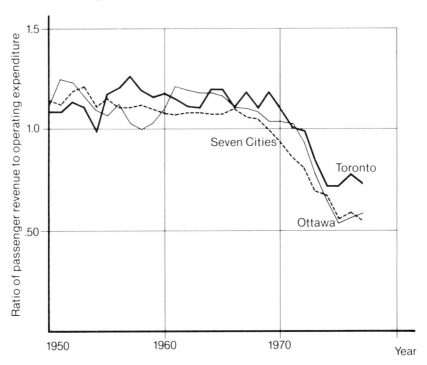

1960s, and then fell precipitously during the 1970s. In Ottawa the ratio averaged 1.12 during 1950-71 and thereafter fell sharply. In Toronto the pattern was similar (Figure 19).

Concluding observations

It is useful to notice some of the relationships between the curves in Figures 12 through 19, particularly in the case of changes that occurred after 1970.

The increase in transit ridership after 1970 (Figure 12) coincided with a large increase in vehicle miles of service (Figure 14) and a reduction in real fares (Figure 16). Moreover, Ottawa experienced both the largest percentage increase in ridership and the largest percentage increase in vehicle miles of service.

In spite of the reduction in real fares, the percentage increase in ridership after 1970 was less than the percentage increase in vehicle miles of service, i.e. revenue passengers per vehicle mile declined. With declines in the real fare and in the number of revenue passengers per vehicle mile, real passenger revenue per vehicle mile declined. At the same time, real operating expenses per vehicle mile increased, except in Ottawa (Figure 18). Thus, the ratio of passenger revenue to operating expense declined dramatically (Figure 19). Obviously this situation was possible only because of the substantial growth in provincial and municipal government subsidies for urban transit during the 1970s described in Chapter 6.

EXPLANATIONS OF TRANSIT TRENDS AND THE EFFECTS OF SUBSIDIES

This section seeks to explain the trends described above, and particularly to analyse the effects of subsidies on fares, service, and ridership. The discussion will be based on an implicit model of urban transit operations similar to the explicit one developed in Chapter 8 and tested in Chapter 10. We assume here that the demand for transit rides (per capita) depends on the number of vehicle miles of service (per capita), the real fare, automobile ownership (per capita), and other variables, and the absolute value of the fare-elasticity of demand is less than one. The levels of vehicle miles of service and the real fare are determined by the transit system to maximize an objective function subject to a budget constraint.

In this model our interpretation of the evidence[8] is that transit systems were affected by four important exogenous changes beyond their control (apart from government intervention, which will be discussed below) during the period from 1950 to 1978:

– The demand for transit rides per capita declined because of an increase in automobile ownership per capita (see Table 25), due in large part to an increase in real income per capita.[9]
– The demand for transit rides per capita declined because of the suburbanization of employment and residences and the advantages of automobiles in serving travel patterns not oriented to the central business district.
– The real cost per vehicle mile of transit service increased considerably (Figure 18), primarily because of an increase in the real wage of transit employees (Table 26).

8 Although the explanation offered here is essentially consistent with the available data and the model tested in Chapter 10, the statistical tests do not permit us to reject all the alternative hypotheses. Further research might modify the explanation.
9 Actually, the assumption that automobile ownership is exogenous and not dependent on transit fares or service is questionable. But it probably does not affect the conclusions seriously, and it simplifies the discussion. For a study in which automobile ownership and choice of mode are determined simultaneously, see Train (1980).

TABLE 25

Automobile registrations per capita in Ontario

Year	Registrations per capita
1951	0.22
1956	0.26
1961	0.29
1966	0.32
1971	0.35

SOURCES: Statistics Canada (Cat. 53-219) and *1971 Census of Canada* (Cat. 92-702, Table 2)

- There was an increase in the total population of most urban areas. However, the vast majority of this population increase occurred in suburbs not served by transit in 1950, and in some intervals in some urban areas the population actually declined in the areas served by transit in 1950.

Because of the decline in the demand for transit rides per capita resulting from increased ownership of automobiles and suburbanization, there was a gradual reduction in the total demand for transit rides in the areas originally served. At the same time, the real cost per vehicle mile of transit service increased, largely because of wage increases. Consequently, if transit service and real fares had been left unchanged, there would have been a decline in the total number of revenue passengers and in the ratio of passenger revenue to operating expenditure.[10] Moreover, at these real fares the revenues earned by extensions of service into new suburbs would generally not have been sufficient to cover the costs of the services (even if zone fares had been charged). As a result, in the absence of government subsidies, transit systems would have been forced to change their vehicle miles of service and real fares in order to satisfy their budget constraints.

The most obvious reaction would have been to reduce vehicle miles of service or raise real fares. This reduction in service or increase in fares would in turn have led to a further decline in the total number of revenue passengers, until a

10 Other factors contributed to the deteriorating financial position of transit systems beyond those touched upon in the somewhat simplified discussion in the text. For example, during the 1950s the demand for transit apparently declined because of the reduction in the work week from six days to five. Moreover, the demand for transit became subject to increased peaking, i.e. the ratio of peak to off-peak demand increased, which raised the average cost per vehicle mile. Finally, transit systems came under increasing pressure to offer fare concessions to senior citizens, to switch from zone-fare to uniform-fare pricing systems, and to offer monthly transit passes.

TABLE 26

Real hourly wage of transit operators in London

Year	Real wages (1978 dollars)
1951	3.05
1956	4.07
1961	4.60
1966	4.95
1971	6.50
1976	7.08
1977	7.15
1978	7.02

NOTE: Excludes fringe benefits, which probably increased faster than wages
SOURCE: Unpublished data from the Canadian Urban Transit Association and the London Transit Commission

new equilibrium satisfying the budget constraint was reached. However, an alternative reaction would have been to raise real fares sufficiently to satisfy the budget constraint even with a higher level of vehicle miles of service.

In fact, during the 1950s transit systems generally (e.g. in Seven Cities and in Ottawa after 1951) reduced their vehicle miles of service, increased their real fares, and experienced a substantial decline in ridership. Even in this period transit systems tended to rely more on raising real fares than on reducing service to satisfy their budget constraints; the percentage change in real fares was greater than the percentage change in vehicle miles of service.

The pattern was generally different during the 1960s than during the 1950s. During the 1960s most transit systems simultaneously expanded total vehicle miles of service (mainly in new subdivisions and suburbs) and increased real fares.[11] This occurred even in the absence of government subsidies, and it appears that riders in the older, more dense parts of the urban areas were called upon to bear the increasing costs of cross-subsidizing new suburban services.

11 The pattern in Toronto was somewhat different. Expansion of transit services began in 1954, and about 40 per cent of the increase in service between 1960 and 1970 was in non-suburban areas. This was due in large part to the extension of the subway system, and it occurred with government subsidies after 1959. However, in percentage terms the expansion of service was much greater in suburban areas than in non-suburban areas. Between 1960 and 1970, suburban service increased by about 150 per cent while non-suburban service increased by only about 25 per cent. Furthermore, according to the Toronto Transit Commission (1966, 12), 'most of the routes in outlying Metro districts lose money for several years and must be supported by the rest of the system.'

While government subsidies for urban transit were negligible in the early 1950s, they increased in importance afterwards, especially during the early 1970s. During the 1960s government subsidies increased the rate at which transit service was expanded and moderated the rate at which real fares were increased. During the 1970s subsidies led to a substantial increase in transit service and a significant reduction in real fares, and consequently a higher level of revenue passengers than would otherwise have prevailed.

CONCLUDING REMARKS

The financial problems of transit systems which led to government subsidies were a result of three basic factors: the exogenous decline in demand for transit, due largely to increased automobile ownership and decentralization of urban areas; the increase in the cost per vehicle mile of transit service, due largely to an increase in the real wages of transit employees; and the pressure to provide transit service in new subdivisions and suburbs, in spite of low ridership per vehicle mile on such routes (see Sewell 1978a; b).

Whereas increased use of automobiles, suburbanization, and rising wages were for the most part, if not entirely, beyond the control of the governments and transit authorities involved,[12] this was not true of providing new service. If the provincial government, the municipalities, and the transit authorities had demonstrated less enthusiasm in expanding suburban and commuter transit services, there would have been less expansion of subsidies during the 1970s, less pressure to raise real fares for inner-city riders in the late 1970s, and less reason for concern over how to finance public transit in Ontario during the 1980s.

---

12 These changes are exogenous in our implicit model. Of course, government road pricing, transportation investment, and land use policies may have had significant effects on the demand for transit.

10

An econometric model of subsidy effects in Ontario

This chapter develops and estimates an econometric model of an urban transit system in order to determine empirically the effects of alternative forms of subsidy on transit fares, service, and ridership. The model, which describes transit operations in a city by a set of equations which determine the aggregate annual city-wide levels of transit ridership and service and the average fare, could also be used to predict the cost to the government of a subsidy program or to explain past trends in urban transit.

Econometric models of urban transit systems have previously been estimated by Nelson (1972), Veatch (1973), Garbade and Soss (1976), Frankena (1978a; b), Anderson (1979), and Gaudry (1980). The model presented here, a refinement of the ones used by Nelson and Frankena, is estimated using data for London, Canada, for the period 1951-77.[1]

THEORETICAL MODEL

The econometric model used in this chapter is based on the theoretical model developed in Chapter 8, modified to take account of non-fare revenue and the problems that arise when the transit firm finances its capital accumulation without borrowing. Both of these modifications involve elaboration of the transit firm's budget constraint.

Non-fare revenue
Net non-fare revenue N, which includes income from investments, advertising, and charter and sightseeing services, is assumed to be exogenously determined. It

---

1 Crude estimates of the transit-demand, vehicle-mile, and fare equations using data for twenty-two urban areas in Canada for 1966-76 are presented in Frankena (1978b) and summarized in TEE Consulting Services (1979).

is accommodated in the model by including the variable N in the budget constraint.

Capital accumulation
The theoretical model developed in Chapter 8 can be thought of as a description of a transit system in which the firm leases the capital it uses. The model requires significant modification to describe the operation of a typical transit firm in Ontario, because most transit firms own the capital they use and finance all capital accumulation from revenues (including subsidies) without borrowing. Moreover, the province subsidizes expenditures on capital goods rather than the costs of using capital. These practices force us to expand the theoretical model to allow for capital accumulation, albeit in a rather crude way.

We assume that the transit firm operates subject to a more complex budget constraint, which includes imputed income on capital I_1, net capital accumulation I_2, and capital subsidies I_3, which are based on net capital accumulation. Thus, an alternative budget constraint to equation (5) in Chapter 8 is

$$(F + S_3)R + N + S_1 + I_1 - I_2 + I_3 - (1 - S_2)CM = 0. \tag{6}$$

A glossary of variables is given in Appendix D.

Of course one could go on to develop an intertemporal model of transit firm behaviour using an intertemporal objective function and making net capital accumulation as well as the fare and vehicle miles of service subject to choice by the transit firm. But that would lead to an unmanageable empirical model. Instead, we assume that I_1, I_2, and I_3 are exogenous. While this is short of ideal, and may introduce a simultaneous-equation bias in the empirical estimates, it nevertheless leaves us with a model which takes account of features that have been ignored by previous models of urban transit systems.

ASSUMPTIONS

To use the theoretical model outlined above as the basis of an econometric model requires a number of assumptions. To the extent that these assumptions do not hold in reality, the inferences based on the model must be regarded with a corresponding degree of caution.

The most fundamental assumption made in developing the theoretical model is that government transit subsidy formulas are exogenous, so that the transit firm determines the fare and level of service subject only to its budget constraint. This assumption would be violated if any level of government imposed a binding constraint on the fare or service level[2] or if the local government itself determined transit operating policies. In the latter case, only senior-level government subsidy formulas could be taken as exogenous, while the fare, the level of service, and the level of local government subsidies would be determined simultaneously by the local government.

A second assumption is that the gross-of-subsidy cost per vehicle mile of transit service is independent of the transit subsidy policy. This assumption would be violated if transit subsidies influenced the labour contract terms or equipment prices or the capital intensity of the transit firm.[3] Thus, to use the model developed here to analyse the effect of capital cost subsidies, which subsidize the use of capital but not non-capital inputs, requires the assumption that the elasticity of substitution between capital and non-capital inputs in transit is zero.

A third assumption is that transit operations can be described by the average fare, total vehicle miles of service, and total ridership, and that one can ignore variations among passengers, during the year, and across the city in the fare, service, and the demand for rides.[4]

THE ECONOMETRIC MODEL: PRELIMINARY REMARKS

The theoretical model of a transit system outlined above consists of the objective function (equation 3), the demand function (equation 2), and the budget constraint (equation 6). The model contains three endogenous variables: the fare F, vehicle miles of service M, and ridership R.

This theoretical model yields an econometric model which consists of the demand equation (2), the budget constraint (6), and two reduced-form equations describing the determination of vehicle miles of service and the fare[5]:

2 For example, in 1963 the municipal government gave the Toronto transit system an operating subsidy of $2.5 million conditional on cancellation of a 17 per cent increase in the fare, and between April 1974 and March 1975 the provincial government imposed a freeze on nominal transit fares as a condition for operating subsidies for all transit systems in the province.
  In his research on the Montreal transit system, Gaudry (1980) assumes that the fare is exogenous. Consequently, in his model the transit firm simply sets vehicle hours (rather than miles) of service at the level which satisfies the (expected) budget constraint.
3 The available information on the effects of subsidies on labor contract terms, equipment prices, and capital intensity is discussed in Chapter 7.
4 The existence of variations of the types ignored will lead to aggregation bias in the estimates (see McFadden and Reid 1975).
5 Because this is a monopoly model, there are no structural supply equations, i.e. the parameters of the vehicle-mile and fare equations depend, among other things, on the behaviour of transit riders.

$$M = M(C', S_3, Z), \tag{7}$$
$$F = F(C', S_3, Z), \tag{8}$$

where

$$C' = (1 - S_2)C, \tag{9}$$
$$Z = N + S_1 + I_1 - I_2 + I_3. \tag{10}$$

The exact specification of the equations used in our econometric work will be discussed below.

DATA

We estimate the parameters of the econometric model using annual time series data for London, Canada, for the period 1951-77, excluding 1975 when there was a strike. During this period, the London transit system used only conventional motor buses, and the population served by the transit system increased from 95 000 to 237 000. All monetary variables were converted to 1978 dollars.

While most of the data came from annual reports and unpublished records of the London Transit Commission (LTC) and from Statistics Canada publications, some of the series had to be constructed more or less from scratch. In particular, LTC data on capital stock, depreciation, and interest costs could not be used because they followed conventional accounting practices and do not .measure the relevant economic magnitudes. Series were constructed for analytical purposes using what were considered to be workable assumptions concerning rates of depreciation on different assets, the real rate of interest, and so on. However, capital costs account for only about 10 per cent of the total costs of urban bus transit, so that one would not expect the empirical analysis to be very sensitive to the precise assumptions made in constructing the capital cost series.

ADAPTATION OF THE ECONOMETRIC MODEL TO LONDON

Several modifications are required to adapt the econometric model to London, mainly because the time series data were for a period of twenty-seven years, during which the population of the city, the area served by the transit system, and real income per capita grew continually. In addition, in 1961 the City of London annexed a large amount of land adjacent to the city in all directions and extended bus service to a number of subdivisions that already existed in the annexed territory.

To take account of the changing population and area of the city and changing incomes, modifications were made in the specification of the demand equation:

- The dependent variable in the demand equation was defined as the natural logarithm of the number of revenue passengers *per capita* in the area served by the bus sysem, ln (R/P).
- The independent variable in the demand equation measuring vehicle miles of transit service was defined as population in the area served per vehicle mile P/M. I used $P/M \equiv (M/P)^{-1}$, rather than the more obvious alternative of M/P, because a specification was needed that would be consistent with the assumption made in Chapter 8 that the elasticity of demand with respect to vehicle miles of service decreases as the level of vehicle miles of service increases. *Population* per vehicle mile was used, rather than the more appealing alternative of *area* per vehicle mile, for reasons discussed in Frankena (1978, 281).
- An independent variable Y, measuring income per capita (actually wage and salary income per worker), was included in the demand equation.
- A dummy variable A was included as an independent variable in the demand equation to take account of changes related to the 1961 annexation ($A = 0$ for 1951-60 and $A = 1$ for 1961-77).

Because the vehicle-mile and fare equations are reduced form equations, P, Y, and A were also included in them as independent variables.[6]

Some variables have not been included in the model because of lack of data. The most obvious omissions are two variables that are generally believed to have caused a secular decline in the demand for transit rides, namely measures of automobile ownership and of suburbanization of travel origins and destinations. Statistics Canada data on automobile registrations in London are not accurate, and there are no data on the intra-urban location of jobs and similar travel destinations. The use of a time trend to approximate either of these variables as well as population, income, and the annexation dummy appears to introduce problems of collinearity. In any case the omission of automobile ownership and suburbanization variables is likely to bias the coefficients of income in the model.

During the period covered by this study, the London transit system received four major subsidies. It is important to understand how these were treated in the

6 P does not appear as a separate variable in the demand equation because the demand equation is expressed in per capita terms. P appears as a separate variable in the vehicle-mile and fare equations because the latter equations are not in per capita terms.

estimation of the model. First, the transit system received provincial government capital grants equal to 75 per cent of the capital expenditures from 1973 through 1977. The capital grant was treated as a 75 per cent subsidy for the capital costs of current operations plus a residual subsidy equal to the difference between the capital grant received and the subsidized portion of the capital costs of current operations. The subsidy for the capital costs of current operations was treated like a cost subsidy applying to all inputs (at the appropriate lower percentage rate), under the assumption that the elasticity of substitution between capital and non-capital inputs in transit was zero; thus, it enters the model through S_2. To the extent that a capital cost subsidy would in fact induce a transit firm to substitute capital for non-capital inputs, the empirical estimates will be biased. The residual subsidy was treated as a lump sum and enters the model as I_3. Treatment of I_3 as exogenous in the estimation could be a source of simultaneous equation bias because of the way I_3 is computed.

In 1977 the London transit system received a provincial government subsidy equal to 17.5 per cent of its operating costs. As in the case of the capital cost subsidy, this subsidy was converted into a cost subsidy applying to all inputs and hence enters the model through S_2.

The system received a provincial government subsidy covering 50 per cent of its operating deficit between 1971 and 1976. In the present model an operating deficit subsidy acts as a matching grant for any operating subsidies which the transit system receives from other levels of government. Consequently, the provincial operating deficit subsidy must be treated in the same manner as the municipal operating subsidy, which is discussed next.

Between 1972 and 1977 the system received a municipal operating subsidy. No explicit formula was used to determine this subsidy. Instead, it appears that each year the municipal government specified a lump-sum target for the 50 per cent of the operating deficit that was not covered by the provincial operating deficit subsidy. Thus, if the transit system took the provincial operating deficit formula and the municipal operating subsidy target as exogenously given, and if the transit system satisfied its target budget constraint exactly, then the provincial operating deficit subsidy and the municipal operating subsidy would both be lump-sum subsidies. This is the way they have been treated here; the actual dollar amounts received enter the model as S_1.

There is a problem with this last assumption. Since the actual deficit, and hence the actual subsidies received, are dependent upon the fare, the level of service, and ridership, the measure of S_1 will in fact be endogenous, and the treatment of S_1 as exogenous will introduce a simultaneous-equation bias into the estimates. One way around this would have been to use the target rather than the actual level of subsidies in determining S_1, but the information necessary to do this was not available.

During the period covered by this study the London transit system did not receive passenger subsidies. Consequently, S_3 has been omitted from the econometric model.

ECONOMETRIC MODEL: SPECIFICATION ADOPTED

The specification of the econometric model is as follows:

$$\ln(R/P) = \alpha_0 + \alpha_1 F + \alpha_2(P/M) + \alpha_3 Y + \alpha_4 A + \epsilon_1, \tag{11}$$
$$M = \beta_o + \beta_1 C' + \beta_2 Z + \beta_3 P + \beta_4 Y + \beta_5 A + \epsilon_2, \tag{12}$$
$$F = \delta_o + \delta_1 C' + \delta_2 Z + \delta_3 P + \delta_4 Y + \delta_5 A + \epsilon_3, \tag{13}$$
$$F \cdot R + Z - C' \cdot M = 0, \tag{14}$$

where $C' = (1 - S_2)C$ is the net-of-subsidy cost per vehicle mile of service and $Z = N + S_1 + I_1 - I_2 + I_3$ is net non-passenger revenue. The complete model consists of (11), either (12) or (13) – since one of them is redundant given the demand function and the budget constraint – and (14).

Equations (12) and (13) have been linearized. Given the demand equation and equation (12), which determines M, the equation for F that would be consistent with the budget constraint would be a great deal more complicated than equation (13) and would have to be estimated by non-linear techniques. Similarly, if we started with equation (13), the equation for M could not actually have the functional form specified in (12).

COMPARISON WITH EXISTING MODELS

Readers should note the major differences between the econometric model outlined here and other models of transit systems that have been estimated. Since there is nothing new in our demand equation, we will be concerned exclusively with the vehicle-mile and fare equations. There are four differences worth noting in this model.

The fare F has not been included here as an independent variable in the vehicle-mile equation, whereas Gaudry (1980) includes F in his vehicle-hours equation. This is because we treat F as endogenous while Gaudry treats it as exogenous. Whether endogenous or not, this difference in specification is important because the inclusion of F as an independent variable would affect the estimates and the interpretation of the coefficients of the remaining variables if F

is correlated with them. For example, if political authorities simultaneously impose a low value of F and give large lump-sum subsidies (when F is exogenous), or if transit authorities respond to large lump-sum subsidies by reducing F (when F is endogenous), then the variable Z which includes lump-sum subsidies will be negatively correlated with F in the vehicle-mile equation. Consequently, the estimated coefficient on Z and its interpretation will depend on whether F is included in the vehicle-mile equation.

It should be noted that if F is exogenous there is no interest in estimating a vehicle-mile equation, since the level of vehicle miles would be fully determined by the demand equation, the budget constraint, and the exogenous fare level.

The number of transit rides R is not an independent variable in the equation determining vehicle miles M, as it is in Nelson (1972), or in the fare equation.[7] Entering R as an endogenous independent variable in the M or F equations is conceptually different from entering M and F as endogenous independent variables in the equation determining R. While each individual transit rider does take M and F as given in deciding whether to ride transit, the transit firm cannot take R as given in determining M and F, because the transit firm's own choice of M and F will have a significant effect on R.

A simple attempt has been made to deal with several problems that arise because the transit firm invests in durable capital goods. Previous studies have ignored these complications.

Lump-sum and cost subsidies are distinguished. The treatment of subsidies in previous models has been more rudimentary; for example, Anderson (1979) treats all subsidies as lump sums.

EXTRANEOUS INFORMATION ON THE OBJECTIVE FUNCTIONS OF TRANSIT FIRMS

Chapter 8 demonstrates that the effect of a transit subsidy depends on the objective function of the transit firm. Consequently, it is useful to summarize some of the inferences that can be made about transit firm objective functions before outlining our empirical hypotheses concerning the effects of transit subsidies. There are three sources of information on this issue: econometric

---

7 Similarly, Veatch (1973) includes number of riders (assumed to be endogenous) in the vehicle-mile equation, and Garbade and Soss (1976) include both the fare (exogenous) and the number of riders (endogenous) as independent variables in the equation determining vehicle miles of service.

studies of transit demand functions, econometric studies of transit vehicle mile and fare equations, and institutional descriptions. We will consider these in turn.

The transit demand functions
If a transit firm maximizes $U(F, M, R) = M$, i.e. if it selects the combination of fare and vehicle miles which maximizes vehicle miles of service, then the following condition would hold regardless of whether there were no subsidies, lump-sum subsidies, or cost subsidies:

$$0 < -E_M < -E_F = 1, \tag{15}$$

where E_M and E_F are the elasticities of the demand for transit rides with respect to vehicle miles of service and the fare respectively.

Almost without exception, empirical studies of the demand for transit have found the following condition to hold:[8]

$$0 < -E_F < E_M < 1. \tag{16}$$

Consequently, the empirical evidence is inconsistent with the hypothesis that the typical transit firm maximizes vehicle miles of service. Instead, both the fare and vehicle miles of service are set below the levels which would maximize vehicle miles of service.

The vehicle-mile and fare equations
Based on empirical research on transit vehicle mile and fare equations, Nelson (1972) concludes that transit firms do not maximize vehicle miles of service. This conclusion is based on the inference that changes in demand and cost affect not only vehicle miles of service but fares as well.[9]

Institutional descriptions
In 1975 the London, England, transit system adopted an objective of maximizing the total number of passenger miles, which is a variation on maximization of

---

8 See Frankena (1978a, Tables 1 and 2). However, studies do not generally report whether $-E_F$ and E_M are significantly different.
9 Nelson (1972, 71). Nelson argues (52-3) that one cannot distinguish empirically between maximization of R and maximization of $f(R, M)$, but he does not exploit the conditions on demand elasicities. Nor does he consider objective functions in which F is an argument.

ridership, and the National Bus Company, British Rail, and a number of local bus companies in the United Kingdom have also considered adoption of this objective. In 1979 the Toronto Transit Commission was considering adoption of maximization of ridership as an explicit objective. Maximization of ridership will be achieved at fare and vehicle mile levels below those which would maximize vehicle miles of service.

Conclusions
Based on the available evidence, we conclude that transit firms do not maximize vehicle miles of service. The empirical hypotheses presented in the following section are based on this conclusion.

EMPIRICAL HYPOTHESES

Of greatest interest are the hypotheses concerning the coefficients of cost per vehicle mile and net non-passenger revenue in the vehicle-mile and fare equations, because the primary motivation for this econometric study is to estimate the effects of cost and lump-sum subsidies on transit operating policies.

The demand equation
It is hypothesized that the coefficient on the fare in the demand equation is negative, i.e. $\alpha_1 < 0$. Furthermore, since transit firms do not maximize vehicle miles of service, it is hypothesized that the fare-elasticity of demand at observed fare levels is less than one in absolute value. We are also interested in testing the 'Simpson-Curtin' rule-of-thumb that the fare-elasticity of demand is -0.33.

It is hypothesized that, other things equal, an increase in vehicle miles of service would lead to an increase in ridership, i.e. $\alpha_2 < 0$.

No hypothesis is made concerning the effect of income on demand for transit, i.e. concerning α_3. On one hand an increase in income seems to lead to an increase in the total number of trips by all modes combined. On the other hand an increase in income seems to lead to an increase in the value of travel time and in automobile ownership and hence a decline in the share of trips made by public transit. But the net effect of an increase in income on number of trips by transit is not known. The reader is reminded that since we do not have an automobile ownership variable in the demand equation, income will serve, among other things, as a proxy for automobile ownership.

No hypothesis is made about the effect of the annexation dummy on the demand for transit rides per capita when population per vehicle mile of service and the fare are held a constant, i.e. concerning α_4. On one hand the annexation of a populated suburban area, accompanied by an increase in vehicle miles of service sufficient to maintain P/M unchanged, could lead to an increase in rides per capita by people previously served by transit, because the transit system would serve more destinations. On the other hand one would probably expect rides per capita by people in the annexed suburban area to be lower than the pre-annexation level of rides per capita in the area served by transit before the annexation. The net effect of the annexation dummy on the demand for rides per capita is not known.

The vehicle-mile and fare equations

The effects of subsidies
The rate of the cost subsidy S_2 enters the econometric model through the variable which measures the net-of-subsidy cost per vehicle mile of transit service, $C' = (1 - S_2)C$. Lump-sum subsidies S_1 enter through net non-passenger revenue, $Z = N + S_1 + I_1 - I_2 + I_3$. Consequently, the effects of subsidies on transit operating policies depend on the coefficients of cost per vehicle mile and net non-passenger revenue in the vehicle-mile and fare equations, i.e. on β_1, β_2, δ_1, and δ_2.

Our hypotheses concerning these coefficients are based on the conclusion that transit firms do not maximize vehicle miles of service and on the theoretical analysis of the effects of transit subsidies in Chapter 8. Given reasonable restrictions on the demand function (for instance, assuming the specification in equation 11), it is hypothesized that an increase in the cost per vehicle mile of transit service would lead to a reduction in vehicle miles and an increase in the fare, and that an increase in net non-passenger revenue would lead to an increase in vehicle miles and a reduction in the fare, i.e. $\beta_1 < 0$, $\beta_2 > 0$, $\delta_1 > 0$, $\delta_2 < 0$.

Furthermore, on the basis of the comparative analysis in Chapter 8 of cost and lump-sum subsidies for a transit firm which does not maximize vehicle miles of service, it is hypothesized that

$$\left| \frac{\beta_1}{\delta_1} \right| > \left| \frac{\beta_2}{\delta_2} \right| . \tag{17}$$

This condition implies that a cost subsidy would have a larger effect on vehicle miles of service and a smaller effect on the fare than a lump-sum subsidy with the same cost to the taxpayer would have.

Other variables
The equations determining vehicle miles of service and the fare are reduced-form equations. Consequently, the exogenous variables in the demand equation

appear in the vehicle-mile and fare equations as well. Any variable that influences the demand for transit rides will thereby influence transit revenues and hence the transit system's feasible set of operating policies. The way these variables influence the feasible set of operating policies obviously depends upon how they influence the demand for transit. Consequently, our hypotheses concerning the effects of these variables on vehicle miles and the fare will be linked to the effects of these variables on the demand for transit.

The specification of the demand for transit rides is in per capita terms. Population served P appears in the vehicle-mile and fare equations because the population affects the total demand for transit and hence the level of passenger revenue. It is hypothesized that an increase in population would lead to an increase in transit revenue, and hence to an increase in vehicle miles of service and a reduction in the fare, i.e. $\beta_3 > 0$, $\delta_3 < 0$.[10]

If income Y appeared in the vehicle-mile and fare equations only because it appears in the demand equation, we would hypothesize that its coefficient in the vehicle mile equation would have the same sign as its coefficient in the demand equation, while its coefficient in the fare equation would have the opposite sign. However, as incomes increase, one might also expect the objective function of the transit firm $U(F, M, R)$ to change. For example, given the transit firm's budget constraint, as incomes and hence the value of people's travel time increase, one might expect quasi-political pressure to be exerted on the transit system to adopt an operating policy involving a higher level of service (and a higher fare), i.e. one might expect the coefficient on income in the vehicle-mile and fare equations to be positive. Consequently, it is hypothesized that if the coefficient on income in the demand equation is positive, the coefficient on income in the vehicle-mile equation will also be positive and the coefficient on income in the fare equation will be ambiguous; if the coefficient on income in the demand equation is negative, the coefficient on income in the vehicle mile equation will be ambiguous, and the coefficient on income in the fare equation will be positive.

If the annexation dummy A appears in the vehicle-mile and fare equations only because it appears in the demand equation, we would hypothesize that its coefficient in the vehicle mile equation would have the same sign as its coefficient in the demand equation, while its coefficient in the fare equation would have the

10 This hypothesis is appropriate if there are changes in the population in the area served by the transit system, but not necessarily if the change in population is due to a change in the area.

opposite sign.[11] However, one might also expect annexation to lead to quasi-political pressure on the transit firm to adopt an operating policy involving more vehicle miles, and a higher fare given the transit firm's budget constraint. Consequently, it is hypothesized that if the sign of the coefficient on the annexation dummy in the demand equation is positive, the sign of the coefficient on the annexation dummy in the vehicle-mile equation will also be positive, and the sign of the coefficient on the annexation dummy in the fare equation will be ambiguous; if the sign of the coefficient on the annexation dummy in the demand equation is negative, the sign of the coefficient on the annexation dummy in the vehicle-mile equation will be ambiguous, and the sign of the coefficient on the annexation dummy in the fare equation will be positive.

Finally, it is hypothesized that each of the error terms $\epsilon_i (i = 1, 2, 3)$ follows a first-order autoregressive scheme of the usual type.

ESTIMATION TECHNIQUE

Because of significant positive first-order autocorrelation of residuals (see the t-statistics for ρ in Tables 27 and 28), with one exception all equations in the model are estimated using the Cochrane-Orcutt technique. The exception is the fare equation, which was estimated using ordinary least squares because there was not significant first-order autocorrelation of residuals.

One expects that P/M and F are correlated with the error term ϵ_1 in the demand equation and hence that the use of a simultaneous equation estimation technique is required in order to obtain consistent estimates of the parameters of the demand equation. The problem is that some of the same variables (e.g. automobile ownership per capita) have been omitted from both the demand equation and the equations determining M and F. Consequently, the demand equation was estimated using two-stage least squares in order to purge P/M and F of their correlations with ϵ_1.

We have seen that, given the demand equation and the budget constraint, the fare equation is fully determined by the vehicle-mile equation, or vice versa, i.e. one of the two equations is redundant. Nevertheless, because a considerable number of assumptions are required to derive the budget constraint, and because the demand equation may be mis-specified, the vehicle-mile and fare

---

11 It should be recalled that the demand equation is in per capita terms and that population enters the vehicle-mile and fare equations as a separate variable. Consequently, the effect of annexing a populated territory depends on the coefficients of both the population variable and the annexation dummy.

equations are estimated independently rather than using the budget constraint, and the results for both equations are presented. For the same reason any correlations between the error terms in the different equations have also been ignored.

EMPIRICAL RESULTS

The empirical results are presented in Tables 27 and 28.

The demand equation
The coefficient on fare is negative as hypothesized and significantly different from zero at the 1 per cent level. The fare-elasticity of demand calculated at the sample mean is -0.28, which is within the normal range of results for empirical studies of transit demand, significantly different from -1.0 at the 1 per cent level, and not significantly different from -0.33 (the Simpson-Curtin rule) at the 10 per cent level.

The coefficient on population served per vehicle mile is negative as hypothesized and significantly different from zero at the 5 per cent level. The elasticity of demand with respect to vehicle miles of service, holding population served constant, is 0.39 at the sample mean.

The coefficient on wage and salary income per worker is negative and significantly different from zero at the 1 per cent level. The income elasticity of demand for transit at the sample mean is -0.37.[12] Since there is no automobile ownership variable in the demand equation, presumably the negative sign of the coefficient on income is largely a reflection of the fact that over the period 1951-77 the number of automobiles per capita increased along with (and largely because of) the increase in incomes, and increasing automobile ownership per capita reduced the demand for transit rides per capita. Thus, the negative coefficient on income should probably be interpreted as support for the hypothesis that the demand for transit rides per capita has declined over time because of the combination of increasing incomes, increasing automobile ownership per capita, and suburbanization of urban areas.

Finally, the annexation dummy is negative and significantly different from zero at the 1 per cent level.

Overall, the empirical results for the demand equation are reasonably consistent with the existing literature, much of which is summarized in Frankena

12 Because wage and salary income per worker reflects the opportunity cost of travel time, the estimated income elasticity includes both income and substitution effects.

TABLE 27

Estimates of the demand equation

Independent variables	Coefficient	Elasticity
Constant	5.83^d	–
	(44.7)	
F Fare	-0.912^a	-0.28
	(-3.79)	
P/M Population served per vehicle mile	-8.90^b	-0.39
	(-2.03)	
Y Income	-0.00199^d	-0.37
	(-3.50)	
A Annexation dummy	-0.325^d	–
	(-5.30)	
Other statistics		
R^2	0.997	
$F_{(4, 19)}$	1770	
R^2 in terms of first differences	0.962	
ρ rho for Cochrane-Orcutt	0.747^a	
	(5.51)	
D.W. Durbin-Watson statistic	1.75	
Number of observations	24	

a significantly different from zero at 1 per cent level, one-tailed test
b significantly different from zero at 5 per cent level, one-tailed test
c significantly different from zero at 10 per cent level, one-tailed test
d significantly different from zero at 1 per cent level, two-tailed test
e significantly different from zero at 5 per cent level, two-tailed test
NOTE: Estimation technique is two-stage least squares with Cochrane-Orcutt. t-statistics are in parentheses. A one-tailed test is applied if there is a hypothesis about the sign of the coefficient; a two-tailed test is applied if there is not. Elasticities are calculated at the sample means.

(1978a; 1979), although the elasticity of demand with respect to vehicle miles is usually estimated to be about 0.50 to 0.60.[13]

However, the aggregation in the model leads to some ambiguity in the interpretation of the results. For example, the level of transit service and changes in service were not uniform across the urban area, and one suspects that the

13 By comparison, the computer simulation model used by the Toronto Transit Commission assumes a fare elasticity of demand of -0.165 and a vehicle-miles elasticity of demand of 0.226. See Joint Metro/Toronto Transit Commission Transit Policy Committee (1979b, 18).

TABLE 28

Estimates of the vehicle-mile and fare equations

Independent variables	Vehicle mile equation	Fare equation
Constant	3139.0^d	-0.123^d
	(7.65)	(-2.92)
C' Net-of-subsidy cost per vehicle mile	-1595.0^a	0.150^a
	(-5.53)	(3.32)
Z Net non-passenger revenue	0.177^a	-0.0000520^a
	(3.00)	(-7.06)
P Population served	9.87^b	-0.000553^c
	(2.32)	(-1.38)
Y Income	6.18	0.00153^d
	(1.51)	(3.63)
A Annexation dummy	-290.0	0.0627^e
	(-1.08)	(2.58)
Other statistics		
R^2	0.982	0.946
F (degrees of freedom)	192 (5, 18)	70 (5, 20)
R^2 in terms of first differences	0.726	–
ρ	0.638	–
	$(4.05)^a$	–
D.W. Durbin-Watson statistic	1.66	1.59
Number of observations	24	26

NOTE: Estimation technique is Cochrane-Orcutt for the vehicle-mile equation and ordinary least squares for fare equation. The value of D.W. lies in the indeterminate zone for a 5 per cent significance level for the one-tailed test against the alternative of positive autoregression. For the superscripts see the note to Table 27.

allocation of changes in service between central and suburban areas may play an important role in determining the estimate of the elasticity of demand with respect to vehicle miles of service. The fact that service improvements were concentrated in the suburbs in the 1960s and 1970s might account for our relatively low estimate of this elasticity.

In any event, the demand equation is not of primary concern in this study, because many other estimates of demand equations, some based on superior data, are available in the literature. Of much greater interest are the vehicle-mile and fare equations discussed below, since relatively little work has previously been done on these, and the present data and equation specifications have some advantages over those used by other researchers.

The vehicle-mile and fare equations
As noted above, given the budget constraint and demand equations, either the vehicle-mile equation or the fare equation is redundant. Moreover, given the budget constraint and the functional form of the demand equation, the functional forms assumed for the vehicle-mile and fare equations, (12) and (13), are not consistent with each other. Nevertheless, estimates for both (12) and (13) are presented to avoid carrying over mis-specifications in the budget constraint or demand equation into the estimates for either the vehicle-mile or the fare equation.

Since the vehicle-mile and fare equations are not independent, we shall examine them together, variable by variable.

Cost per vehicle mile and the cost subsidies
As we hypothesized, the coefficient on cost per vehicle mile, $C' = (1 - S_2)C$, is negative in the vehicle-mile equation and positive in the fare equation. Each coefficient is significantly different from zero at the 1 per cent level.

Since C' includes the effect of cost subsidies, these results can be used to determine the effect of alternative rates of cost subsidy on the expected values of vehicle miles and fares. The results imply that an increase in the rate of cost subsidy would lead the transit firm to increase its vehicle miles of service and to reduce its fare. Our estimates of the demand equation imply that these changes would lead to an increase in ridership.

Net non-passenger revenue and the lump-sum subsidies
The coefficient of net non-passenger revenue Z is positive in the vehicle-mile equation and negative in the fare equation, as hypothesized. Each coefficient is significantly different from zero at the 1 per cent level.

Since Z includes lump-sum subsidies, these results imply that an increase in lump-sum subsidies would lead to an increase in vehicle miles of transit service, a reduction in the fare, and an increase in ridership.

Cost subsidies vs lump-sum subsidies
Chapter 8 demonstrates that if the transit firm does not maximize vehicle miles of service, then a cost subsidy would have a larger effect on vehicle miles of service and a smaller effect on the fare than a lump-sum subsidy with the same cost to the taxpayer. This was formulated as hypothesis on β_1, δ_1, β_2, and δ_2 (see equation 17). Condition (17) does in fact hold for the estimates in Table 28.

Population served
As hypothesized, the coefficients on population served in the vehicle-mile and fare equations are positive and negative respectively, and both are significantly different from zero at the 10 (or 5) per cent level.

Income
We have seen from the estimate of the demand equation that the income elasticity of demand for transit is negative. Based on this consideration alone we would hypothesize that the coefficient on income in the vehicle-mile equation would be negative and the coefficient on income in the fare equation would be positive. However, it was also hypothesized that as incomes increase there will be quasi-political pressure on the transit system to provide a higher level of service (financed by a higher fare).

In fact, the coefficient on income in the fare equation is positive and significantly different from zero at the 1 per cent level, which is consistent with either or both of the above hypotheses. The coefficient on income in the vehicle-mile equation is also positive. While it is not significantly different from zero at the 10 per cent level in a two-tailed test, its sign lends some modest support to the hypothesis that there was quasi-political pressure on the transit system to increase service (and the fare) as incomes increased.

Annexation dummy
The coefficient on the annexation dummy is negative but not significantly different from zero at the 10 per cent level in the vehicle-mile equation. This result is consistent with the fact that the coefficient of the annexation dummy in the demand equation is negative.

This does not mean that the transit firm responded to the annexation by reducing or leaving unchanged the total number of vehicle miles of service. The annexation also led to an increase in population, and population has a significant positive coefficient in the vehicle-mile equation. The net effect of the annexation through the annexation dummy and the population variable was in fact to increase vehicle miles of service.

The coefficient on the annexation dummy is positive and significantly different from zero at the 5 per cent level in the fare equation. This result is also consistent with the fact that the coefficient of the annexation dummy in the demand equation is negative. Of course the annexation also led to an increase in population, which has a negative but not significant coefficient in the fare equation. The net effect of the annexation through the annexation dummy and the population variable was still to increase the fare.

These results do not shed any light on the hypothesis that annexation led to quasi-political pressure to expand service (and increase the fare to finance the higher level of service). The results for the vehicle-mile and fare equations are consistent with the coefficients in the demand equation and hence can be interpreted as describing the response of the transit firm to changes in the feasible set of operating policies without any change in its objective function as the result of quasi-political pressure.

Nevertheless, the results suggest that annexation of adjacent populated suburbs did induce the transit firm to expand its service and to raise its fare in order to finance the higher level of service.

CONCLUSIONS

Based on the estimated coefficients and elasticities of the variables in the econometric model, we conclude the following:

The theoretical model of an urban transit system analysed in Chapter 8 is essentially consistent with the data for London, Canada. Of course alternative models not tested might prove to be superior.

Provincial and municipal government lump-sum and cost subsidies for urban transit during the 1970s led to a significant increase in vehicle miles of service, a significant reduction in the fare, and a significant increase in ridership in London, Canada.

A cost subsidy has a larger effect on vehicle miles of service and a smaller effect on the fare than a lump-sum subsidy with the same cost to taxpayers would have.

The transit firm did not maximize vehicle miles of service subject to its budget constraint. If the transit firm maximized vehicle miles of service, the fare elasticity of demand would not be significantly different from one in absolute value.[14] The levels of fare and vehicle miles chosen were below the ones which would have maximized service.

Annexation of adjacent suburban areas led to an increase in the number of vehicle miles of transit service, financed in part by an increase in the fare. Given the uniform fare system that has generally been in effect, fares were raised for all

---

14 Also, if the transit firm maximized vehicle miles of service, and if equation (11) is the correct specification for the demand function, one would expect that the coefficients of cost per vehicle mile and net non-passenger revenue in the fare equation would not be significantly different from zero.

transit users, including low-income central city residents, in order to provide increased service in the new subdivisions.

As real incomes and the real value of travel time increased, the transit system responded by increasing the number of vehicle miles of service, again financing this by an increase in the real fare.

11

Implications for public policy

Irrespective of the economic merits of road pricing, it is doubtful that any scheme for comprehensive pricing of road use on the basis of marginal social cost will be politically feasible in Ontario in the foreseeable future. This is partly because of opposition to road pricing by people who (correctly or incorrectly) believe that road pricing would make them worse off, partly because of lack of confidence in what the government would do with this new source of revenue, partly because of concern over the possibility that road pricing would benefit high-income motorists at the expense of low-income motorists, and partly because of the costs involved in collecting road user charges. The discussion of road pricing in this study has therefore been kept relatively brief.

Chapter 2 showed that if collection of road user charges did not involve any transaction costs, then to achieve efficient use of existing urban roads, road user charges should be set so that road users paid the marginal social costs of their trips. These charges per vehicle trip would be equal to the sum of the three marginal external costs imposed by an extra vehicle trip: marginal congestion, pollution, and road maintenance costs. In large urban areas marginal social cost pricing of urban road use by private automobiles would probably involve a charge ranging between 0 and about 50 cents a mile for congestion, a pollution charge averaging about one cent a mile, and a charge of around one cent a mile for road maintenance and related government services.

Among the various technologies available for collecting urban road congestion charges, supplementary licences probably have the greatest practical potential for large urban areas. Vehicles travelling in the downtown area during congested periods would be required to display on their windshields a sticker sold by the city government. The cost of a sticker valid for one day would probably be between $1.50 and $3.00, depending largely on city size. However, any such road pricing scheme would have to be tested in a carefully monitored demonstration project to permit evaluation of its benefits and costs in practice, since no urban area apart from Singapore has implemented such a policy.

While imposition of such road user charges would presumably lead to an increase in the efficiency of resource allocation, at least in the largest urban areas in Ontario, charging for the use of roads would probably increase the inequality of income, unless the revenues from road user charges were used in ways which would substantially benefit lower-income people, such as to reduce income tax rates for low-income people and to provide income supplements for low-income people with no taxable income.

Short of imposing comprehensive road user charges, motor fuel taxes and registration fees could be set at higher rates in large urban areas than elsewhere in the province as a crude way of imposing congestion charges in cities. Another possibility would be to charge a tax based on mileage for cars registered in cities.

Parking in urban areas should be priced on the basis of marginal social cost. Among other things, this means that the government should eliminate the existing tax incentive to provide free employee parking by including the value of parking provided by employers in taxable income. Municipal governments should also consider imposing parking surcharges on cars arriving at parking locations in congested areas during the morning peak period.

Special incentives should not be provided for car pools, because these seem to me likely to promote inefficient car pooling, e.g. diversion from public transit to car pools, and hence are unlikely to have positive net social benefits.

URBAN TRANSIT FARE POLICIES

Transit fares should be set so as to promote economic efficiency and, perhaps, to reduce income inequality. Maximization of ridership is not an appropriate objective for urban transit systems. This conclusion is in conflict with the thrust of the recommendations made in 1979 by the Joint Metro / TTC Transit Policy Committee.

Considerations of efficiency indicate that transit rides should be priced below marginal social cost because the use of automobiles is priced below marginal social cost, and hence transit fares too should be set below the marginal congestion costs imposed by the additional transit riders.

Apart from fare collection costs, it would be efficient to charge higher fares during peak periods than during off-peak periods, to base fares in part on distance travelled during peak periods, and to charge for transfers. None of these changes would have serious adverse effects on income inequality.

Some of the efficiency gains from more complex fare structures might be offset by higher fare collection costs. This would be particularly true in smaller cities where automobile and transit congestion are limited. However, a number of innovations in fare collection methods lower fare collection costs substantially for any of the fare structures under consideration. Additional research on the economics of fare collection is necessary, and provincially subsidized demonstrations of options such as semi-automatic fare collection and honour fare collection should be considered for medium-to-large urban areas in Ontario.

One method of reducing fare collection costs is to introduce monthly passes. More research on the efficiency of monthly passes should be undertaken. Until such studies are done, other transit systems in Ontario should not introduce monthly passes, unless this is part of a carefully designed demonstration project. Before passes were introduced in Toronto the TTC did not believe that transit passes would lead to an increase in average vehicle operating speeds; if this is true it is unlikely that introduction of passes was justified on efficiency grounds in Toronto.

THE JUSTIFICATION FOR URBAN TRANSIT SUBSIDIES

There are strong economic arguments for subsidizing urban transit. The economic efficiency case for subsidizing conventional public transit rests almost entirely on two considerations: the existence of increasing returns to scale in public transit, and the practice of pricing automobile trips below their marginal social cost. Each of these arguments has been carefully evaluated. Mohring estimated that increasing returns to scale alone could justify a subsidy of roughly 50 to 60 per cent of the total costs borne by a bus system in a large U.S. urban area, and Glaister and Lewis estimated that failure to charge automobile users for their marginal congestion costs alone could justify a subsidy of 27 per cent of the total costs borne by the bus system in London, England.

There is an economic efficiency argument for subsidizing competent research and relevant demonstration projects in the field of urban transit, on the grounds that the results of such research and demonstration projects would be a public good (information). Of course subsidies are justified by this argument only to the extent that the projects are expected to generate external benefits.

There is also an income distributional argument for subsidizing urban transit, on the ground that in urban areas low-income people spend a larger share of their income on urban transit that do high-income people.

Thus on one hand there are strong economic arguments for subsidizing urban transit. On the other hand in practice the efficiency and income redistribution gains from transit subsidies may be less than the potential gains indicated above.

In order to finance transit subsidies the government must levy taxes; these taxes reduce the efficiency of resource allocation elsewhere in the economy, because they raise prices above marginal social costs for other goods and services. This important consideration will limit the size of socially optimal transit subsidies.

The fact that a case can be made for some form of subsidy for urban transit on both efficiency and income distributional grounds does not mean of course that *existing* subsidy programs contribute to efficiency or reduce income inequality. The subsidy will not necessarily be used to enable the transit firm to select the optimal services and fares. The transit firm might use it to introduce a new route in a high-income suburb where the demand does not justify the cost of providing the service. In this case the subsidy could bring about a less efficient allocation of resources and a less equal distribution of income.

URBAN TRANSIT SUBSIDIES IN ONTARIO

The level of government subsidies for urban transit in Ontario increased continually over the past two decades, at least until the late 1970s, in both nominal and real dollars, whether measured by a total dollar amount, an amount per vehicle mile or per passenger, or as a percentage of total costs. The percentage rate of increase in government subsidies was greatest during the first half of the 1970s. In descending order of importance, the sources of subsidies are the provincial, municipal, and federal governments.

Provincial and municipal grants to urban transit in Ontario amounted to about $260 million in 1976. However, the subsidy value of subsidized loans and tax exemptions has not been possible to estimate accurately.

Provincial and municipal lump-sum and cost subsidies for urban transit led to a significant increase in transit vehicle miles of service, a significant reduction in the real fare, and a significant increase in transit ridership during the 1970s.

Cost subsidies have a larger effect on vehicle miles and a smaller effect on real fare per subsidy dollar than do lump-sum subsidies.

Our review of transit subsidy policies in Ontario reveals two serious weaknesses. First, existing subsidy programs are heavily capital-biased. Capital costs are generally subsidized at a higher percentage rate than non-capital costs for a given public transit mode (e.g. bus transit) in a given urban area. Moreover, in Toronto, where there are several public transit modes, municipal and provincial subsidies for the more capital-intensive subways and commuter railways have been at higher percentage rates than for the less capital-intensive buses. Capital-biased subsidies may induce transit firms to substitute heavily subsidized capital for other inputs which are less heavily subsidized (e.g. by reducing vehicle maintenance, scrapping vehicles early, and opting for rail rapid transit rather than buses) and hence to increase the average social cost of supplying transit service. Any increase in the level of transit service or reduction in fares that would be brought about by a capital-biased subsidy could be achieved at a lower cost to the taxpayer by a neutral subsidy, so that capital-biased subsidies lead to a waste of resources. All levels of government should therefore revise their subsidy policies so that any subsidy given for transit costs should apply to all inputs at a uniform percentage rate.

Furthermore, existing subsidies appear to be used to an excessive degree for suburban and commuter services, including GO Transit. It appears likely that the efficiency of resource allocation could be increased and the inequality of the income distribution could be reduced by raising fares or reducing vehicle miles for these services and reducing fares or increasing vehicle miles on more centrally located services.

APPENDIX A

Distributional effects of road pricing

INTRODUCTION

Richardson (1974) recently discussed the distributional effects of road congestion charges. He considers three results of congestion pricing which have distributional implications: (1) the money cost of using congested roads would increase; (2) the time cost of using congested roads would decrease; and (3) because revenue would be raised from congestion charges other taxes would be reduced or additional public services would be provided. Richardson is primarily concerned with effects (1) and (2), presumably because (3) depends on a separate policy decision concerning the disposition of the revenue. For the same reason, the following analysis ignores (3) and deals only with (1) and (2).

Richardson does not explicitly analyse the direction of the *combined* effect on the well-being of road users of the changes in money and time costs of travel which would result from congestion charges. Consequently, while he concludes that 'road pricing must be regressive between motorists,' he is not explicit about whether high-income motorists could gain in *absolute* terms or about the circumstances under which they would gain. This appendix provides an economic model of road use which can be used to analyse these aspects of the combined effect of changes in money and time costs for different income groups.

A model of road use with homogeneous vehicle flow
Before considering a model of road use which recognizes different income groups, it will be useful to review the implications of the standard textbook analysis of congestion charges for the well-being of road users. That analysis

This appendix is based on Frankena (1975). A number of the same points were arrived at independently by Layard (1977).

assumes that the vehicle flow is homogeneous and that the private cost of road travel per vehicle trip of given length C, is the sum of vehicle operating expenses (excluding road user charges) per vehicle trip E, road user charges per vehicle trip P, and the value of travel time per vehicle trip. The value of travel time per vehicle trip is the product of the value of travel time per vehicle hour V and vehicle hours per vehicle trip T. Both E and T are assumed to be increasing functions of vehicle flow per hour F for vehicle flows greater than F_0, where F_0 is the level of vehicle flow at which congestion sets in.[1] V is assumed to be a positive constant.[2] Thus

$$C = E(F) + P + VT(F), \qquad (A.1)$$

where E', $T' > 0$, for $F > F_0$.

In addition, it is assumed that the quantity of vehicle trips demanded per hour Q is a decreasing function of C:

$$Q = D(C), \qquad (A.2)$$

where $D' < 0$.

The condition for equilibrium road use is

$$Q - F = 0. \qquad (A.3)$$

It is assumed that the initial equilibrium prior to imposition of a congestion charge occurs at $F > F_0$.

Taking the total differentials of equations (A.1) to (A.3) and solving, the model yields the following comparative static derivative of C with respect to P:

1 This assumption rules out the 'bottleneck case' discussed by Walters (1961) in which an increase in the number of vehicles per mile leads to a reduction in the flow of vehicles per hour.

2 V could be treated as an endogenous variable, equal to the product of the value of travel time per person hour and the vehicle occupancy rate. The occupancy rate could be treated as an increasing function of the money cost per vehicle trip, and vehicle hours per vehicle trip could be treated as an increasing function of both the vehicle flow per hour and the occupancy rate.

$dC \,/\, dP = 1 \,/\, (1 - E'D' - VT'D') > 0.$

Thus, the combined effect of the changes in money and time costs of travel which result from imposition of a congestion charge in this model is to make everyone using the road at the initial equilibrium worse off (whether or not they reduce their use of the road after the congestion charge is imposed) by increasing the cost per vehicle trip. The indirect gain for road users from reduced congestion is less than the direct loss due to the congestion charge.[3] The explanation for this result is that in order to bring about a reduction in travel time a congestion charge must reduce vehicle flow, and to do this it must raise the cost per trip.

It should be emphasized that the conclusion that road users would be worse off depends on the assumptions of the model and the partial equilibrium nature of the analysis.[4] This conclusion ignores gains from the disposition of the revenue from the congestion charge.

A model of road use with two income groups
Suppose now that one distinguishes between two groups of road users with different incomes. Let members of Group 1 have higher incomes than members of Group 2. Assume that the value of travel time per vehicle hour is higher for

3 In addition, road users might be required to bear some costs of collection, such as the costs of meters or electronic identifiers on their vehicles. However, assuming that such costs are not excessive and that there are no second-best complications, one would expect the aggregate gain for taxpayers or consumers of public services who benefit from the revenue raised by the optimal positive congestion charge to be greater than the aggregate loss borne by road users, compared to a situation with no congestion charge. In any event, if all households in an urban area were identical and achieved the same utility level in equilibrium, a general equilibrium analysis would lead to the conclusion that all households would be better off as a result of efficient congestion pricing. For a general equilibrium analysis of congestion tolls, see Oron, Pines, and Sheshinski (1973).

4 The conclusion reached in the text concerning the well-being of road users ignores general equilibrium effects including shifting and capitalization and revenue from the congestion tax, which might be used to reduce other motor vehicle taxes or to expand the road system. Also, even if vehicles are homogeneous, this conclusion does not hold in three cases which have been excluded by the assumptions of the model: the bottleneck case referred to in footnote 1; the situation referred to in footnote 2 where occupancy rate is very elastic with respect to money cost and vehicle hours is very elastic with respect to vehicle flow; and the situation analysed by Henderson (1974) in which commuters have the same desired arrival time and must choose the time at which to start their trips. In these three cases, all road users could benefit from congestion pricing, even if the disposition of the tax revenue were ignored.

Group 1 than for Group 2, $V_1 > V_2$,[5] but that the other determinants of cost per vehicle trip for the two groups C_i are the same:[6]

$$C_i = E(F) + P + V_i T(F), \qquad (i = 1, 2). \tag{A.4}$$

In addition, assume that the quantity of vehicle trips demanded per hour for each income group Q_i is a decreasing function of C_i:

$$Q_i = D_i(C_i), \qquad (i = 1, 2). \tag{A.5}$$

The condition for equilibrium road use is

$$Q_1 + Q_2 - F = 0. \tag{A.6}$$

Again, assume that the initial equilibrium occurs at $F > F_0$.

Taking the total differentials of equations (A.4) to (A.6) and solving, the model yields the following values for the comparative static derivatives of C_i with respect to P:

$$dC_2 / dP = [(V_1 - V_2)T'D'_1 - 1] / A > 0,$$

$$dC_1 / dP = [(V_2 - V_1)T'D'_2 - 1] / A,$$

where $A = (E' + V_1 T')D'_1 + (E' + V_2 T')D'_2 - 1 < 0$.

Thus, the combined effect of the changes in money and time costs of travel which result from a congestion charge is to make low-income road users worse off by raising C_2, the cost per vehicle trip to them.

However, the combined effect of these changes on the well-being of high-income road users cannot be determined without further assumptions about the magnitudes of the parameters. Depending on the values of the parameters, for

5 Other things equal, this assumption is consistent with the findings of empirical studies of the value of travel time for the journey to work. These studies typically indicate that on average the value per person hour of travel time is an increasing function of the wage rate. However, if low-income people have a higher vehicle occupancy rate or make trips for different purposes than high-income people, this assumption might not always describe the real world accurately.

6 This assumption rules out differences between the vehicles used by the two income groups and between the congestion charges paid per vehicle trip.

high-income road users the direct loss due to the congestion charge may (or may not) be more than offset by the indirect gain from the reduction in congestion which occurs when members of the low-income group reduce their use of the road. High-income road users gain from congestion charges if the absolute values of $V_2 - V_1$, T', and D'_2 are large enough that $(V_2 - V_1)T'D'_2 > 1.$[7]

In order for either group to gain from the congestion charge the total vehicle flow must be reduced. Consequently, the cost per trip must rise for at least one group. It follows that the cost will rise for the low-income group, since the change in money cost will be the same for both groups while the value of the reduction in travel time will be lower for the low-income group. Hence, the number of trips made by the low-income group will decline.

Whether the high-income group benefits depends on the value of its travel time. For the high-income group to gain, the value per hour of its travel time must be sufficiently high relative to that of the low-income group that the money value of the equilibrium time savings exceeds the change in money cost for the high-income group but not for the low-income group. For given values per hour of travel time, this is more likely to occur if travel time is highly sensitive to the cost per trip for the low-income group, i.e. if travel time is highly sensitive to the vehicle flow and the demand for trips on the part of the low-income group is highly sensitive to the cost per trip.

Further implications of the second model
In this model the essential result that some road users can gain from congestion charges while others lose depends upon the existence of differences in the value of time per vehicle trip. While it was assumed above that differences in V result from differences in income, obviously they may be related to other factors, such as differences in trip purpose and in vehicle occupancy rates. For example, other things equal, V will be higher for vehicles making trips during work time rather than leisure time and for vehicles with a larger number of occupants. Consequently, in addition to high-income motorists, users of taxis and car pools would be among the groups using passenger cars which would be most likely to gain from congestion charges.

So far the analysis has assumed that $E(F)$, $T(F)$, and P are the same for all vehicles, but the analysis could be extended to vehicles which have different E

---

7 Thus, unless he is restricting himself to the case where the vehicle flow is homogeneous, Sharp (1966, 811) is not justified in asserting that 'without a compensating tax reduction motorists continuing to use the congested roads will be worse off, since the congestion tax must be greater than the benefits gained from the reduced level of congestion.'

and T functions and different levels of P. Thus, even if commercial vehicles and buses bore higher congestion charges than passenger cars because they impose more congestion, users of commercial vehicles and buses would also be among the groups most likely to gain from the combined money and time effects of congestion charges because of relatively high levels of V, and also perhaps because their E and T functions are relatively elastic with respect to F.[8]

Implications for empirical research

At the empirical level, the most important implication of the present analysis is that one cannot evaluate the distributional effects of taxes on road use the same way as one evaluates taxes on goods and services not subject to congestion. The incidence of a tax on road use depends not only on the income elasticity of demand for travel but also on the effect of the tax on the cost of travel for members of different income groups.

---

8 Because of improvements in bus service, some motorists who were almost indifferent between using private cars and buses at the initial equilibrium would gain from congestion pricing by switching from cars to buses. However, if the number of vehicle hours of bus service remained unchanged, some of the gains for bus users would be offset by increased congestion of buses because of the increase in bus ridership.

APPENDIX B

Second-best pricing of public transit with unpriced automobile congestion

Consider a simplified case in which the following assumptions are made.[1] There is only one time period. The value of travel time is the same for all individuals. Automobile and public transit passenger trips are perfect substitutes from the consumers' point of view. Hence there is a single market demand curve for trips, labelled D^* in Figure B.1b. Each individual will choose the mode of travel with the lowest private cost, considering value of travel time and money outlays on vehicle operating expenses and fares; the condition for an equilibrium in which some people travel by each mode is that the marginal *private* cost of a trip is equal on the two modes. Neither mode causes pollution, and automobiles do not impose congestion on public transit vehicles and vice versa. We are concerned with the short run, a period in which the sizes of rights-of-way and the number of transit vehicle hours of service are fixed,[2] and each mode is subject to congestion. The marginal private cost and short-run marginal social cost curves for transit passenger trips and automobile passenger trips are given by MPC_t, MSC_t, MPC_a, and MSC_a in Figure B.1, where subscript t stands for transit and subscript a for automobile. The marginal private cost curves do not include any transit fares or road user charges.

---

1 Sherman (1971, 1972) considers the case in which automobile and transit passenger rides are not perfect substitutes and automobiles impose congestion on transit vehicles and vice versa. He assumes that an automobile passenger trip imposes more congestion on both other automobile users and transit riders than does a transit passenger trip and investigates the circumstances under which a reduction in the transit fare would lead to a decrease in transit congestion.

2 If we assume that the sizes of the rights-of-way and the number of vehicle hours of service are fixed at the second-best-efficient levels, the analysis would apply in the long run as well.

Figure B.1
Second-best transit fare with unpriced automobile congestion

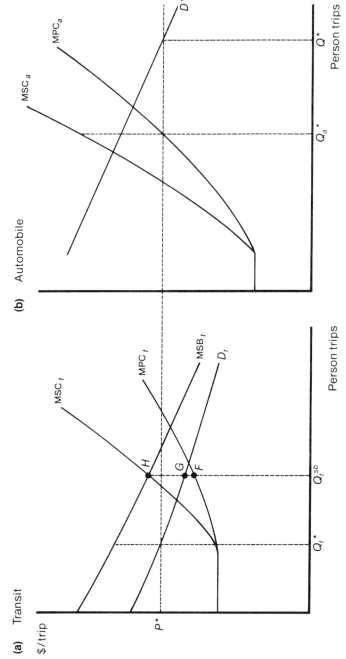

(a) Transit

(b) Automobile

Note: The marginal private cost curves, MPC_t and MPC_a, measure the average variable social costs of travel by transit and automobile respectively.

To determine the second-best-efficient level for the transit fare in this situation when automobile congestion is unpriced, we must now derive two additional curves. First, we need the demand curve D_t for transit rides, conditional on the demand curve D^* for trips by all modes and on the option of travel by automobile, which is characterized by the private cost curve MPC_a when no congestion tolls are charged. Second, we need the marginal social benefit curve MSB_t for public transit in the same situation.

To derive D_t we ask the following question: At each price P (including value of travel time and fare) per trip by transit, how many transit trips would be demanded? The answer is $D^*(P) - MPC_a^{-1}(P)$, where MPC_a^{-1} is the inverse of the MPC_a function. In other words, the number of transit trips that would be demanded at the price (not fare) P per trip would equal the total number of trips by all modes demanded at the price P per trip minus the number of trips people could take by automobile with a private cost of P per trip. Geometrically, at each value of dollars per trip along the vertical axis the horizontal distance between D_t and the vertical axis in Figure B.1a equals the horizontal distance between D^* and MPC_a in Figure B.1b.

Ordinarily we assume that at each level of output the height of the demand curve for a commodity tells us the marginal social benefit of an extra unit of output. However, this assumption is appropriate only when certain conditions are met, one of which is that there are no unpriced externalities affecting the demand curve so that what consumers are willing to pay for the good provides a measure of all the benefits of increasing the production and consumption of that good.[3] This assumption is reasonable for D^*, but it is not appropriate for D_t because, when there is unpriced automobile congestion, the willingness to pay for transit trips on the part of a person who is choosing between use of automobiles and transit would not reflect the benefits to other automobile users of reduced automobile congestion if that person would go by transit.

In geometric terms, the demand curve for use of transit for trips that would be taken by automobile in the absence of the transit option would be a mirror-image of the portion of MPC_a to the left of the intersection of MPC_a and D^*. However, the marginal social benefit curve for use of transit for these trips would be a mirror-image of the corresponding segment of MSC_a. The vertical difference between these two curves is the unpriced marginal congestion cost of a person trip by automobile.

Thus, if D^* were perfectly inelastic, i.e. if all transit trips were trips diverted from automobiles, the relevant marginal social benefit curve for transit trips would be simply the mirror-image of MSC_a described above. However, because

3 Another assumption is that there is no income effect on demand.

we assume in Figure B.1b that D^* is not perfectly inelastic, some trips taken by transit would not be taken at all if no transit service was offered. The demand for these trips is represented by D^* to the right of the intersection of MPC_a and D^*, and the height of D^* is an appropriate measure of the marginal social benefit of these transit trips. Since D_t is derived from D^*, as far as these trips are concerned the height of D_t measures the marginal social benefit of transit trips.

Thus, we come to the conclusion that the marginal social benefit of transit trips MSB_t is a *weighted* average of the heights of the relevant portions of MSC_a and D^*, where the weights are the proportions of trips attracted to transit from automobile travellers and from non-travellers respectively. Thus, to find the height of the curve representing the marginal social benefit of transit trips MSB_t at any given level of transit trips such as Q_t^*, find P^* such that $D_t(P^*) = Q_t^*$. Then find $Q_a^* = MPC_a^{-1}(P^*)$. From the above it follows that

$$MSB_t(Q_t^*) = [\alpha_1 / (\alpha_1 + \alpha_2)] \cdot MSC_a(Q_a^*) + [\alpha_2 / (\alpha_1 + \alpha_2)] \cdot P^*,$$

where $\alpha_1 = dMPC_a^{-1} / dP$ and $\alpha_2 = - dD^* / dP$.

It follows from this derivation that if automobile congestion is unpriced MSB_t lies above D_t. At the same time if D^* is not perfectly inelastic, then the vertical distance between D_t and MSB_t will be less than the vertical distance between MPC_a and MSC_a at the corresponding level of automobile travel.

Now that all the necessary curves have been derived, we can use Figure B.1a to determine the second-best transit fare when automobile congestion is unpriced. The second-best-efficient level of transit trips is determined where MSC_t and MSB_t intersect, i.e. at Q_t^{sb}. In order to attain this level of transit use, the fare must be set at FG, the vertical distance between MPC_t and D_t at the output level Q_t^{sb}.

It should be noted that with the fare FG, the private cost of transit trips including the fare is less than the marginal social cost by the amount of GH. The second-best fare is less than the marginal congestion cost FH imposed by the last transit rider. This illustrates the basic point that when use of roads is priced below marginal social cost, use of transit should also be priced below marginal social cost if the two modes are (gross) substitutes.

Efficiency of alternative transit objectives and subsidy formulas

This appendix considers whether the operating policy selected by a transit firm which maximizes vehicle miles of service or ridership would be economically efficient, whether provision of a subsidy to such a firm would increase efficiency, and which subsidy formula would be most efficient.

EFFICIENCY OF VEHICLE MILE AND RIDERSHIP MAXIMIZATION

Suppose that the theoretical model presented in Chapter 8 accurately represents the behaviour of a transit firm. We define the efficient operating policy as the combination of fare F and vehicle miles M which maximizes the net social benefit from transit service given the transit firm's budget constraint. The net social benefit is measured by the total amount of money that transit users would be willing to pay for their rides (excluding the value of their own time) minus the total cost of operating the buses used to produce these rides. We assume that there are no externalities and that the transit firm is required to break even.

Corresponding to each level of M is a different demand curve for transit rides, $R = R(F, \overline{M})$, in (R, F) space. As M is increased, the demand curve shifts outward. Figure C.1 shows demand curves corresponding to four different levels of M ($M_1 < M_2 < M_3 < M_4$).

Also corresponding to each level of M is a level of total cost CM, where C is the cost per vehicle mile of transit service, and hence a level of total fare revenue FR which is necessary to break even. Along a given demand curve there will typically be two points which yield a given level of fare revenue, corresponding to points on the upward-sloping and backward-bending portions of ZZ' in Figure 8. We are concerned only with points on the upward-sloping portion. The letters A, B, D, and E indicate the points along the demand curves at which the transit firm would break even. For other levels of M between M_1 and M_4 the break-even points would lie on the dashed line $ABDE$.

Along line $ABDE$, point E (which is located where the fare-elasticity of demand is -1) would be chosen by a firm maximizing vehicle miles of service, and point D would be chosen by a firm maximizing ridership. By contrast, a firm maximizing the net social benefit would choose point B. At point B the net social benefit, or consumer surplus in the case at hand, is measured by the shaded triangle F_2BG.[1] This shaded triangle is larger than the corresponding triangle for any other point along line $ABDE$.[2]

Thus, in the example given in Figure C.1, a transit firm which maximizes either vehicle miles of service or ridership would set F and M above the efficient levels and hence would waste resources. However, the location of the efficient operating policy compared to that of the policy that would maximize ridership depends upon the assumptions one makes about the demand function. In Figure C.1 the demand curve becomes flatter as M increases. If the slope of the demand curve does not change as M increases and the demand curve shifts out, the operating policies corresponding to ridership maximization and efficiency would coincide. If the demand curve becomes steeper as M increases, the efficient operating policy would involve a higher level of F and M than the policy which would maximize ridership.

Intuitively, how the slope of the demand curve changes as M increases depends upon how inframarginal users value the increase in vehicle miles of service or the resulting savings in travel time compared to marginal users. For example, given the level of vehicle miles of service, suppose that if the fare is high only low-income people who place a low value on their travel time would ride buses. Suppose that if the fare is reduced the new riders would be higher-income people who place a higher value on their travel time. If the level of vehicle miles of service is now increased, the demand will shift up. However, the left end of the demand curve might not rise very much, because low-income (inframarginal) riders may not be willing to pay much for improved service. By contrast, the right end of the demand curve might rise a good deal, because higher-income (marginal) riders may be willing to pay much more for improved service. In this

1 One should use income-compensated demand curves for this purpose.

2 To prove this, observe that at any point (R_i, F_i) at which the transport firm would break even, the net social benefit V_i is determined by $V_i = 0.5(G - F_i)R_i$. All break-even points with a consumer surplus equal to that at B therefore must lie along the line TT', which is a rectangular hyperbola when viewed with respect to an origin located at point G and axes formed by the lines $R = 0$ and $F = G$. Since the locus of break-even points $ABDE$ and TT' are tangent at B, all break-even points other than B would yield lower net social benefits than B.

Figure C.1
Comparison of operating policies for alternative objectives

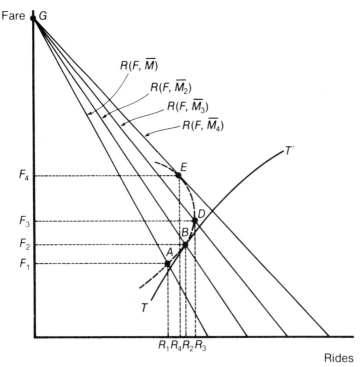

case the demand curve would become flatter as vehicle miles of service increase, as in Figure C.1. In this case a transit firm which maximizes ridership offers more than the efficient level of service (and charges more than the efficient fare) because of the disportionately large valuation placed on improved service by marginal users. This extra service is not efficient because it costs more per rider than the average user would be willing to pay for it.

Furthermore, the information about demand behaviour required to determine the efficient operating policy is greater than that required to maximize ridership. To determine the efficient policy, one must know how all inframarginal users value improved transit service or the resulting reduction in travel time, while to maximize ridership one needs information only on the relevant marginal users. This helps to explain why transit firms find it more convenient to maximize ridership than to maximize net social benefits.

Our basic conclusion is that while vehicle-mile maximization is clearly inefficient, neither of the other simple objective functions considered in Chapter 8 (ridership maximization or any particular specification of low fare preference) will lead to an efficient allocation of resources for all specifications of the demand function. Moreover, the direction of any deviation from efficiency which would result from the ridership maximization or low fare preference objectives cannot be determined without more specific information about, or restrictions on, demand behaviour.

REFORMULATION USING THE SPENCE-SHESHINSKI MODEL

The analysis of a non-profit monopolistic transit firm which selects a combination of fare, vehicle miles of service, and ridership is similar to the analysis carried out independently by Spence (1975) and Sheshinski (1976) for a profit-maximizing monopoly which selects a combination of price, product quality, and product quantity. This section modifies some of the assumptions made in Chapter 8 so that our transit model corresponds more precisely to the general model analysed by Sheshinski. The only remaining difference between the transit model analysed here and Sheshinski's model is the monopoly's objective function. While vehicle miles of service in our model plays the role of product quality in Sheshinski's model, one could replace vehicle miles of service by a more general scalar index or vector of quality variables including in-vehicle travel time, walking and waiting time, comfort, and adherence to schedules.

Assume that the inverse demand function facing the transit firm is $F = F(R, M)$ and that $F_R < 0$ and $F_M > 0$, where F is the fare per ride, R is number of rides, M is vehicle miles of service, and F_R and F_M are partial derivatives. Also assume that the total production cost function is $c = c(R, M)$ and that $c_R > 0$ and $c_M > 0$. (By comparison, in Chapter 8 and in the preceding section we assumed that $c = CM$, so that $c_R = 0$.)

The net social benefit of transit service (assuming there are no externalities of the type that would arise if there were unpriced automobile congestion) is

$$V(R, M) = \int_0^R F(Z, M)dZ - c(R, M). \tag{C.1}$$

The first-order conditions for maximization of V with respect to R and M are

$$V_R = F - c_R = 0, \tag{C.2}$$

$$V_M = \int_0^R F_M(Z, M)dZ - c_M = 0. \tag{C.3}$$

We assume that the second-order conditions hold globally. For any given value of M, equation (C.2) determines the level of R which maximizes the net social benefit. Similarly, for any given value of R, equation (C.3) determines the level of M which maximizes the net social benefit.

Since we want to analyse this model geometrically, we now want to identify the locus of points (R, M) which satisfy equation (C.2) and similarly the locus for equation (C.3). To do this, we must specify the sign of $(F_M - c_{RM})$, and we assume that it is positive, as it would be for the model in Chapter 8 where $c_{RM} = 0$ (see Sheshinski 1976, 130). This gives us the case in Sheshinski's Figure 1. In this case, the loci for $V_R = 0$ and $V_M = 0$ in Figure C.2 both slope upwards and $V_R = 0$ is steeper at the intersection, point H, which is the combination of R and M which maximizes the net social benefit. Around this intersection we have added the iso-net social benefit contour $V(R, M) = \bar{V}$.

We now wish to add to Figure C.2 the locus of combinations of R and M which satisfy the transit firm's break-even budget constraint in the absence of subsidies:

$$F(R, M)R - c(R, M) = 0. \tag{C.4}$$

This can be regarded as an iso-profit contour defined by the firm's profit function:

$$\pi(R, M) = F(R, M)R - c(R, M). \tag{C.5}$$

Consequently, in order to locate the points which would satisfy (C.4), it is helpful to find the combination of R and M which would maximize the transit firm's profit. The first-order conditions for profit maximization are

$$\pi_R = F + F_R R - c_R = 0, \tag{C.6}$$

$$\pi_M = F_M R - c_M = 0. \tag{C.7}$$

We assume that the second-order conditions hold globally.

To add to Figure C.2 the locus of points which satisfy equation (C.6) and similarly the locus for equation (C.7) we must specify the sign of $(F_M + F_{RM} R - c_{RM})$; we assume that it is positive (ibid.). We must also specify the sign of F_{RM}, which determines how the slope of the transit demand function changes as M increases. We assume $F_{RM} > 0$, which is the assumption made in Figure C.1. The assumptions give us the case analysed by Sheshinski in his figure 1a. The loci for $\pi_R = 0$ and $\pi_M = 0$ both slope up, and $\pi_R = 0$ is steeper at the intersection, point N, which is the combination of R and M which maximizes the transit firm's profits. Furthermore, $\pi_R = 0$ lies to the left of $V_R = 0$, and $\pi_M = 0$ lies above $V_M = 0$.

Figure C.2
Efficiency of alternative objectives

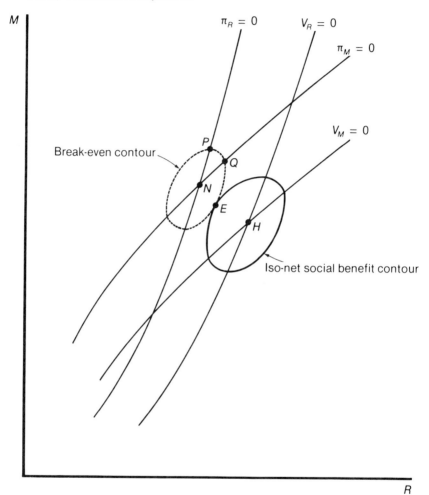

We can now add the transit firm's break-even contour (C.4) to Figure C.2. While Sheshinski's profit-maximizing monopolist operates at point N, a non-profit monopolistic transit firm would choose the point along the break-even contour which maximizes its utility function $U = U(F, M, R)$. If the transit firm maximizes vehicle miles of service, that is $U = M$, it will select point P where the break-even contour and the locus $\pi_R = 0$ intersect. If the transit firm maximizes ridership, that is $U = R$, it will select point Q where the break-even contour and the locus $\pi_M = 0$ intersect. If the transit firm has an objective function characterized by what was defined in Chapter 8 as 'low fare preference,' it would choose a point along the break-even contour right of $\pi_R = 0$ and below $\pi_M = 0$.

In order to achieve an efficient allocation of resources given its budget constraint, the transit firm should operate at point E, where it is on the highest attainable iso-net social benefit contour. Under the assumptions made in Figure C.2 (notably the assumption that $F_{RM} > 0$), the points that would maximize vehicle miles of service and ridership both involve an inefficiently high level of F and M. The reasoning behind this result was discussed in the preceding section. In the case at hand an objective function involving a particular specification of low fare preference could have led the transit firm to choose point E. However, one could not specify what transit objective function characterized by low fare preference would achieve this result unless one knew the transit demand and cost functions.

If we changed one of the assumptions made above and assumed that $F_{FM} < 0$, we would obtain a new diagram similar to Figure C.2 except that the locus $\pi_M = 0$ would lie below the locus $V_M = 0$ (see Sheshinski's Figure 1b) rather than above it. With this change, the tangency between the break-even contour and the iso-net social benefit contour would lie between the points of maximum vehicle miles and maximum ridership along the break-even contour. In that case, ridership maximization would lead to inefficiently low levels of F and M. Finally, if $F_{RM} = 0$, the tangency would coincide with the point of maximum ridership. In this very restrictive case, ridership maximization would be efficient given the budget constraint.

EVALUATION OF THE EFFICIENCY OF TRANSIT SUBSIDIES

Chapter 5 explained the economic arguments for transit subsidies. We saw that if the objective of a transit firm is to achieve an efficient allocation of resources, and if the transit fare is above the marginal social cost of transit rides because of economies of scale, then a lump-sum subsidy will lead to an increase in the efficiency of resource allocation. Unfortunately, if the transit firm's objective function departs from efficiency or maximization of net social benefits, it no longer follows that a subsidy will necessarily increase efficiency even if the fare is above the marginal social cost of transit rides. Consequently, in practice one cannot justify a transit subsidy on efficiency grounds without reference to empirical information about the transit firm's objective function, demand function, and cost function.

Figure C.3
Efficiency of subsidy

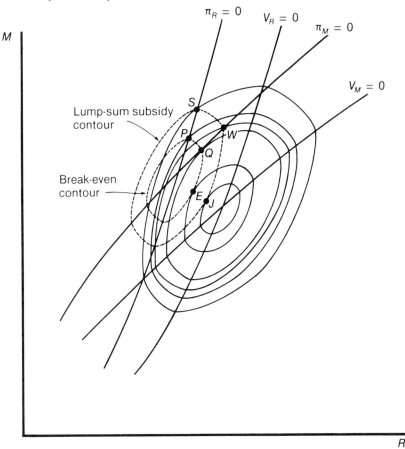

This point is illustrated in Figure C.3, which repeats Figure C.2 with additional iso-profit and iso-net social benefit contours. We assume that the transit firm receives a lump-sum subsidy which shifts the firm's constraint from the break-even contour to the lump-sum subsidy contour, which is tangent to a higher iso-net social benefit contour. If the firm maximizes net social benefits, it will move from point *E* to point *J* as a result of the subsidy, and net social benefits will increase. However, if the firm maximizes vehicle miles of service it will move from *P* to *S*, and if it maximizes ridership it will move from *Q* to *W*. In either case, given the explicit and implicit assumptions on which Figure C.3 is based, net social benefits will decrease. However, under some other assumptions about the demand and cost functions, one would find that a subsidy to a transit firm which maximizes ridership would increase net social benefits, even when ridership maximization is not an efficient objective.

The net social benefits resulting from a subsidy with a given cost to taxpayers will depend not only on the objective function of the transit firm and the demand function but also on the subsidy formula used. If the transit firm maximizes net social benefits subject to its budget constraint, a lump-sum subsidy will be most efficient. It will be more efficient than a subsidy based on vehicle miles of service or (unless $F_{MR} = 0$, so that ridership maximization and efficiency coincide) a passenger subsidy.

There are, however, circumstances under which a subsidy based on vehicle miles of service, such as the cost subsidy analysed in Chapter 8, would be more efficient that a lump-sum subsidy. For example, if the transit firm maximizes ridership and if $F_{MR} < 0$, then in the absence of subsidies the transit firm will choose a point along the budget constraint where F and M are below the efficient levels. Since a subsidy based on vehicle miles of service would induce the firm to increase F and M more than a lump-sum subsidy with the same cost to taxpayers (see Chapter 8), in this case a subsidy based on vehicle miles of service might produce higher net social benefits than a lump-sum subsidy.

SUMMARY

The results of this appendix are essentially negative. Unless one has information on the demand and cost functions, one cannot determine whether ridership maximization would lead to fare and vehicle-mile levels below, equal to, or above those which would be efficient given the budget constraint, and one cannot determine whether a subsidy to a firm which maximizes ridership would increase or reduce efficiency even though fares exceed marginal social costs. Also, unless one has information about the transit firm's objective function, demand function, and cost function, one cannot determine which subsidy formula would be most efficient.

A final qualification is in order. The analysis in this appendix has assumed that there are no relevant externalities such as unpriced road congestion.[3] If some transit riders were diverted from using roads priced at less than marginal social cost, the net social benefit of transit service would be greater than that

---

3 The analysis also ignores the costs imposed by an extra transit rider on the other transit riders and on other road users, such as when an extra rider delays a transit vehicle while boarding.

indicated by equation (C.1). The principal effect of this would be to shift $V_R = 0$ to the right in Figure C.2. This in turn would shift the tangency of the break-even iso-profit contour and the iso-net social benefit contour in the direction of the point of maximum ridership (regardless of the sign of F_{RM}). However, while this would reduce the magnitude of the efficiency loss resulting from ridership maximization, it would not have much effect on the qualitative problems raised.

Glossary of variables

A Annexation dummy. $A = 0$ for 1951-60; $A = 1$ for 1961-77.

C Gross-of-subsidy cost per vehicle mile for bus service in 1978 dollars

C' Net-of-subsidy cost per vehicle mile for bus service in 1978 dollars, or $(1 - S_2)C$

F Fare or passenger revenue per revenue passenger in 1978 dollars

I_1 Imputed income on capital in thousands of 1978 dollars

I_2 Net capital accumulation in thousands of 1978 dollars

I_3 Capital subsidies (net of subsidies for the capital costs of current operations) in thousands of 1978 dollars

M Vehicle miles in thousands

N Other net revenue in thousands of 1978 dollars

P Population served in thousands

R Riders or revenue passengers in thousands

S_1 Lump-sum subsidies in thousands of 1978 dollars

S_2 Rate of cost subsidy as a decimal

S_3 Rate of passenger subsidy in dollars per rider

Y Real income or weekly wage and salary income per worker in 1978 dollars

Z Net non-passenger revenue in thousands of 1978 dollars, or $N + S_1 + I_1 - I_2 + I_3$

Bibliography

Allen, G.L. (1975) 'Optimal and second-best pricing of urban transportation services,' PH D thesis, Department of Economics, University of Minnesota

Anderson, S.C. (1979) 'The economic effects on urban bus transit of public ownership and Urban Mass Transportation Administration capital grants.' PH D thesis, Department of Economics, University of California, Los Angeles

Armour, R.F. (1980) 'An economic analysis of transit bus replacement' *Transit Journal* 6, 41 – 54

Arnott, R.J. and J.G. MacKinnon (1978) 'Market and shadow land rents with congestion.' *American Economic Review* 68, 588 – 600

Barnum, D.T. (1972) 'Collective bargaining and manpower in urban mass transit systems.' PH D thesis, University of Pennsylvania

Baumol, W. and D. Bradford (1970) 'Optimal departures from marginal cost pricing.' *American Economic Review* 60, 265 – 83

Ben-Akiva, M. and T.J. Atherton (1977) 'Methodology for short-range travel demand predictions: analysis of carpooling incentives.' *Journal of Transport Economics and Policy* 11, 224 – 61

Bhatt, K. (1974) *Road Pricing Technologies: A Survey* (Washington DC: Urban Institute)

Bhatt, K., J. Eigen, and T. Higgins (1976) *Implementation Procedures for Pricing Urban Roads* (Washington DC: Urban Institute)

Bly, P.H. (1976) *The Effect of Fares on Bus Patronage* (Crowthorne, Berkshire, England: Transport and Road Research Laboratory)

Bly, P.H., F.V. Webster, and S. Pounds (1980) *Subsidisation of Urban Public Transport* (Crowthorne, Berkshire, England: Transport and Road Research Laboratory)

Boadway, R.W. (1974) 'The welfare foundations of cost-benefit analysis.' *Economic Journal* 84, 926 – 39

Boiteux, M. (1956) 'Sur la gestion des monopoles publics astreints à l'équilibre budgétaire.' *Econometrica* 24, 22 – 40

Bös, D. (1978) 'Distributional effects of maximization of passenger miles.' *Journal of Transport Economics and Policy* 12, 322 – 9

Braeutigam, R.R. (1979) 'Optimal pricing with intermodal competition.' *American Economic Review* 69, 38 – 49

Brown, G. (1972) 'Analysis of user preferences for system characteristics to cause a modal shift.' *Highway Research Record* 417, 25 – 36

Bureau of Management Consulting (1977) *The Ottawa Bus-Pass System: An Examination of Effects* (Montreal: Transport Canada)

Canada, Department of Finance (1976) *Working Paper on Urban Transportation* (Ottawa)

Canadian Inter-Mark (1976) *A Research Survey on Attitudes and Uses by Riders and Non-Riders of the Toronto Transit Commission* (Toronto)

City of Toronto, Department of Public Works (1973) *Parking Policies for Central Toronto* (Toronto)

City of Toronto Parking Authority (1976) *Carpool Incentive Experiment* (Toronto)

City of Woodstock Transportation Service (1970) *Annual Report for 1969* (Woodstock, Ontario)

Commission de Transport de la Communauté Urbaine de Québec (1977) *Normalisation des Services* (Montreal: Transport Canada)

Complan Research Associates Ltd (1979) *Executive Summary: 1978 Survey on Attitudes and Uses for the Toronto Transit Commission* (Toronto)

Comptroller General of the United States (1979) *Analysis of the Allocation Formula for Federal Mass Transit Subsidies* (Washington DC: United States General Accounting Office)

Cooter, R. and G. Topakian (1980) 'Political economy of a public corporation: pricing objectives of BART,' *Journal of Public Economics* 13, 299 – 318

Cundhill, M.A. and P.F. Watts (1973) *Bus Boarding and Alighting Times* (Crowthorne, Berkshire, England: Transport and Road Research Laboratory)

DeLeuw, Cather (1978) *Honour Fare: A Study of Practical Application in Ontario* (Downsview, Ontario: Ministry of Transportation and Communications)

De Vany, A. and T.R. Saving (1980) 'Competition and highway pricing for stochastic traffic.' *Journal of Business* 53, 45 – 60

Dewees, D.N. (1974) *Economics and Public Policy: The Automobile Pollution Case* (Cambridge, Mass.: MIT Press)
- (1977) 'Changes in urban accessibility: a preliminary analysis of Metropolitan Toronto, 1964 – 1971.' Centre for Urban and Community Studies, University of Toronto
- (1978) 'Simulations of traffic congestion in Toronto.' *Transportation Research* 12, 153 – 61
- (1979) 'Estimating the time costs of highway congestion.' *Econometrica* 47, 1499 – 512
Dewees, D.N., E. Hauer, and F. Saccomano (1979) *Urban Road User Subsidies: A Review of Theory and Measurement.* Joint Program in Transportation, University of Toronto–York University, Toronto.
Dewees, D.N. and L. Waverman (1977) 'Energy conservation: policies for the transport sector.' *Canadian Public Policy* 3, 171 – 85
Faulhaber, G.R. (1975) 'Cross-subsidization: pricing in public enterprises.' *American Economic Review* 65, 966 – 77
Feldstein, M.S. (1972a) 'Distributional equity and the optimal structure of public prices.' *American Economic Review* 62, 32 – 6
- (1972b) 'Equity and efficiency in public sector pricing: the optimal two-part tariff.' *Quarterly Journal of Economics* 86, 175 – 87
Frankena, M. (1973) 'Income distributional effects of urban transit subsidies.' *Journal of Transport Economics and Policy* 7, 215 – 30
- (1974) 'Distributional effects of urban transportation investments.' Metropolitan Toronto Transportation Plan Review, Toronto
- (1975) 'Distributional effects of road pricing: further analysis.' Department of Economics, University of Western Ontario, London
- (1978a) 'The demand for urban bus transit in Canada.' *Journal of Transport Economics and Policy* 12, 280 – 303
- (1978b) 'Conceptual framework for transit deficit forecasting.' TEE Consulting, Ottawa
- (1979) *Urban Transportation Economics: Theory and Canadian Policy* (Toronto: Butterworths)
- (1980) 'The effects of alternative urban transit subsidy formulas.' Department of Economics, University of Western Ontario, London
Garbade, K.K. and N.M. Soss (1976) 'Fare policies for mass transit deficit control: analysis by optimization.' *Transportation Research* 10, 237 – 47
Gaudry, M. (1975) 'An aggregate time-series analysis of urban transit demand: the Montreal case.' *Transportation Research* 9, 249 – 58
- (1978) 'Seemingly unrelated static and dynamic urban travel demands.' *Transportation Research* 12, 195 – 211

- (1980) 'A study of aggregate bi-modal urban travel supply, demand and network behavior using simultaneous equations with autoregressive residuals.' *Transportation Research* B14, 29 – 58

Gillen, D.W. (1977a) 'Alternative policy variables to influence urban transport demand.' *Canadian Journal of Economics* 10, 686 – 95

- (1977b) 'Estimation and specification of the effects of parking costs on urban transport mode choice.' *Journal of Urban Economics* 4, 186 – 99

Glaister, S. (1974) 'Generalised consumer surplus and public transport pricing.' *Economic Journal* 84, 849 – 67

- (1979) 'On the estimation of disaggregate welfare losses with an application to price distortions in urban transport.' *American Economic Review* 69, 739 – 46

Glaister, S. and J.J. Collings (1978) 'Maximization of passenger miles in theory and practice.' *Journal of Transport Economics and Policy* 12, 304 – 21

Glaister, S. and D.L. Lewis (1978) 'An integrated fares policy for transport in London.' *Journal of Public Economics* 9, 341 – 55

Gomez-Ibanez, J.A. and G.R. Fauth (1980) 'Downtown auto restraint policies: the costs and benefits for Boston.' *Journal of Transport Economics and Policy* 14, 133 – 53

Hamermesh, D. (1975) 'The effect of government ownership on union wages.' In *Labor in the Public and Non-Profit Sectors* (Princeton NJ: Princeton University Press) 227 – 55

Haritos, Z. (1973) *Rational Road Pricing Policies in Canada* (Ottawa: Canadian Transport Commission)

Harmelink, M.D. (1977) *Transit Fare Systems in Europe* (Downsview, Ontario: Ministry of Transportation and Communications)

Hedlin Menzies and Associates Ltd (1972) *Urban Transit Fare Study: Volume 1 – Findings and Analysis* (Downsview, Ontario: Ministry of Transportation and Communications)

Henderson, J.V. (1974) 'Road congestion: a reconsideration of pricing theory.' *Journal of Urban Economics* 1, 346 – 65

- (1977) *Economic Theory and the Cities* (New York: Academic Press)

Hilton, G.W. (1974) *Federal Transit Subsidies* (Washington DC: American Enterprise Institute for Public Policy Research)

Jannson, J.O. (1979) 'Marginal cost pricing of scheduled transport services.' *Journal of Transport Economics and Policy* 13, 268 – 94

- (1980) 'A simple bus line model for optimisation of service frequency and bus size.' *Journal of Transport Economics and Policy* 14, 53 – 80

Johnston, G.H. and G.R. McMillan (1978) 'Transit finance policies.' *RTAC Forum* 1, 40 – 7

Joint Metro/Toronto Transit Commission Transit Policy Committee (1979a) *Fare Structure* (Toronto)

– (1979b) *Transit Financing* (Toronto)

Keeler, T.E., G.S. Cluff, and K.A. Small (1974) 'On the average costs of automobile transportation in the San Francisco Bay area.' Institute of Urban and Regional Development, University of California, Berkeley

Keeler, T.E., and K.A. Small (1975) *The Full Costs of Urban Transport: Part III: Automobile Costs and Final Intermodal Cost Comparisons.* Institute of Urban and Regional Development, University of California, Berkeley

– (1977) 'Optimal peak-load pricing, investment, and service levels on urban expressways.' *Journal of Political Economy* 85, 1–25

Kraft, G., and T.A. Domencich (1972) 'Free transit.' In M. Edel and J. Rothenberg, eds, *Readings in Urban Economics* (New York: Macmillan) 459–80

Kraus, M., H. Mohring, and T. Pinfold (1976) 'The welfare costs of nonoptimal pricing and investment policies for freeway transportation.' *American Economic Review* 66, 532–47

Kulash, D. (1974a) *Congestion Pricing: A Research Summary* (Washington DC: Urban Institute)

– (1974b) *Income-Distributional Consequences of Roadway Prices* (Washington DC: Urban Institute)

– (1974c) *Parking Taxes as Roadway Prices: A Case Study of the San Francisco Experience* (Washington DC: Urban Institute)

– (1974d) *Parking Taxes for Congestion Relief: A Survey of Related Experience* (Washington DC: Urban Institute)

Layard, R. (1977) 'The distributional effects of congestion taxes.' *Economica* 44, 297–304

Lee, N. and I. Steedman (1970) 'Economies of scale in bus transport.' *Journal of Transport Economics and Policy* 4, 15–28

Lewis, D. (1977) 'Estimating the influence of public policy on road traffic levels in Greater London.' *Journal of Transport Economics and Policy* 11, 155–68

London Transit Commission (1974) *1973 Annual Report* (London, Ontario)

Lurie, M. (1960) 'Government regulation and union power: a case study of the Boston transit industry.' *Journal of Law and Economics* 3, 118–35

May, A.D. (1978) 'Supplementary licensing: an evaluation.' *Urban Transportation Economics* (Washington DC: National Academy of Sciences)

McFadden, D., and F. Reid (1975) 'Aggregate travel demand forecasting from disaggregated behavioral models.' *Transportation Research Record* 534, 24–37

228 Bibliography

Miller, D.R. (1970) 'Differences among cities, differences among firms, and costs of urban bus transport.' *Journal of Industrial Economics* 19, 22 – 32

Miller, R.U., C.A. Olson, and J.L. Stern (1978) 'Labor costs and collective bargaining in urban mass transit.' In *Urban Transportation Economics* (Washington DC: National Academy of Sciences)

Mills, E.S. (1972) *Urban Economics* (Glenview, Illinois: Scott-Foresman)

Mohring, H. (1970) 'The peak-load problem with increasing returns and pricing constraints.' *American Economic Review* 60, 693 – 705

– (1972) 'Optimization and scale economies in urban bus transportation.' *American Economic Review* 62, 571 – 604

– (1976) *Transportation Economics* (Cambridge, Mass.: Ballinger)

– (1979) 'The benefits of reserved bus lanes, mass transit subsidies, and marginal cost pricing in alleviating traffic congestion.' In P. Mieszkowski and M. Straszheim, eds, *Current Issues in Urban Economics* (Baltimore: Johns Hopkins University Press) 165 – 95

– (1981) 'The role of minibuses in American urban transportation.' Department of Economics, University of Minnesota, Minneapolis, Minnesota

Mohring, H.D. and M. Harwitz (1962) *Highway Benefits* (Evanston, Illinois: Northwestern University Press)

Morlok, E.K. (1976) 'Supply function for public transport: initial concepts and models.' *Lecture Notes in Economics and Mathematical Systems* 118 (Berlin: Springer-Verlag) 322 – 67

Mouzet, J. and F. Torjussen (1979) *Rationalisation of Fare Collection – Scope and Limitations* (Brussels: 43rd International Congress, International Union of Public Transport)

Nash, C.A. (1978) 'Management objectives, fares and service levels in bus transport.' *Journal of Transport Economics and Policy* 12, 70 – 85

Nelson, G.R. (1972) *An Econometric Model of Urban Bus Transit Operations* Paper P-863 (Arlington, Virginia: Institute for Defense Analyses)

Newhouse, J.P. (1970) 'Toward a theory of non-profit institutions: an econometric model of a hospital.' *American Economic Review* 60, 64 – 74

Oi, W.Y. (1971) 'A Disneyland dilemma: two-part tariffs for a Mickey Mouse monopoly.' *Quarterly Journal of Economics* 85, 77 – 96

– (1973) *Alternative Formulas for a Federal Operating Subsidy Program for Transit*, Paper P-943 (Arlington, Virginia: Institute for Defense Analyses)

Olsson, M. and G. Miller (1978) *Parking Discounts and Carpool Formation in Seattle* (Washington DC: Urban Institute)

Ontario, Ministry of Transportation and Communications (1971 – 72 to 1976 – 77) *Annual Report* (Toronto)

– (1978) *Ontario Municipal Transit* (Downsview, Ontario)

Ontario, Ministry of Treasury and Economics (annual) *Public Accounts* (Toronto)

Ontario, Royal Commission on Metropolitan Toronto (1977) *Report, Volume 2: Detailed Findings and Recommendations* (Toronto)

Oron, Y., D. Pines, and E. Sheshinski, (1973) 'Optimum vs equilibrium land use pattern and congestion toll.' *Bell Journal of Economics and Management Science* 4, 619 – 36

Patriarche, J.C.D. (1979) *Provincial Subsidy Programmes* (Ottawa: Roads and Transportation Association of Canada)

Peskin, H.M. (1973) *An Analysis of Urban Mass Transit Subsidies*, Paper P-793 (Arlington, Virginia: Institute for Defense Analyses)

Pozdena, R.J. (1975) 'A methodology for urban transport project selection.' PHD thesis, Department of Economics, University of California, Berkeley

Pozdena, R.J. and L. Merewitz (1978) 'Estimating cost functions for rail rapid transit properties.' *Transportation Research* 12, 73 – 8

Precursor, Ltd (1978) *A Study of Transit Fare Policies, Fare Structures and Fare Collection Methods* (Montreal: Transport Canada)

Puccini, R. (1979) *Urban Transit Operations: An Introduction* (Downsview, Ontario: Ministry of Transportation and Communications)

Ramsey, F.P. (1927) 'A contribution to the theory of taxation.' *Economic Journal* 37, 47 – 61

Recon Research Consultants (1968) *Benchmark Household Survey* (Toronto: Metropolitan Toronto and Region Transportation Study)

Richardson, H.W. (1974) 'A note on the distributional effects of road pricing.' *Journal of Transport Economics and Policy* 8, 82 – 5

Sage Management Consultants (1978) *Labour in Urban Transit Operations: Profile and Prospects* (Montreal: Transport Canada)

Segal, D. and T.L. Steinmeier (1980) 'The incidence of congestion and congestion tolls.' *Journal of Urban Economics* 7, 42 – 62

Segelhorst, E.W. and L.D. Kirkus (1973) 'Parking bias in transit choice.' *Journal of Transport Economics and Policy* 7, 58 – 70

Sewell, J. (1978a) 'Public transit in Canada: a primer.' *City Magazine* 3, 40 – 55

– (1978b) 'Transit authority in trouble.' *City Magazine* 3, 6 – 7

Sharp, C. (1966) 'Congestion and welfare – an examination of the case for a congestion tax.' *Economic Journal* 76, 806 – 17

Sherman, R. (1967) 'Club subscriptions for public transit passengers.' *Journal of Transport Economics and Policy* 1, 237 – 42

– (1971) 'Congestion interdependence and urban transit fares.' *Econometrica* 39, 565 – 76

- (1972) 'Subsidies to relieve urban traffic congestion.' *Journal of Transport Economics and Policy* 6, 22–31
Sheshinski, E. (1976) 'Price, quality and quantity regulation in monopoly situations.' *Economica* 43, 127–37
Shortreed, J.H., ed., (1974) 'Urban bus transit: a planning guide.' Department of Civil Engineering, University of Waterloo
Shoup, D.C., and D.H. Pickrell (1979) 'Free parking as a transportation problem.' School of Architecture and Urban Planning, University of California, Los Angeles
Small, K.A. (1976) 'Bus priority, differential pricing, and investment in urban highways.' PH D thesis, Department of Economics, University of California, Berkeley
- (1977) 'Estimating the air pollution costs of transport modes.' *Journal of Transport Economics and Policy* 11, 109–32
Spence, A.M. (1975) 'Monopoly, quality, and regulation.' *Bell Journal of Economics* 6, 417–29
Spielberg, F. (1978) *Transportation Improvements in Madison, Wisconsin* (Washington DC: Urban Institute)
Statistics Canada (Cat. 62–010, quarterly) *Consumer Prices and Price Indexes* (Ottawa)
- (Cat. 72–002, monthly) *Employment, Earnings and Hours* (Ottawa)
- (Cat. 62–003, monthly) *Prices and Price Indexes* (Ottawa)
- (Cat. 62–544, 1974) *Urban Family Expenditure Survey* (Ottawa)
- (Cat. 53–003, monthly) *Urban Transit* (Ottawa)
- (Cat. 53–216, annual) *Urban Transit* (Ottawa)
Straszheim, M.R. (1979) 'Assessing the social costs of urban transportation technologies.' In P. Mieszkowski and M. Straszheim, eds, *Current Issues in Urban Economics* (Baltimore: Johns Hopkins University Press) 196–232
Strotz, R. (1964) 'Urban transportation parables.' In J. Margolis, ed., *The Public Economy of Urban Communities* (Baltimore: Johns Hopkins University Press) 127–69
Tebb, R.G.P. (1978) *Differential Peak / Off-Peak Bus Fares in Cambria*, (Crowthorne, Berkshire, England: Transport and Road Research Laboratory)
TEE Consulting Services (1978) *Review of Transit Subsidy Mechanisms* (Ottawa: Ministry of State for Urban Affairs and Transport Canada)
- (1979) *Urban Public Transit Subsidy Levels and Effects* (Ottawa: Ministry of State for Urban Affairs and Transport Canada)
Toronto Area Transit Operating Authority (1979) *Annual Report for the Year Ended March 31, 1979* (Toronto)
Toronto Transit Commission (1966) *Annual Report* (Toronto)

- (1976) *Transit in Toronto* (Toronto)
- (1977) *Transit Revenue Policy Study* (Toronto)
- (1978) *A Study of Monthly Passes* (Toronto)

Train, K. (1980) 'A structured logit model of auto ownership and mode choice.' *Review of Economic Studies* 47, 357–70

Transport Canada (1978) *The Effects of the Imposition of Parking Charges on Urban Travel in Ottawa: Summary Report* (Montreal)

Turvey, R. and H. Mohring (1975) 'Optimal bus fares.' *Journal of Transport Economics and Policy* 9, 280–6

Tye, W.B. III (1969) 'The economic costs of the Urban Mass Transportation capital grants program.' PH D thesis, Department of Economics Harvard University, Cambridge, Mass.

Tzedakis, A. (1980) 'Different vehicle speeds and congestion costs.' *Journal of Transport Economics and Policy* 14, 81–103

Veatch, J.F. (1973) 'Cost and demand for urban bus transit.' PH D thesis Department of Economics, University of Illinois, Urbana-Champaign

Vickrey, W.S. (1963) 'Pricing in urban and suburban transport.' *American Economic Review* 53, 452–65

Wabe, J.S., and O.B. Coles (1975) 'The peak and off-peak demand for bus transport: a cross-sectional analysis of British municipal operators.' *Applied Economics* 7, 25–30

Walters, A.A. (1961) 'The theory and measurement of the private and social cost of highway congestion.' *Econometrica* 29, 676–9

Watson, P.L. and E.P. Holland (1978) *Relieving Traffic Congestion: The Singapore Area License Scheme* (Washington DC: World Bank)

Watts, P.F. (1974) *Passenger Handling Performance of One-Man Buses* (Crowthorne, Berkshire, England: Transport and Road Research Laboratory)

Waverman, L. (1980) 'The invisible hand: the pricing of Canadian oil resources.' In *Energy Policies for the 1980s: An Economic Analysis* Vol. 1 (Toronto: Ontario Economic Council) 25–58

Webster, F.V. (1977) *Urban Passenger Transport: Some Trends and Prospects,* (Crowthorne, Berkshire, England: Transport and Road Research Laboratory)

Werz, H. (1973) *Automatic Fare Collection in Surface Transport* (Brussels: 40th International Congress, International Union of Public Transport)

Westin, R.B. and D.W. Gillen (1978) 'Parking location and transit demand: a case study of endogenous attributes in disaggregate mode choice models.' *Journal of Econometrics* 8, 75–101

Wheaton, W.C. (1978) 'Price-induced distortions in urban highway investment.' *Bell Journal of Economics* 9, 622–32

Wilbur Smith and Associates (1975) *Ottawa Parking Study Final Report* (Ottawa)

Woods, Gordon (1971) *Financial Assistance for Urban Transit* (Downsview, Ontario: Ontario Department of Highways)

Zerbe, R.O. and K. Croke (1975) *Urban Transportation for the Environment* (Cambridge, Mass.: Ballinger)